POLICE ORGANIZATIONS AND CULTURE

NAVIGATING LAW ENFORCEMENT IN TODAY'S HOSTILE ENVIRONMENT

CHIEF SCOTT SILVERII, PHD

Copyright © 2011 Scott Silverii, Ph.D. Updated 2019
All rights reserved.

No part of this book may be reproduced or transmitted in any form or by any means, electronic or mechanical, including emailing, photocopying, recording, or by any information storage and retrieval system, without permission in writing from the author.
Produced by Scott Silverii at Five Stones Press.

DEDICATION

This work is dedicated to those who have worn the badge, those who are wearing the badge, and those who will wear the badge.

No matter what my Brothers and Sisters, don't tarnish our badge. Always do the right thing.

Yes, it's just that simple.

For he is God's servant for your good. But if you do wrong, be afraid, for he does not bear the sword in vain. For he is the servant of God, an avenger who carries out God's wrath on the wrongdoer.

Romans 13:4

CONTENTS

Preface   ix

1. The Blue Line Mystique   1
2. Special Operations Groups   13
3. Studying a Secret Culture   27
4. History of Policing in America   39
5. Occupational Socialization   59
6. Why Cops Quit   67
7. Anti-Diversity In the Ranks   77
8. Police Culture   85
9. State Sponsored Violence   105
10. Policing the Police   117
11. Cop Culture and OMC   125
12. Driving Drunk Behind the Badge   141
13. Silent Suffering   153

PART I
STRESS

PART II
DEPRESSION

PART III
SUICIDE

14. Investigative Strategies   171
15. Just the Facts   187
16. Hating Others   213
17. Final Shades of Blue   229
18. Final Verdict   241
19. Igniting Change   257

Appendix Introduction	271
Appendix A	273
Appendix B	279
Appendix C	285
Appendix D	291
Appendix E	297
Appendix F	303
Appendix G	307
Afterword	313
Acknowledgments	315
About the Author	317
INSERTS & CREDITS	319
Bibliography	321
Notes	337

PREFACE

I vividly recall completing my application for the local sheriff's office in the late 1980s. There was no check box asking if I wanted to be a good cop or bad cop. There were no requirements that I be or become socially cynical, emotionally detached or personally uncaring. I was not even asked to write a paragraph about becoming disenfranchised with the ideals of public service, or joining other officers in a cultural divide against the civilian population. There were no written test questions asking preferences for divorcing my spouse, drinking excessively, committing petty theft or engaging in major corruption.

The final evaluation phase of the hiring process includes an oral review board. Consisting of ranking members of the agency, each officer was dressed so professionally that I was naturally nervous within their presence. Although intimidated by their stature, I am one hundred percent positive not one of those officers asked when I planned to commit suicide, beat my wife, begin using illegal drugs or enjoy abusing my authority against a civilian public.

A question that has plagued me for years is "Why do good cops go bad?" For the sake of this work, I refer to going "bad" in the widest expanse of actions ranging from professional apathy to criminal behavior, or the "darkest shade of blue." From the once idealistic rookie cop who now lets the drunk drive away because he doesn't want to get stuck doing the paperwork, to former cops committing murder, what changes?

What is it that transforms individuals signing up for public service to believe it is suddenly okay to take cash from a crime scene, accept sex while on duty in exchange for a warning instead of a citation, and that it is no longer socially acceptable to "protect and serve?"

This work focuses specifically on the dynamics responsible for creating the environment of change. The change does not always have to result in negative behaviors. It very often produces positive changes in the personality and character of the individual. One thing is without escape; change will occur. This phenomenon is the process of "becoming blue," or more formally termed; occupational socialization. The process is not taught in the academy, but does originate the day a police cadet enters the classroom to begin a career dreamed of for a lifetime. Experiencing and becoming enmeshed within the cop culture, becoming blue, has the potential for a rewarding profession. It is also fraught with dangers, temptations and subcultures powerful enough to seduce the most faithful in the service.

Relational Association

This work is by no means an autobiography, though there are personal accounts of my experiences over more than the last two decades. I do believe it is critical that I share pieces of my life, my experiences, and my vision for several practical purposes. Unless we break down the initial personal perceptions serving as barriers between police and the public, the effectiveness of this book is lost. Despite the uniforms, weapons, policies and assumed authority granted through the commissioning of each officer; what we are ultimately discussing is humanity.

Preface

Spending years researching the content of this work, I have added to the applied social science field work with intense academic theoretical studies focusing on the anthropological aspects of cop culture. What does this mean for the reader? I believe it presents a unique opportunity for experiencing the realities of police work and life behind the badge from a perspective rarely afforded. This work is not a tell-all like the police dramas portrayed in media and myth; it is about the men and women taking the same oath with the similar ideals to protect and serve the communities within our country. It is about cop culture. It is about why good cops go bad.

Most officers will stop to wonder why. Why is the socialization process so mystical, so secretive and so misunderstood? Why as a society do we hesitate to question it, as a research body we struggle to quantify it, or as a fraternity we refuse to unveil it. This work ask the questions and reveals the reasons why?

Equally important to discovering why, is the reality that this work is not an indictment on the profession or community of law enforcement. Like every gathering of people, whether it's for work or play, there are some who will take the path of least resistance and succumb to committing actions that bring concern for all. The dynamics of socialization effect every officer, but to neglect the moral obligation for discovering the instances when the price paid for fitting in becomes detrimentally expensive for the officer, agency and community, is a disservice to all.

Discovering "Why" in a Crisis

Spending my entire adult life serving others and proudly wearing the shield has afforded experiences like none other. Obviously there have been amazing times, and like the singularly well-placed golf shot after only 18 holes, you wait with anticipation for your next tour of duty. There have been times not so amazing, but still for the sake of doing the "job," they are acceptable and you move forward.

This book is about each of those times and how they contribute to becoming blue. It will however, primarily address the disquieting question of do once idealistic public servants transform into professional deviants. The fraternal expectancy demands that while the job's experiences of highs are very high, the lows must never be revealed for the sake of protecting the "blue." Crises and suffering in silence are dominant variables in the going "bad" dynamic, so allow me to go back to a pivotal moment in my career that began this journey of cultural revelation. The following section is important because I want fellow officers to know the experiences we share behind that badge are similar. It is also vital that civilians also understand that our experiences with occupational socialization, or "fitting in" are not that different from their reality of entering a work, school or a social ecology.

The Reality

I sat there in full uniform admiring the electric blue of the shirt created by applying too much starch before ironing it for duty. The badge still shined after all the years of polishing and handling on duty and off. I remember looking downwards to my chest, off to the left and noticing the multicolored rows of service ribbons I had earned through the years. I always took pride in pinning each ribbon on before duty, as they served a reminder of where my career achievements. The Medal of Valor, Purple Heart, the Distinguished Service, Marksmanship and the Hurricane Katrina ribbons mixed in with others to illustrate a long and decorated career.

Slightly hunched where I sat, laboring to breath, my eyes scanned across the front of my duty belt to check my weapon's security as I had thousands of times before during retention drills at the academy, trainings and street encounters. I was reassured of its presence and readiness to engage.

As I continued to assess my status, both eyes lifted and caught a glimpse of the shiny gold-colored nameplate that read SCOTT SILVERII as it lay on my upper right chest above the standard uniform pockets with their gold decorative buttons. Above the nameplate was the issued American flag pin serving as a constant reminder of the country I loved and was proud to serve. Finally, as I continued determining the cause of the discomfort, I was reassured by the coveted SWAT eagle pin I had earned as an operator for over sixteen years. It was going to be the skills and hardening acquired during these years that got me through this ordeal.

The navy blue epilate boards and their gold stitched double bars hung loosely from atop each of my shoulders as I continued to regulate my breathing in an effort to grasp a situation spiraling out of control. Then it hit me, I looked down towards my holster and lifted my right arm and then my left arm, and saw the pools of blood staining the newly issued electric blue uniform shirt. All I could think about was after all the SWAT calls and undercover deals and arrests, I was going to go out like this.

In times of crisis, people revert to various tactics for rationalizing the severity of the situation. My system for coping began by going back to the "why," and how did I arrive at this point. Why had I allowed the process of becoming blue have such a powerful effect on my personal and professional life? I was well trained, educated, solid believes and moral anchors, yet I sat there alone. Bleeding.

The Rationalizing

My dad was a high school teacher for over thirty years. He had been retired another twenty years, but people still speak to him and always ask my family and I, how is Coach? Tell him I said hello. My mom, having passed away for over a decade still draws kind comments and the sharing of stories illustrating her caring, loving character while establishing herself in the community as a compassionate business owner.

My niece on the other hand shared with me that her friend thinks I'm a prick. This teenaged girl does not know me, but only her perception of an officer. Therefore, I go back to the "why?" Why does a profession serving the public share such a bi-polar relationship with the very people we swore to serve? Why does the socialization process of this profession not encourage community engagement but isolationism, and yes, of course, why do well-intended cops just stop caring or go bad?

The Recollection

Allow me to try to answer the question of why people become cops despite the threats to public safety and challenges to personal integrity. I assume that my life is no different from most people, and that's why I believe you will relate better to the following discoveries once I strip away any preconceived notions about law enforcement officers being pricks. However, some are!

No one in my family has ever been and with the impression I get, no one will ever be a cop. That is okay. I recall as a young boy, afternoons and evenings running and playing in a typical rural south Louisiana sugarcane town. The neighborhood consisted of scattered single-family middle class working people surrounded by what seemed like miles and miles of sugarcane fields.

It was the perfect playground for a rambunctious group of boys and the occasional tag-along tomboys. When the cane was growing, it was camp outs and hide and seek games. After the harvesting, it was motto-cross bicycle races and dirt throwing wars between our hastily dug "fox holes." The muddier the better. I remember my mom telling us in the mornings, "be back before the street lights come on." We seldom did.

I lived about five houses from the railroad track, and during the day we would chase the trains as they lumbered along the rails with their boxcars loaded with what we thought were mysterious goods. Many times we dared each other to hop on and see what adventures befell us. Most often, we relinquished the idea in lieu of placing pennies on the track for the immediately flattened Abraham Lincoln effect. The problem with bringing your newly shaped penny home to show your mom was that she now knew you had not heeded her warning against playing on the tracks.

We had the "longest street" in the world running through our parish, Bayou Lafourche. The bayou ran down the middle of the parish from one end to the other, about 90 miles later. The thought of paddling a pirogue all that way and into the swamps was so foreign and exciting, but not so much as to ever attempt it. Anyway, all that playing and open space could have led to mischief, but mostly didn't. What we loved to play was army and SWAT. Not just regular cops and robbers, but a full-blown special weapons and tactics team with training grounds. I was glued to the 1970s "SWAT" television series. Hondo, Deke and Lucas were my heroes and I wanted to be just like them.

I organized the neighborhood kids and we began our training. We scaled the walls of our families' homes and dared each other to jump from the rooftops. All was fine until the day I sent Mark H. on a surveillance mission into a tree across the street from our command post. Fine that was, until he forgot to follow the kid rule of looking both ways before crossing the street. He got clipped along the way and ended up in the hospital. The team was deactivated, but my passion was ignited.

It wasn't until many years later that I befriended a police recruiter who reignited that childhood flame. Until then I never thought of myself as officer material. Honestly, I had no clue what it took, or who actually became cops. One thing I did know, was that I wanted to be a good cop and make my family, friends and community proud. What initially inspired me to become a cop? Maybe it is an innate attraction, or a rational career choice after researching other options. Maybe it was the childhood years of playing and imaging the "what ifs." Despite the reason and my call to duty, we are not that different. Even though there may be a few pricks among us.

Preface

The Revelation

I believe the call to duty is inherent. Some people heed it, while others avoid it. Still, others having never experienced it are drawn to the job for various and less than altruistic motivations. The public servant spirit is nothing to be defined in a catchall phrase, but its depth of understanding by those who have experienced the draw cannot deny the power. This is the core of my work; the powerfully irresistible call to duty that envelops new recruits, inspires seasoned officers, and fragments institutional subcultures from the organizational ideals of duty, honor, and service. Despite this mystical call to serve the public, still some officers do go bad. Why?

Discovering "Why"

The pooling of blood should have triggered a physical alarm, but at that moment seeing the crimson ruining my favorite tailored uniform shirt, it set off a firestorm of questioning, regretting and bargaining. Today, I believe I've answered my questions, resolved my regrets and characteristically never compromised my core values as a bargaining position. The research questions challenge the larger picture of policing, not just the daily operating procedures making for interesting reading and unrealistic movies. What is the social, fraternal and occupational culture of policing, and why is the process of "fitting in" so overwhelming to those heeding the call?

After collecting data over the course of several years from cops across the country, I discovered the following key elements concerning the culture of policing, the mysteriously powerful process of "fitting in", and possible effects of becoming a darker shade of blue.

Discoveries About Policing's Culture

From the moment a person decides to pursue a career in law enforcement, there are six phases they may experience before reaching a point of "becoming dark blue." As the individual becomes enmeshed in the unique culture of policing, the potential exist for separating themselves from prior familial, social and communal anchors. The self-assumption that "no one understands me," begins to isolate the individual from exterior accountability relationship.

If the officer joins a special operations group (SOG) such as undercover or SWAT, they may even become more distanced from traditional police officers like Patrol or Detectives. Finally, because the important part of becoming socialized is "fitting in," the individual surrenders what makes them unique for the sake of becoming like the others surrounding them. While the officer assumes comfort and privilege through sameness, there is actually a harmful affect associated with this type of organizational sub-culture.

This investigation ploughed through the complex and complicated forces of not just the sociology of workplace dynamics, but the psychology of organizational institutions and the cultural mores of anthropology. The combination of strategies including observations, interviews, literature reviews and theoretical examinations reveal four key points about the cop culture, the challenges for avoiding the pitfalls of policing and effecting professional and personal change for sustaining a positive and productive service environment. The following points recapture the descriptions above for the sake of illustrating this perspective;

- Six liminal benchmarks track the career of an officer from civilian to fully socialized SOG.
- Individuals may devolve into a deviant subcultural fraternity once separated from the mainstream population of moral civilian anchors.
- The SOG subculture is a reflection of specialized skill sets, a collection of personal characteristics transformed during periods of liminal opportunities inspired by the unique SOG mission, and the institutionally independent operational environment of violence, silence and risk.
- *Detrimental homogenetic entitlement* occurs when people of

influence, exercise force or intimidation to protect a false sense of deviant entitlement or privilege.

Figure P.1: Author on post-Katrina SWAT patrols in metro-New Orleans area. *Source:* Original photograph property of Dr. Scott Silverii.

1
THE BLUE LINE MYSTIQUE

"Once they (SOG) trust you, everything is possible and you are always in. You never rat. Never! It doesn't matter what you see or do. No one talks. This is the way things should be."
(SWAT cop, Colorado, 2010)

The culture of law enforcement is an all or nothing proposition with no gray area where membership into this society is concerned. Either you are "on the job" or you are not. Even references among officers to "the job" indicate there is only one job. Likened to a secret handshake, that initial phrase if answered correctly opens the door to instant fraternal acceptance, get out of violation passes, and the many other assumed privileges of belonging.

The profession of law enforcement is held in the highest level of societal esteem. It rises to the point of possessing a powerful mystification[1] described as the "sacred canopy." It is further asserted that, "the police role conveys a sense of sacredness or awesome power that lies at the root of political order, authority, and the claims a state makes upon its people for deference to rules, laws and norms"[2]. This is a lofty accolade bestowed upon a collective body of mostly dedicated, but primarily fragmented individuals, agencies and jurisdictions.

Because conditions of employment often involve long hours, low pay, high risk and detrimental stress, it is vital that the profession is seen as a calling to serve more than a career. This attachment to an altruistic ideal contributes to the mystery of a fraternal history steeped in tradition, symbolism and ritualism. It is also an oxymoronic combination of reliance upon doing the job "by the book," and conforming to a cultural code of expectant behaviors undocumented within any official police manual. Much of this tradition is bound by a code of silence that serves to protect the vested authority for serving as the state's arm of violence for exacting societal conformance to laws. The "code" and the abstract concept of the "thin blue line" solidify participant loyalties, while excluding the served public from engagement or accountability purposes.

These elements make policing unique to all other American occupations. The autonomy of operations involved with the profession creates a social barrier protected by the officers' code of silence. Operating in this vacuum apart from public accountability sometimes fosters an environment for behavior outside of the same laws the institution is charged with enforcing. While previous works have explained the code of silence as a by-product of the policing culture, this examination identifies it as fundamental for maintaining the covenant of the dark blue fraternity. It is this same "code" that contributes to the perpetuation of illicit and illegal behaviors encouraging good cops to go bad.

While policing may share similarities with other hierarchical-based professions separating individuals into groups based on skill-set, specialization and assignment, it remains unique in its authorization to use force, deadly force if justified upon the very citizens sworn to protect. This creates an institutionalized confliction causing distress of loyalties to the organizational objectives. In actuality, the confliction of purpose begins the very day the cadet enters an academy setting that stresses uniformity and singular focus of mission. Upon graduation, that same rookie officer is mentored by seasoned officers encouraging them to forget the academy instruction for the sake of maintaining an established status quo. Throughout the career, the officer is assigned into a multiplicity of segregated "pockets" within the agency's structure.

Each fragmented section expects behavior most conducive to their immediate goals, while the organizational vision comes secondary at best. This progressively diminishes the institutional commitment of the individual officers and the effectiveness of the organization's service delivery system. This organizational segregation decreases the esprit de corps enjoyed earlier in an officer's career. Once an officer moves into a high-skill set assignment with a special operations group (SOG), they become even further separated from the central ideals of duty, honor and service and adopt informal oaths to the fragmented subcultures.

This investigation shows the process of occupational socialization and segregation as ushering officers into a state of "becoming blue," or the enculturation of expectant behavior and actions. The process of becoming blue is defined as civilians becoming informally indoctrinated into the fraternity of law enforcement's restricted access society separating idealistic public servants from SOG Operators enmeshed in a destructive cycle of subcultural self-allegiance. The further distancing of individual officers from the organizational core ideals into specialized assignments without appropriate monitoring measures fosters deviant subcultures. These informal alliances separate the officer from the institutional mission[3] and encourage a self-serving ethos identifying officers with a labeling of deviance. It is not uncommon for officers to create informal clubs or subcultures where behaving badly become the norm, i.e... The Bad Boys.

Figure 1.1: is an illustration marketing the SWAT warrior mindset. *Source*: Reprinted with permission from Special Forces Gear, online at www.specialforces.com

How badly the boys behave depends more on the degree of commitment to the subculture than the professional assignment. Before blaming the officers too harshly, it is important to understand the external influences at work. There is a powerfully seductive phenomenon drawing people into the world of policing and consumes them like an intoxicating drug. There are studies[4] showing that once a person shares certain experiences, it is difficult for them to wholly return to the person they once were. The process of occupational socialization (fitting in) involves transitioning phases, like passage ways throughout the journey of one's career. These transitions are referred to as liminal stages, and are complex periods leading to sometimes dramatic changes in a personality, behavior or professional ethos.

Liminality

The concept of liminality is important to discuss at this point because it was the development of this classic anthropological term that shed the light on processes of officers sliding into the darkest shades of blue, and potentially becoming bad. To understand this concept is to establish a foundation for gaining an answer to the question; "Why do good cops go bad?"

The original term "limen" in Latin means "threshold." It was first used to describe a state of ambiguous transition during rituals where a perceptual, attitudinal or conceptual change was expected to result by completion of the act. Participants caught in the "threshold" between where they were prior to the ritual, and not yet where they would be, found themselves at this liminal stage. Theoretically, the individual experiencing this transition becomes open or vulnerable about alternatives to their current state of comprehension and reality. The phenomenon of liminality is further and formally described in an anthropological context as a period of transition where normal limits to thought, self-understanding, and behavior are relaxed - a situation which can lead to new perspectives. It refers to the phase as a "betwix and between" period.[5]

An officer may transition through six phases during their career along the path to becoming fully socialized, or darkest blue. These transitional phases include passages through occupational, social, ethical, and experiential thresholds. Each of these phases has the potential for reversing previously preconceived postures and understandings about particular fraternal expectancies involved in the profession of policing or the cop culture. This includes the effects on individuals transitioning from civilian life to policing and also the officers moving from traditional policing roles into the irregular subculture of the SOG.

A practical example includes a former police academy cadet trained to protect and serve her community. She is instructed on the detection and apprehension of impaired drivers and knows the dangers of alcohol abuse. Having no history of personal alcoholism, it is inconceivable that this officer would engage in that destructive behavior. Although trained and certified to carry a firearm in the course of her duties, the reality is this officer has no level of experience with the taking of another person's life.

This officer responds to a call in progress and is presented with a dangerous situation involving a violator brandishing a firearm. The duly trained officer justifiably uses her firearm and neutralizes the threat. The suspect is killed; the officer is cleared through administrative channels and a district attorney's grand jury. It would be logical to welcome the officer back to duty with the respect and appreciation of her peers.

That welcome back scenario is often an unrealistic docudrama. The reality is that this officer has entered the threshold between the public servant she was and the killer she has become. She is ostracized by her peers, misunderstood by her family and personally torn by the transitioning phases of where she was comfortable in existence, and where the confliction of self is forcing her. This is liminality, and she is vulnerable to the temporary dissolution of her once high ethical standards and the continuation of potentially detrimental behavior leading to alcoholism, depression or suicide.

This is an unfortunate but extreme instance. Other daily examples of the liminal phases of transitions leading moral public servants into abnormal behaviors include exchanging leniency for gratuities, sex or cash payments. A final example is the officer who uses excessive force while executing an arrest, but receives no reprimand. The immediate peer approval creates a conflict of obligation between moral and legal behavior versus the cultural expectations required for fitting in by using excessive force. The officer becomes vulnerable to the transformational phase for committing to a path of continued illicit behavior for the sake of social acceptance.

The threshold between what was done correctly, and what is inappropriately expected has a powerful influence on affecting the future behavior of individuals. It is important that liminality is discussed early in this work, as the remainder of the investigation is based upon the principle. For the cop or civilian reader, it is also like the cheating spouse who escaped undetected; they will always have that guilt of being unfaithful, or fear of getting caught. The liminal transition they experienced was having become weak. Maybe there was never intention to stray, yet the seduction of power, sex, notoriety or money has a way of clouding one's judgment, and that spouse, caught or not is never the same.

Though the effects of liminality on the SOG vary by degrees of tension and separation from institutional ideals, this urban affairs project shows an associational relationship between liminality and the trajectory of socialization and the potential for going bad. This state of transition may present itself as a continuing evolution beginning with the civilian-to-officer assimilation and continue as the officer moves beyond the thin blue line from traditional policing assignments and into the covert or specialized environments. This holds true for cops who take an oath serving as society's protector, their strength, and moral entrepreneur. Gradually, they begrudgingly discover their frailty veiled in the mystique of the thin blue line. They are reminded, though acceptance does not come easily, that they are indeed; human

Standing at the Threshold of the Thin Blue Line

This transformational process from unrealistic expectations to unimaginable cultural demands has the potential to occur each time a person decides to join law enforcement. They have an anticipation of what they think the job involves based on faulty perceptions shaped by media and movies. Once they enter the profession and attend a police academy, their idea of policing changes drastically.

The person's opinions and attitudes begin changing rapidly, and they become very similar to the officers training them. That is the idea behind enculturation. To introduce others into the formal and informal ways of performing within a group so that they "fit in." This process of shape changing does not stop once out of the academy. It continues throughout a career. The degree to which officers become entrapped in the subculture where deviance is the rule and living on the edge is the standard depends upon the individual's assignments and depth of commitment to the attraction of behaving badly.

Because an assignment into the SOG usually involves operating autonomously, and socializing less with traditional officers such as Patrol and Detectives, Operators tend to sink deeper into the nonconformity that remains hidden behind the thin blue line. They also separate more quickly from the agency's core ideals while committed to the covert environment of the SOG. Once a detachment from those ideals begins through the phases of liminality, the good officer begins to go bad.

Behaving Badly

The "thin blue line" is an abstract concept commonly used to represent the position law enforcement holds in society standing between honest citizens and criminals. Standing in this gap for protecting society, places SOG Operators on the legal, ethical and societal fringe where temptations become the standard. Deviance is associated with behaviors differing from the traditional norms of society and policing. Examples of decadent behavior include alcohol consumption, violence, sex, discriminatory practices and risk-taking and societal fringe lifestyles encroaching upon criminal activities and placing officers upon a slippery slope.

The image of a slippery slope[6] describes the social and psychological process where once ethical candidates for the police service begin to experiment with abnormal behaviors. If the officer is not held accountable or reprimanded for this behavior, it opens the door for a continuation and increase of frequency and severity. The matrix of decision and consequences is influential for serving as a deterrent to unethical or illegal behavior. Yet many of the introductory actions of fringe behavior are not illegal and only boarder line infractions of policy. It is the decision without consequences fostering the perception that the behavior is acceptable, though not justified. The continuation of this behavior without consequence does not always equate to an increase in the level of illicit behavior, but does fail to detect and deter future activities. Officers experiencing a depth of aberration find themselves bumping up to criminality.

Grass-Eaters versus Meat-Eaters

The metaphor of the slippery slope illustrates bad behavior on various degrees of severity referred to as either grass-eaters or meat-eaters[7]. The less threatening officers falling into a fringe subculture classified as grass-eaters may get involved with acts such as using alcohol on duty, sex, and execution of unjustifiable violence. Does becoming a grass-eater mean the officer has gone badly? Well, it does mean they have become a product of their immediate environment.

A specific environment or police beat may have previously established deep roots of deprivation. The tempted rookie officer may be just become one of generations of officers who have become socialized to understand that to fit in with their squad, precinct or partner, it is an expected behavior. Other low-level fringe behavior may also be a once or rare occurrence involving a brief sexual affair, or an arrest with an application of unjustifiably excessive force used to "teach the perp a lesson." Either way, the cop culture provides protection for officers choosing to engage in the dishonest behaviors through the conceptual virtues of the line and the code.

This is not a broad brush stroke indictment of all officers. It is vital to understand the frailty of human temptation and the constant barrage of "offers" made to officers in an atmosphere of moderate accountability and high operational autonomy. This level of illicit offerings may range from free coffee at a convenience store, to illegally gained pain medication to help make it through shift work wearing a heavy gun belt with an injured back. Where is the line drawn between a generous showing of appreciation and unethical conduct?

The meat-eaters are the more dangerous, as they have become committed to living a life outside the law and within the criminalistic fringe lifestyle. They participate in bribe taking, accepting favors for preferential treatment, extortion, or even murder. These officers do not think their behavior is unethical or even illegal. They attempt to rationalize deviant behavior by using their "vocabularies of motive[8]." This is a tactic referred to as "neutralization theory," where an individual may use distorted logic to explain irregular behaviors. An example used by a thief might be; because he had two cars and I have none, it is okay that I take one.

The dynamics of groupthink[9] also influence the behaviors, attitudes and actions of multiple individuals engaged in similar activities. The profession of policing is hinged upon homogeneity, so it is vital that officers look, act and respond the same way. The groupthink dynamic is nearly synonymous with the standardized practices of a singularly focused law enforcement organization. It also serves as a form of cultural assurance against officers causing friction by reporting illegitimate behaviors committed in violation of those standardized policies.

We have covered social science theories heavily saturated in anthropology and sociology particular to law enforcement's direct applications to liminality, neutralization and groupthink. This is not a cop only phenomenon. The following section is to demonstrate the powerful draw of external social influencers when the "perfect storm" brews, and susceptible victims are mistreated for the sake of hedonistic desire.

Priests, Prostitutes and Penn State

Police are not the only ones behaving badly. The dynamic of groupthink and deviance is the same in other mainstream cultures where a group of similar people use force, threats, intimidation or power to gain influence over others. This is done so their assembly may enjoy whichever vice they please, no matter how decadent, illegal or damaging to their victims, organizations or the public trust.

Recently, high profile scandals bring professions into the public light such as priests (ex: Catholic Church sex abuse cases), coaches (ex: Penn State football sex abuse scandal), federal employees and military (ex: U.S. Secret Service/ Army's Cartagena, Colombia prostitution scandal.) These environments are dominated by homogeneous people in positions of influence. The deviating subculture of "hegemonic masculinity" is where control over others is exercised. They justify their antisocial behavior as necessary, and are willing to risk the positive purposes for which the original culture began.

One of the four primary observations made about cop culture and its influence on deviant behavior is the term coined, "detrimental homogenetic entitlement." It reflects a deviant culture dominated by a select group of similar race, alpha males operating behind a veil of secrecy who inject force or intimidation as a resource for securing the desired outcomes of the cohesive group. There is a negative outcome associated with operating within this culture of assumed entitlement as the select individuals become vulnerable to personal and professional damages. The subculture of the SOG fosters this homogenous membership of alpha male Operators, who by the covert nature of their assignment are allowed extending degrees of latitude.

This is not a comparative analysis between law enforcement, sport coaches, priests, prostitutes and military. It is presented as an illustration that the same dynamics of liminality, occupational socialization and institutionalized specialization without core value accountability and transparency, produces similar results in seemingly divergent areas. Beyond these examples used for their high profile coverage and societal shock, every group has the potential to experience sub-sets fragmenting from institutional ideals that degenerate into forbidden practices.

Looking through a lens of cultural anthropology allows an opportunity to examine the links between liminality and law enforcement's informal processes for fitting in, and the path for good cops to go bad. The theories of neutralization, groupthink and liminality provide a foundation for the remainder of this work. Now that we have a sense of what the goal is, let's examine the focus of the study and how the SOG came to be included.

2

SPECIAL OPERATIONS GROUPS

"If Not Us, Who?"
(Louisiana SWAT unit motto)

Understanding the informal processes of socialization, and how fitting in affects idealistic recruits, cadets and officers who succumb to the pressures of expected illicit or illegal behavior helps us comprehend the ethical slide. The unit selected as the focus of this project has the greatest potential for experiencing the transformations of liminality. The examination of liminality should not be viewed as something mysterious. Instead it is studied in the context of a series of logical progressions through the occupational trajectory of a career. Most frequently an officer realizes these stage changes because of a failure of the institution to properly supervise and hold the individual responsible. A series of "If This, Then That" logic matrixes better serves to illustrate the points of transition. In an institution founded upon strict adherence to policies and regulations for efficiency, effectiveness and safety; supervision and management are critical. The absence of these promotes an atmosphere for irregular behaviors based on a lack of consequences for improper decisions.

Table 2.1 - The "If This, Then That" model, illustrates the effects of failed supervisor accountability on discouraging bad behavior. *Source* :(original figure produced by Dr. Scott Silverii for *Cop Culture: Why Good Cops Go Bad*.)

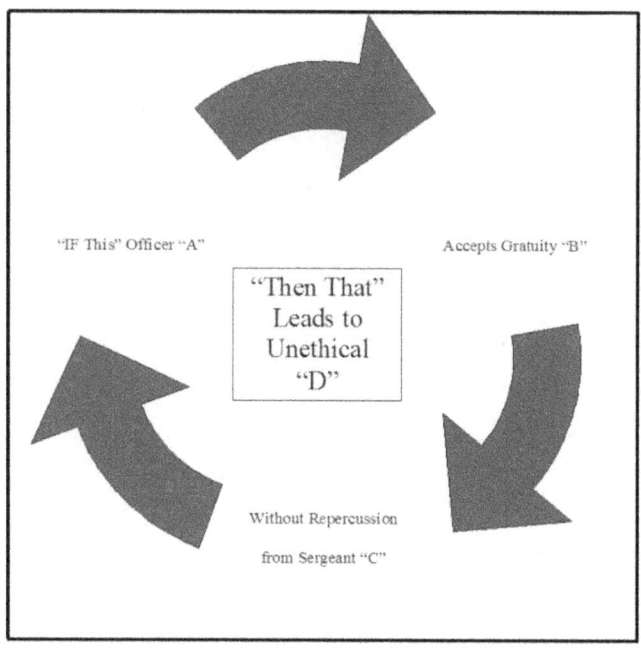

To facilitate this social science experiment, I select a unit of analysis entrenched in an environment of temptation potential and need for strict adherence to rules of accountability and transparency. A finite sample of officers (SOG) who exemplify deep levels of fraternal unity, while experiencing great exposure to environments of temptations is selected as the focus of this work. Law enforcement's special operations groups include many areas of concentration and degrees of collective associations. Although the SOG represents a small percentage of the total policing population, the observations and conclusions are universally applicable through this and other institutions with similar ecologies of work environments because of the shared variables of socialization. These units offer the example of individuals having successfully completed the application and hiring process, the initial indoctrination process, job-related field training and have moved onto become fully socialized to have earned the ability to achieve additional assignment or recognition in their particular field.

Focus Group

The selection of the Special Operations Group (SOG) for examination was purposeful. There are many assignments in law enforcement falling under the category of SOG to include; K-9 teams, counter-terrorism units, water patrol units, explosive ordnance disposal, divers, mounted divisions, motorcycle patrols, mountain search and rescue teams and air patrol units just to name a few. My work uses the Special Weapons And Tactics (SWAT) and Narcotics Operators as the sample population. Cops use the term "Operator" for officers in the SOG. Operators mostly call themselves by this term as a distinction and a way to further separate themselves from the non-SOG officers such as Patrol and Detectives. The extra closeness between Operators comes as a result of their mission focus, and that their performance and very survival depends on the ability to work as a singularly cohesive unit.

These two units (SWAT and Narcotics) differ from the other SOG work primarily because their missions often demand operational autonomy, covert training, secreted assignments, and supervisory authority outside the typical chain-of-command. They also require depersonalization by concealing their identities (SWAT – heavy armor and Nomex balaclava, Narcotics – undercover identities); the use of long surveillance periods followed by brief, potentially violent actions (SWAT hostage rescue or Narcotics undercover purchase of illegal drugs or weapons from dangerous felons) and regularly operate segregated from the assistance of non-SOG officers such as Patrol and Detectives. Many local law enforcement agencies do not support a full-time SWAT unit, and therefore combine special operations assignments. Narcotics assignments include the execution of high risk operations requiring the activation of SWAT and therefore many SWAT Operators are also Undercover Agents.

The selection of Narcotics Operators was also decided because of their uniquely pre-emptive nature in the policing profession. The fascinating uses of modern undercover operations have their roots in Europe's eighteenth century. France's Francois Vidocq, a former fugitive from justice, turned detective understood that to catch a criminal, the police have to think and act on their level. He coined the term "it takes a thief to catch a thief" and utilized that philosophy successfully by hiring secret detectives who were former criminals. The idea that crime can only be fought by criminals allowed him tremendous success in making significant arrests in the Paris underworld by making use of role-playing to allow officers to become indistinguishable from criminals[1]. The United States law enforcement milieu does not make a practice of hiring criminals as detectives, so who are the SOG Operators and how are they chosen from among the 683,396 full- time state and local law enforcement officers in the United States?

Since World War II, the government has worked to identify characterizes of a successful undercover agent for national and law enforcement interests. The conflict begins when an officer is recruited based on performance measures to include good judgment and integrity, and then asked to falsify their identity to misrepresent themselves to others for the sake of detecting crime.

Undercover Agents proactively seek out drug dealers in an effort to engage them for conducting illegal transactions for narcotics. This policing style rests at the opposite end of the response spectrum as compared to a Patrol Officer who reactively responds to calls for service because a crime has already been committed. As we continue into this work, a deeper and more complex description and explanations of the nature of Narcotics operations will be discussed as it relates to the process of fitting in.

The selection of SWAT is also useful because many of the other disciplines of SOG fall within the umbrella of a SWAT operation. This may include K-9 teams searching for fugitives, explosive ordinance disposal units clearing suspicious packages, or water and mounted patrol units searching for a missing person. Unlike the isolated Narcotics operation, SWAT allows an ebb and flow of resources as required by mission objective. Ironically, it is this introduction of "outsiders" that uniquely contributes to the fraternal bonds of SWAT Operators uniting against them, and shall also be further examined.

Why SOG?
The most practical explanation for selecting SWAT and Narcotics Operators as the focus of investigation is because I spent the majority of my career assigned to both SOG units. I served 12 years working undercover and supervising a multi-jurisdictional drug task force. This service also includes 3 years assigned full-time to a Drug Enforcement Administrations (DEA) Task Force.

SWAT service includes 16 years collateral duty that began in 1991 and extended through the evolution of tactical responses ranging from blue jeans and badge chains to sophisticated tactical equipment and advanced training. I have experienced the gamut from drug warrants, active school shooter, fugitive barricade apprehension, hostage rescue, Hurricane Katrina response and Commission on Accreditation for Law Enforcement Agencies (CALEA) accreditation of policies and procedures.

SWAT and Narcotics Operators are what and who I know best. There would be no way of gaining access into their closed circles had I not been in this world for so many years. I earned my stripes, my ink, and their trust in the margins of the SOG, and anyone trying to twist the truth about experiences shared with me would be detected as fiction. Conducting a study of this depth requires a keen sense of slicing through the "war stories" cops love to share, and revealing the truth about the great things we do, and the things we must do better.

Figure 2.2 – Author participating in advanced SWAT "Officer Rescue" training. *Source:* Photograph is original property of Dr. Scott Silverii

There is a bond between SOG Operators beyond what I've experienced with any other discipline in law enforcement. It's not better, just different. Until you have known the experience of completing a drug deal and your only protection is your partner listening to the body wire; you have not understood. Until you have willingly taken the point position in a tactical stack and are willing to engage the initial volley of gun fire for the sake of your team's safety; you have not understood. Until you look your brother in blue in his worried gray face, and he tells you he is going to take his life; you have not understood.

This is by no means an attempt to romanticize of the SOG lifestyle. Living on the edge in these often risk-all assignments create elevated levels of danger and adrenaline. This is part of the elixir of the SOG's intoxication and passageways into bad behaviors. Unfortunately, this also means Operators often live alone or spend time away from family and civilian friends. This separation may be harmful to their personal lives and to the effectiveness of their career. And if the tension to your personal life is not overwrought enough, the SOG's exposures to antisocial behavior, violence, drugs, weapons and extreme hazards may prevent the Operator from transferring back into a more traditional, non-SOG role, and ultimately the ability to protect the public.[2]

Interviews and observations of hundreds of cops show that it's hard to back away from the edge and return to traditional policing. The rush of danger attracts, keeps and consumes Operators. After SOG, most else seems boring. While it is easy to see why this life-style is potentially damaging to the individual officer, other questions must be asked. What affect do the negative processes acquired during liminality have on the ability of the organization to provide competent public safety services? In a profession based on uniformity of effort and standardization of response, does the perpetuation of subcultures (detrimental homogenetic entitlement) form cracks in the organization's core? Is there a point of diminishing returns where the fragmentation renders an agency less efficient for or incapable of providing professional domestic protection?

SWAT – Behind the Ballistic Shield

The Special Weapons and Tactics unit referred generically to as SWAT is of particular interest to me other than having spent over half of my career in that discipline. It is unique in many ways and this usually lends itself to erroneous public perceptions associated with excessive force and violence. While this is not an exercise in tactics, it is important to discuss the function of SWAT. The SOG holds a critical role in the creation of fragmenting subcultures within an institution. Unlike Narcotics Operators who are usually segregated from the entirety of the organization, SWAT Operators primarily serve collateral duties in more traditional roles like Patrol Officer, Detective, or K-9 Handler. This creates a duality of conflict for the individual officer as they regularly mingle with the general population of officers, yet experience institutional segregations from the mainstream ideologies and practices of regular policing.

Figure 2.3 – Author's SWAT unit approaching target while wearing chemical suits and SCBA *Source:* Photograph is original property of Dr. Scott Silverii

This element becomes an area of increasing concern as law enforcement in the United States continues to move towards militarization[3]. More officers than ever before are receiving SWAT type training, equipment and duty assignments. Whether a full-time task or part-time participation, the dynamics of socialization becomes engaged and the various degrees of tension affect officers involved in the SWAT ramp up. This group is naturally bound together by the small group tactics required to operate in hostile environments. Homogeneity is critical, as uniformity and total compliance with standard operating procedures drive these operations.

The reliance on team unity, mixed with the adrenaline of training and responding to the most dangerous and complex crimes in progress create a synergy that separates SWAT from traditional policing. While Undercover Agents are looked down upon as being "grey" cops operating within the unethical margins of policing, SWAT Operators are touted as being the best of the very best, but ostracized due to a conception of elitism. The application, mental, physical, shooting, and skills requirements do ascribe these officers into a specialized class, and it is this distinction that begins their journey towards institutionalized segregation.

SWAT Operators are trained to kill. That is the reality of the craft. While administrators promote their life saving and peace-keeping capabilities, Operators spend more time shooting than applying bandages. It is the desensitization to extreme violence, death and weapons of destruction that fuel the anti-social mentality and outlaw gang-like behavioral similarities. Despite the disciplined propensity towards violence and destruction potential these units possess, American law enforcement is progressively moving towards further militarization of policing[4].

A Look Back Before Ahead

Specialized units have been used in times of conflict resolution dating back to the Revolutionary War. Sharpshooters and small group tactics were deployed to counter the traditional military strategies mastered by the British. While not a comprehensive battle plan, the mission specific application of these bands of brothers created confusion amongst the ranks and helped "even the field" against a superior force. This guerilla warfare provided an alternative resource and benefit to the daily standards known to conventional war fighting at that time. The men making up these sniper units and small tactical advance teams were often heralded as heroes.

A brief example of the powerful influence of a singularly well-trained asset is the story of Timothy Murphy (1751 – 1818) who is credited with killing Sir Francis Clerke and General Simon Fraser of the invading British army during a pivotal point in the war for America's freedom at the Second Battle of Saratoga. One of only 500 hand-picked soldiers to join the Sharpshooting Corps, Murphy reportedly killed both influential officers from an unheard of distance of about 300 yards. These sniper shots were taken against high-ranking British officers during a period when conventional military courtesies did not allow for the targeting of certain ranks. Murphy, still celebrated as a hero in his hometown in New York changed that practice and the architecture of war fighting. Like today's SWAT Operator, not better than the others, just different.

Former Los Angeles Police Department (LAPD) Chief Daryl Gates is credited with being the "Father of SWAT." Its formation was an initiative he undertook while serving as an inspector for the agency. While LAPD certainly advanced the concept of a tactical unit made up of a distinctive selection of officers, the origin of the crisis response model began in Delano, California. A special response unit was created to address protests led by a local farm workers' union. LAPD observed the effectiveness of the operation and quickly replicated the model for resolving situations beyond the capabilities of traditional officers. An initial cadre of 60 officers, mostly military veterans, were segregated from the field of regular duty officers and provided special training, equipment and weapons.[5]

In the earliest evolution of SWAT, it is easy to understand the potential for institutional animosity towards the selected group. Extracting officers from among their peers, not only creates an atmosphere of resentment by the officers not chosen, but creates a unique bond by those who are singled out. The additional element of danger included as part of the duty, promotes closeness within the unit. This danger may lead to a risk-all environment and the draw to society's edge. Once individuals are isolated and set apart from the core ideology of the institution without mainstream supervision or accountability, the potential arises for subcultural fringe behavior. The elements required for the application of heterogenic masculinity also became present as these hand-picked officers shared the same characteristics of gender, race, age, and background (military) and were isolated from traditional organizational accountability by creating a separate supervisory channel, Platoon "D."

Despite the risk to the occupational ecology, the LAPD engrained the SWAT model into their institutional practice and psyche following a violent shoot-out with a terrorist faction, the Symbionese Liberation Army (SLA) in 1974. A report following that benchmark incident supported the full-time activation of a specialized tactical response unit based on;

- Riots and civil unrest. Most particularly, LAPD was unprepared, untrained and unequipped to address the Watts Riots.
- Criminals' use of long-range guns causing disorder and chaos was emerging.
- The appearance of the political assassin
- Violent confrontations between LAPD and urban militant groups like the Black Panther Party and the SLA required a specialized response.

The post-incident recommendation report highlighted that using traditional police resources for addressing any of these type situations would increase the likelihood of an officers being killed or injured and the violators escaping apprehension. This official endorsement supporting SOG response capabilities over those of traditional police officers reversed a practice used for centuries, and relegated SWAT to an elite assignment and segregated community of employees.

SWAT has gained media and movie notoriety starting with the short-lived television series of 1975 – 1976, "SWAT." This celebrity, associated with membership added to the further separation from traditional officers, and an autonomous and secretive existence. The mysteriousness of heavily clad and armored officers with their identities concealed by balaclava hoods pursuing society's most violent criminals led to popular movie representations such as the 2003 remake of "SWAT," popular television series "Dallas SWAT" and "Detroit SWAT" and an extremely successful video game series, SWAT as narrated by Chief Gates.

The roots were planted by the LAPD, and seeded by legitimate crisis response calls, but also opportunities for unwarranted over-utilizations. Agencies caught in the lure of media hype or federal grant funding opportunities began creating SWAT units without justification or need. A look at the militarization of American policing demonstrates that the desire often fails to match the demand.

Militarization Culture

SWAT's existence and membership may cause tension within the organization it is intended to serve, but it has definitely become a source of concern for communities across America[6]. The challenge presents itself with gaining political and sociological acceptance because of the dramatic increase in the use of SWAT for conducting specialized risk management as well as traditional policing activities[7]. The practice of militarization within the ranks of the United States' civil law enforcement community continues to reveal the stark contrast and lack of agreement among theory relative to addressing the question of the roles of local law enforcement in emergency management.

Historically the lines between civilian police and the United States military were very clear. Neither shared cross-jurisdictional authority, scope of responsibility or even similar legal justification or doctrine. The only connections between the two were the numbers of men and women who had formerly served in the military and came to work as a police officer. Federal agencies even allow for special veteran status points in competitive hiring processes. Yet the idea of the two forces becoming united to address local issues of crime and deterrence were unthinkable until recent[8].

This normalization of military doctrine into the mainstream policing community can be linked to the metaphors used in the 1980s "War on Drugs". This shift away from community policing and public servants took on the ideology for use of force and domination as an appropriate method of solving problems. To successfully make the shift from routine patrol beats by uniformed community officers, these agencies embraced the "warrior" mentality, and looked to the military for direction in accomplishing the paradigm shift.

The emphasis on military power, hardware and technology became the norm for local law enforcement SWAT units. Federal funding flowed to support the war on drugs and political leaders, who were once opposed to the aggressive militarization of their civil police forces, accepted the monies and the increasingly aggressive nature of specialized tactical units operating within their ranks.

Since the terrorists events of September11, 2001 the increase of SWAT was almost expected and in other studies of local law enforcement agencies' ability to prepare for terrorist threats and incidents, even identify the existence of a SWAT within that agency became a predictor of preparedness[9]. The cultural ideology of agencies has shifted from hosting SWAT as a necessary resource for matching the armed criminal's level of violence, to the post 9/11 first-line of defense for the community and other officers against terrorists.

Over 89 percent of cities with a population of at least 50,000 and 100 sworn officers field a SWAT unit. Of those agencies without a team, over 20 percent suggested they were preparing to start one within the coming years. Additionally, the justification for maintaining this type of expensive resource is based on need. Although call-outs averaged about one per month during the 1980's, the SWAT units demand had increased by 538 percent during the mid-1990's height of the War on Drugs[10]. Despite other research encouraging the Community Oriented Policy (COP) model to address anti-terrorism activities within local jurisdictions, more agencies appear to be embracing the militarization of their police patrols in contrast to public appeal.

From 1982 to 1989 there was an increase of 292 percent in law enforcement agencies incorporating SWAT into daily activity. This continues to show a marked normalizing of militarization of the nation's police forces and the societal acceptance of being patrolled by them. The concern that raises from these types of results show local law enforcement agencies more closely aligning themselves to the military Special Forces ethos of elite small unit tactics without having the practical experience, training or resources to actually manage a crisis situation involving terrorist threats or assaults.

This uncontrolled growth also provided for uncontrolled standards and practices for SWAT Operators and operations. Tactics ranging from kicking in a suspect's door and everyone rushes in; to specialized military style tactics have been employed. Personnel standards included everyone from former military to the best deer hunters. This myriad of standards created an environment for deviance that attracted the most aggressive and violent officers from an agency's force. The early years of SWAT, the 1960's and 70's, promoted Wild West shoot-outs without containment or concern for collateral damage. It was this aggression-fed fraternity that separated the Operators from the community service-minded officers participating in programs focusing on community oriented policing.

These results also demonstrate that this "forced-feed" of the SWAT element into agencies that simply fail to show the need, is unnecessarily and possibly unwittingly promoting the subcultural fragmentation of its own workforce and opening new opportunities for the seductive draw away from the core values of community service policing in lieu of allegiance to the smaller band of SOG Operators. Whether the community's need requires the application of SWAT or not, these units exist and so do the dynamics associated with fitting in. In the next chapter we will look at the challenges of breaching these close-knit communities of SOG Operators for the purpose of studying them.

3
STUDYING A SECRET CULTURE

"With their souls of patent leather, they come down the road. Hunched and nocturnal, where they breathe they impose, silence of dark rubber, and fear of fine sand."
(Federico Garcia Lorca, 1927)

To fully understand how innocent civilians fall prey to these stages of transition by simply accepting a job, we must look at the process as formally examined by researchers. Although best prepared to conduct these types of cultural studies, more than often not, "outsiders" are not welcome behind the badge. Officers refuse to participate, remain silent or give misleading information when interviewed by researchers attempting to understand their occupation and lifestyle.

However, there are several studies helping to explain the way culture works. We will discuss them to make sure this complex environment remains clear. The question of how do ethical "by-the-book" cadets transition from public servants to professional deviants is the focus of this section. The story of those vested to serve as society's moral entrepreneur, yet shifting paradigms for living life on the fringe is fascinating and complex. We will go to the heart of the matter with relevant research on the subject.

As stated, cops do not trust outsiders asking questions. When deciding to undertake this challenge of understanding a subculture to which I once belonged, I was confident my history in the SOG would open doors where others were forbidden. The code of silence prevented other researchers from going inside the subculture, so I knew this would be my opportunity to examine something new, unchartered and mostly; important for the cop culture to understand the external forces affecting it. Anthropology, the study of cultures, became my mechanism for asking the right questions and getting the honest answers. Conducting this ethnography most closely resembles the police work I knew best by conducting investigations into people and occurrences.

I use the lessons from those social science disciplines to design the ethnographic examination. Now, if my old partners heard me using these terms, it would have been a fist fight, but it only refers to investigating the lives of a cultural group by using field study. The SOG calls it surveillance. The best place to begin any investigation is at the core of the issue. The SOG are the darkest of blue, and either live or imitate an outlying lifestyle in their dress, deed and word. Yet, when the proverbial "crap hits the fan," these are the officers you want with you. I lived the SOG life for 16 years, but having distanced myself from the subculture and gaining an academic perspective through theory, I now see it through a different lens.

After years of researching this topic, I am aware that there is a void in the academic body of knowledge about the SOG subculture. This work is the first to combine the unrestricted entrée into the fraternity to an experienced SOG Operator and a formally trained social scientist. It was also because of this earned access to these officers, I have ensured their story, my story, and our story is told with accuracy, honesty, and complete openness. Whether it is watching handcuffs placed on a once great cop, or hearing rookies talk about the sex they had with people they meet on duty, it never benefits a society when good cops go bad.

Investigative Objective

A stated goal for exploring the SOG is understanding how officers evolve from being new cadets with idealistic notions, until they reach a point of accepting illicit or illegal behavior as appropriate. Please understand not every officer transitions along an illicit pathway of occupational trajectory, but everyone experiences changes in their worldview perspective. I wanted to know, and I trust you do too, about this process that demands deviant behavior as a tithing to the brotherhood of blue.

Earlier, I mentioned this book is not just about cops, and that the culture is based on organizational theories relating to other groups with similar dynamics. This investigation into the cop culture relates to any group of employees (members) experiencing changes of perspectives as a result of the pressures to fit in. The SOG demonstrates how subcultures with exposure to specialized, autonomous assignments can lead to them breaking away from the core values, and its ultimate effect on organizational congruity.

By demystifying the SOG, it becomes clear that they are products of organizational division through the process of socialization. To advance our exploration for discovering why good cops go bad, the text is divided into major categories; occupational socialization, police culture, and organizational detection of problematic behavior (policing police), with each holding clues to the final answer.

Challenges for Cultural Research

While studies exist on the topics of organizational structures, deviant behavior and policing, almost no information is available describing the SOG subculture. Failures in past literature[1] often cite the lack of access as the main problem. Researchers struggle with limited entree, forcing them to rely on outside observations, available policies, and agency information made public. Access into the SOG is restricted[2] due to several reasons including the covert nature of the assignment, the disengaged positioning from the public, secreted policing traditions, and an impenetrable code of silence. This causes a misunderstanding of policing's clandestine mission, leaving it a mystery to civilians and researchers.

The main failure in researching cop culture is described in a study of police corruption[3] as it relates to occupational socialization. Although best attempts are made, the civilian researcher[4] is still unable to breach the thin blue line. The code of silence is an unwritten rule among police for not reporting another officer's errors, misconducts or crimes. If questioned about an incident of misconduct involving another officer, the officer may claim ignorance. The code of silence as an expectant mandate[5] among officers to remain quiet about reporting or confronting other officers engaged in illicit, immoral, or illegal activities.

A study by the United States Department of Justice (DOJ) reveals an adversarial culture does exist for honoring the code of silence. This study[6] shows the historical limitation of valid data collection from cops. Officers do not trust anyone outside their circle, and researchers asking questions about corruption results in either limited participation, or unreliable results. Because of this adversarial relationship, institutional mechanisms created to identify the presence of officer behavior non-conducive to the mission of public service falls short in producing a comprehensive matrix for early reporting, intervention and remediation of illegitimate or illegal actions. An example of this problem was witnessed by psychologists[7] examining qualities for selecting successful undercover agents.

The requirements for entering the SOG as a Narcotics Operator are fraught with contradicting characteristics for recruiting ethical candidates for undercover work. Officers are selected based on high-performance and past ethical behavior. Because of the temptations associated with undercover operations, it is critical to identify candidates whose past practices demonstrate an ability to avoid abnormal behavior. In stark contrast to the individual's exemplary work performance leading to an assignment into the SOG, this officer is now trained that conducting undercover operations requires an ability to manipulate and lie to the public as a benchmark of their professional success. This bipolar requirement for success shows how difficult it is for officers to practice ethical behavior[8] and expect to enjoy a healthy career. Instances like these are practiced every day in policing and show how easily these paths lead cops into a fringe existence and to a point of departure from organizational values.

Deficiencies in Current Literature

The three main categories; occupational socialization, police culture and organizational detection of problematic behavior demonstrate the complexity of policing. I use related studies where appropriate for showing connections and comparisons to the policing milieu, the career trajectories and the deviant subcultures leading officers from academy cadet to SOG. With the exception of former police officer, now researcher Librett's[9] access into the professional environment, the cited researchers express difficulties and limitations securing access into the culture. Because the cop culture is secretive and maintains the code of silence, academic studies have failed to produce holistically credible, detailed investigations about the world of the SOG Operator.

Other challenges in conducting my investigation include limited resources for examining the fringe behavior of the SOG, and the pack mentality of groups insulated from outside opinions. The documented psychological tolls[10] affecting Operators during SOG assignments are limited due to Operators refusal to seek mental health assistance or openly speak with researchers. An attempt to study[11] SOG versus non-SOG officers provides a more recent account but results also show issues with factuality as the information provided through interviews directly conflicts with what was observed.

The final major category examines the detection of bad behavior by officers. There are disparities with identifying a standard for referring officers into an early warning system. Although the promotion of aggressive officers fitting the EWS criteria was discovered, there is nothing in current research addressing the SOG's dark blue socialization and labeling of deviance affecting the EWS referral system.

My unlimited access into the SOG allows me to fill in the gaps for a better understanding the cop culture and the SOG subcultures. I have observed and spoken with them in personal and private settings. The material I collected from Operators provides detailed information about their subculture, ideological transitions, individual and collective identities, interpersonal relationships, and their unfiltered reflective perspectives on their path for socialization.

Combined, this information provides a thorough cultural portrait of the individuals belonging to the pack-mentality of SOG. Each of the three main categories benefit from my research to include information explaining how an officer becomes socialized to embrace the fringe existence of SOG, the importance of protecting the autonomy of the blue line fraternity by practicing silence, the risk taking activities and disdain for organizational authority and its inability to detect and correct their countercultural behavior.

Significance of Studying Police Culture

Examining the effects of occupational socialization on the individual, work groups and entire institutions helps with understanding of the elements involved with the occupational socialization of highly trained skill set positions requiring organizational autonomy. Literature relating to the subtleties of workplaces and the effects of peer groups reveal a unique phenomenon within the law enforcement milieu. The autonomous assignment into the SOG creates the potential environment fertile for forbidden and fringe behavior. This fracturing of organizational ideologies[12], promotes a breaking away from the truisms of duty, honor and service. Although officers remaining in more traditional (non-SOG) assignments experience fraternal bonding, the SOG Operators devolve into an allegiance of brotherhood more binding than the oath to the agency; demanding loyalty and adherence to a different code of silence than cops in traditional assignments.

It helps to have an understanding of the elements involved with fitting into highly-trained skill set positions that encourages officers to separate themselves from the core of the agency is important. The information relating to the subtleties of workplaces and the effects of peer groups reveal a unique phenomenon.

Who Does This Affect?

This public service sector is responsible for providing civil order, rule of law and domestic protection. The community of law enforcement is often slow to recognize their vulnerabilities and the detrimental effects on officers who take the oath to protect and serve, but now also owe allegiance to SOG over the agency. The negative effects associated with fitting into the SOG are common for other disciplines associated with similar work ecologies. The difficulties of breaking the tradition of silence is compounded by the extra-ordinary experiences (criminalistic violence, exposure to the drug trade, dangerous criminals and a gun carrying culture) of the stressors placed on SOG Operators. Despite the stress it places on the officer, their family, agency and community, cops see it as breaking the code of silence for seeking professional assistance dealing with problems in their personal and professional lives. They prefer to suffer in silence. This affects everyone!

Asking the Right Questions

As any good investigator or seekers of truth know; to secure the right answers, you have to ask the right questions. Numerous challenges, goals and objectives have been proposed thus far. To ensure this research project maintained clarity of focus and level of specificity relative to conducting a cross-county multiyear study of cop culture, I relied consistently upon four primary questions. I think they provide the foundational tone for seeking answers about what honestly happens in the lives of officers that create so much personal change:

- Does assignment into the SOG cause perceptual changes specific to organizational allegiance that are detrimental to providing quality service to the public?
- Does a liminal state of ideological transition occur during the SOG socialization process that prevents the transfer back into more traditional roles of policing?
- What are the effects of occupational socialization on the personal lives of law enforcement officers assigned to SOG?
- What are the effects of occupational socialization on the professional careers of law enforcement officers assigned to SOG?

Who Benefits from Studying Police Culture?

The benefits of studying cop culture are that it applies to many audiences and disciplines ranging from academic researchers to institutional policy and decision makers. While the SOG is a unique environment, the principles of institutionalized organizations, workforce behavior, groupthink, and the detection of actions non-conducive to professionalism and productivity apply to other groups, organizations and associations.

Looking at the officer's liminal trajectory from traditional officers to countercultural SOG Operator is important because it affects public service institutions, socio-cultural structures, and law enforcement assignments. The research methodology designed for this study also allows replication for future studies. The investigation benefits policing's association with cultural anthropology, the sociology of organizations and institutions, and the psychology of antisocial / deviant workplace behaviors.

Additionally, these revelations benefit public administration and human resource managers responsible for identifying professional behaviors conducive to effective and efficient workplace productivity. The strength of this project lies in my close relationship to the highly restricted subculture of SOG, allowing for thick, rich descriptions of dialogue and observations into a society seldom seen and minimally understood.

Factors Threatening the Investigation

In every study or investigation there are issues limiting total discovery. The first challenge anticipated was the limited amount of information about the SOG subculture. Civilian social scientists have traditionally experienced roadblocks to research. While examining relevant literature in preparation for this project, I was unable to locate information targeting the SOG path along occupational trajectories, or liminality leading to behaving badly. To overcome this hurdle I use parallel literature and similar data for providing a conceptual basis for describing and understanding the culture of organizations.

Another challenge to collecting data in Louisiana and the southern United States involves the events unfolding around the New Orleans metropolitan area concerning law enforcement actions immediately following Hurricane Katrina. Notable events at the time are referred to as the Danzinger Bridge shooting and the Henry Glover murder, involving officers of the New Orleans Police Department (NOPD). During the time of interviewing and observing, six NOPD officers were under indictment by the United States Department of Justice for the deadly police shooting that occurred on the Danziger Bridge.

On Sunday, September 4, 2005, two African-Americans were killed in the gunfire and four other civilians were wounded. It is alleged that the civilians were unarmed and that the officers coordinated in fabricating a cover-up story for their crime. Each officer admitted his role in the cover-up and agreed to cooperate with the prosecution.

Prior to my final research, five NOPD officers pled guilty in the federal trial of this case. Five additional officers were convicted at trial on August 5, 2011, on a variety of charges to include civil rights and firearm offenses for unjustifiably shooting the six civilians on the bridge, and all five defendants were convicted of obstructing justice in the wake of the shooting. One last former officer was scheduled for federal trial at a later date[13].

The Henry Glover murder involved NOPD officers indicted in the death of him. Henry Glover was shot to death in the days following Hurricane Katrina, and his body was burned by officers in an effort to conceal their crime. Three officers were convicted and two were acquitted in a federal trial. Those convicted on federal charges included civil rights violations, obstruction of justice and lying to the FBI[14]. Following the convictions, the United States Attorney's prosecutor Thomas Perez states:

Instead of upholding their oath to protect and serve the people of New Orleans in the days after Hurricane Katrina, these officers violated the law and the public trust" "And while some officers broke through the thin blue line and told the truth under oath, others were rightly convicted for obstructing justice. Today's verdict brought a measure of justice to the Glover family and to the entire city[15].

These cases, and others targeting police officers for criminal indictments are causing the community of law enforcement to become more segregated from the civilian population because the code of silence was broken, and officers were held accountable for illegal actions.

The final major limitation in this study affects the perception of the SOG as having no variations of belief or behavior. I was aware of possibilities for identifying anomalies in the data I collected. I am not claiming the SOG presents itself as one hundred percent homogeneous, but the variations in the data collected were minimal. Operators claiming that they did not share the fringe lifestyle refused to participate in the interviews. This may have caused an impression of total cultural uniformity. Four Operators discontinued the interview and asked that I not mention them. Honoring the requests, there is no mention of their information except that their views were very different from the majority of others.

While acknowledging limitations of the research establishes credibility for the study, the examination of information important to how cops fit into policing's unique culture, and the difficulties of identifying bad behavior establishes the groundwork for past and current research related to these main themes. Today's cop culture is not a new phenomenon. Policing's history plays a major role for influencing the informal mandates and occupational attitudes towards the profession. The next chapter takes a look back at where we were to better understand where we are.

4

HISTORY OF POLICING IN AMERICA

Like many things American, our roots are closely tied to England. This also includes the model for law enforcement. The evolution of the cop culture throughout the history of American policing would be incomplete without an understanding of its origin. Although both organizational objectives are grounded in providing domestic public safety services, they have moved towards different directions in terms of mission and organizational structure. This point of departure will demonstrate the value of examining the history and development of policing in the United States.

English Origin

The very first attempts at organizing a formal system for protecting the community was the English tithing system that included the collective responsibility for maintaining local order. The tithing system required that every male be enrolled for police purposes to enforce the two laws against theft and murder[1]. Upon the commission of one of these two criminal offenses, the "hue and cry" signaled the marshaling of all men. The group's leader, the "reeve" ruled over geographic regions called "shires". As the words resemble, this position evolved into today's American Sheriff.

In 1066, William the conqueror created the Frankpledge system which designated the sire-reeves to conduct law enforcement duties. This innovation in public safety also created a separate branch of the judicial system by appointing judges to hear the criminal cases. By 1100, Henry the Lawgiver divided offenses into felonies and misdemeanors, and by 1154 King Henry II the law enforcement system added the jury to hear and decide over certain offenses[2]. This progression of system specialization continued to reflect today's modern day law enforcement.

Because of London's growth into a large industrialized city, it also experienced unprecedented levels of poverty, disorder, ethnic conflict and crime[3]. This also contributed to a rising crime rate, and as early as the 19th century, the city attempted to prevent crime in contrast to the traditional reactive-based apprehension model. The emergence of London as a populated and global center required the presence of a professional law enforcement organization to reflect a demand for order[4]. The government responded to this increase in crime by improving street lighting, hiring more watchmen, and greatly increasing the severity of punishment for all kinds of crime.

The development of an organized police agency is credited to Robert Peel, known as the "father of modern policing"[5]. In 1829 the English Parliament established the London Metropolitan Police. The officers, known as "Bobbie" in honor of Robert Peel, reflected his vision as an efficient and proactive police force[6].

The London Metropolitan Police, known as the "Met" was the cornerstone for modern policing. Their key features are that they were, public, specialized and professional. Public in that they are a government agency tasked with maintaining public safety, specialized in the sense that they have a distinct mission of enforcement and crime prevention, and professional in the sense that they are full-time, paid employees.

Robert Peel instituted the strategy of high visibility policing to prevent crime before it happens. The Met officers were assigned to fixed "beats" or geographical locations where they familiarized themselves with the people, businesses and criminals in the earliest efforts at community policing. Robert Peel also established para-militaristic organizational structures, uniforms, and authoritarian system of discipline to ensure professionalism and accountability in an effort to combat corruption and provide public safety[7]. Equally important, are his nine foundational principles for honest and accountable police services. These principles were revolutionary when created in 1829, and remain a gold standard even today[8].

Sir Robert Peel's Principles of Law Enforcement 1829

1. The basic mission for which the police exist is to prevent crime and disorder.
2. The ability of the police to perform their duties is dependent upon public approval of police actions.
3. Police must secure the willing co-operation of the public in voluntary observance of the law to be able to secure and maintain the respect of the public.
4. The degree of co-operation of the public that can be secured diminishes proportionately to the necessity of the use of physical force.
5. Police seek and preserve public favor not by catering to public opinion but by constantly demonstrating absolute impartial service to the law.
6. Police use physical force to the extent necessary to secure observance of the law or to restore order only when the exercise of persuasion, advice and warning is found to be insufficient.
7. Police, at all times, should maintain a relationship with the public that gives reality to the historic tradition that the police are the public and the public are the police; the police being only members of the public who are paid to give full-time attention to duties which are incumbent on every citizen in the interests of community welfare and existence.

8. Police should always direct their action strictly towards their functions and never appear to usurp the powers of the judiciary.
9. The test of police efficiency is the absence of crime and disorder, not the visible evidence of police action in dealing with it.

This public service experiment led the way as a model for a developing United States. The earliest days of urbanization and the Industrial Revolution was sweeping into America's northeast where the largest cities of the period where located. With Robert Peel's foundational practices set as the model, the American experience relied upon similar strategies but eventually chose a major shift of paradigm.

Three Eras of American Policing

Policing in the United States has progressed through three major evolutionary eras. While there are sub-sets to each era, these are the overarching periods in our policing history defining how we operate today;

- The Political Era – 1840 – 1930
- The Reform (Professional) Era – 1930 – 1970
- The Community Problem-Solving Era – 1970 – Current

THE POLITICAL ERA

Policing functions were established as quickly as communities settled, and were initially paralleled the British model. In the 1800s, changes in American society forced an evolution in law enforcement practice and ideology. Specifically, the processes of industrialization, urbanization, and immigration changed the country from a primarily homogenous, agrarian society to a heterogeneous, urban one. Citizens left rural areas and flocked to the cities in search of employment. Hundreds of thousands of immigrants came to reside in America's cities.

Unsanitary living conditions and poverty characterized American cities, and the poor, predominantly immigrant urban areas were plagued with increases in crime and disorder. As a direct result, a series of riots occurred throughout the 1830s in numerous American metropolitan areas. Many of these riots were the result of poor living conditions, poverty, and conflicts between ethnic groups. These riots illustrated the need for a larger and better organized law enforcement presence. Both the watch systems[9] in the north and the slave patrols[10] in the south began to evolve into contemporary police organizations.

The British "watch" system initially established to patrol the city for fires, crime and disorder was adopted in 1838 by the City of Boston, the nation's first modern American police force. What started as a mandatory participation for all adult males, evolved into a paid professional position. New York followed suit in 1844, followed by Philadelphia in 1854[11].

While the American northeast may have sponsored the first official professional police forces, it was the slave patrols in Charleston, South Carolina more closely resembling the first modern day police forces. The slave patrols were a distinctive form of law enforcement charged with recapturing runaway slaves and guarding against slave revolt, in 1837 had one hundred officers and was far larger than any northern police departments[12].

The law enforcement developments out west during this period were very different, and mirrored the new American frontier. Settlers originally created marshals and police forces similar to those in the original northern colonies, while settlers from the southern portions of the new frontier adopted the offices of the sheriffs and posse[13]. The sheriff became the most important position and besides peace keeping, they collected taxes, supervised elections and handled many other functions outside the scope of law enforcement. Groups of vigilantes were created in the absence of formal organized law enforcement, as these volunteers joined together to defend against threats to the order of the settlements. These groups of self-appointed law enforcers had a significant influence on collective social norms, including the lack of respect for the law, which had been haphazardly enforced primarily through vigilante violence[14]. The modern police departments "...were born out of urban mob violence."[15] In 1838, an Illinois state legislator, Abraham Lincoln warned of the "increasing disregard for law which pervades the country."[16]

Although law enforcement was enmeshing itself into the national psyche, the quality of the service and professionalism was minimal. Officers were selected primarily on their political affiliations as the positions were rewards for political patronage. The position was a high paying job and one to be desired as most big city police agencies paid officers $900 per year as compared to a factory worker's salary of $450 per year[17]. Local police agencies reflected the ethnic and religious make-up of the reigning political party, and when Barney McGinniskin was hired as Boston's the first Irish-American police officer in 1851, it set off major protest from the English and Protestant establishment.

Beyond the patronage, cops had a job to do. The extreme violence often forced reform in the strategies used by police to quell them. The "baton charge" was the first significant use of an instrument against the public for maintaining force against resistance. The earliest police forces understood their primary responsibilities were to use the physical violence necessary to stop rioters and worker rebellions. This realization of law enforcement serving as the state's arm of violence for exacting societal compliance is sometimes difficult to accept but important to understand.

As more cities created police forces to stem the violence, most were ineffective. Unlike the British system of policing where citizens had no control over the police department, America is much more democratic. American policing became immediately immersed in local politics. While London's Met Police established a level of autonomy meant for protecting officers from political influence and interference, today's practices of American policing have not moved far beyond the central tenants of the Political Era. The decision by government leaders in the 1800's to link police agencies to the control of elected and city leaders were a purposeful scheme. It is a strategy still used today as a mechanism to influence law enforcement operations. This attachment to non-policing political leadership has caused the collective body of officers to bind together for protections against personal or political agendas contrary to the principles of policing.

The New York model dominated the Political Era. New York's state legislature established its first professional police force in 1844 and typical of the era, placed control under city government and elected politicians. Political machines such as the 19th century's "Boss" Tweed and Tammany Hall's running of New York also took advantage of this early practice and effectively protected political and personal interest through the use of force and intimidation exacted by "their" police force. The paid police force was filled with minimally trained officers requiring no standards for hire. There were no scientific investigation capabilities, as even the best forensic techniques could not tell the difference between the bloods of a pig from a human.

An issue of historical significance attributed to this era is the "social worker" paradigm. While the Industrial Revolution created social upheaval within the major cities; the latter 19th century began to experience a settling within the metropolises. Police services focused less on brute force and more on providing social services to the elected officials' constituents. Operating soup lines, finding lost children and locating jobs and housing for new immigrants dominated duties. This is the period remaining endeared in the American consciousness of the friendly Irish beat cop who dutifully patrolled his neighborhood with his trusty rosewood baton while coming to the aid of women and children.

The social servant ideal may have been an idealistic element of the Political Era, but the closeness to politicians, lack of a strong organizational command structure and weak supervision of autonomously operating officers, led to wide-spread corruption. Officers used "curbside" justice and minority discrimination to quiet neighborhood problems. In addition to the immigrant beat cop, images remain from this era of the bungling Keystone cops as an illustration of their uselessness as true public servants. Today, advocates continue to clash over the best purpose for policing. Some feel an emphasis on the "social worker" paradigm is the best utilization of law enforcement resources, while others maintain that the "crime fighter" paradigm of the Professional Era best serves the needs of our communities.

The Professional Era

Policing in America changed dramatically during the twentieth century thanks to three principle forces affecting the movement: the police professionalism movement, modern technologies, and the civil rights movement[18]. If Robert Peel is the father of modern policing, then August Vollmer is the father of American police professionalism.

August Vollmer Leads the Evolution

Led by August Vollmer, an extensive body of literature on policing's purpose, practice and policy emerged. Little known within the circles of modern policing, he served as the chief of police for the city of Berkley, California from 1909 – 1931. He transformed a municipal police department plagued with officers brutalizing the public and partaking in open corruption into the national example for community policing practices, scientific management and investigations. His work to reform the profession also directly attacked the culture of corruption.

An advocate of the "social worker" paradigm, Vollmer was the first chief of police to place officers on bicycles, then motorcycles and finally automobiles. By 1928, his mobile fleet of rapid responders was equipped with radio communications. Requiring his officers to earn college educations, he organized police data into centralized records system and instituted the use of blood, fiber and soil analysis to solve crime. One of the first to use fingerprints to identify suspects, he suggested that the police role is to prevent crime rather than just solve it.

Civil service protections, applicant standards, testing and improved training increased the status of the occupation, but it did not resolve the issues of corruption. Despite the best efforts of skill and knowledge testing, merit-based hiring and promotions and ethics reform, there was still the element of human intervention in each level of decision making.

The limitations on officer discretion were emphasized during this period for minimizing opportunities of corruption and favoritism. While discretion is critical to the humanization of policing and street-level decision-making, it also creates opportunities for an abuse of authority. The most common issues of illicit police behavior occur during traffic stops for minor violations. This unsupervised police action allows the most freedom to exercise discretion, and results in numerous allegations by motorist that officers abused their authority by suggesting bribes, sex or other favors in exchange for a verbal warning instead of a written citation.

Challenges of illicit behaviors did not hinder Vollmer's efforts for advancing the standards of the profession. The adoption of a professional body also saw the first conventions, fraternal orders and benefit societies. While he supported the social worker paradigm, he did not support the political influences adversely effecting policing. He also advocated for workforce diversity by hiring one of the first black and female officers in the country.

Unfortunately, with focus directed to the rapid advancement of scientific investigative techniques, organizational para-militaristic reform and crime fighting, the social worker paradigm and policewoman's momentum suffered. Despite these two challenges, he became so successful at affecting professional changes within historically corrupt organizations that he also helped reorganize the LAPD, Chicago, San Diego, and Dallas Police Departments.

The Wickersham Commission Report

August Vollmer's most ambitious endeavor was writing the 1931 Wickersham Commission Report on Police. The efforts to professionalize the police increased after the 1931 report, which contained vivid descriptions of police misconduct and use of force. The first national study of the criminal justice system in America had a significant impact on the revitalization of the reform movement. This report concluded with a reform agenda of modern management for police departments. A summary of this agenda is provided by listing action items in the Reform Agenda of the Professionalization Movement as;

- Define policing as a profession
- Eliminate political influence from policing
- Appoint qualified chief executives
- Raise personal standards
- Introduce principles of modern management
- Create specialized units.[19]

In addition to the Wickersham, the 1955 National Institute on Police and Community Relations also suggested renewed emphasis placed on police-public communications. The Institute was abolished by 1969, and the culture of policing maintained the thin blue line's segregation from the public.

O.H. Wilson

Professionalization continued under the direction of O. W. Wilson, one of Vollmer's protégés. Wilson was the chief of police in Wichita, Kansas, from 1928 to 1935, a professor of criminology at the University of California, and Chief of the Chicago Police Department in the

1960s. Wilson had a significant impact on organizational changes within police departments during this time, largely through his 1950 textbook *Police Administration*. Utilizing scientific principles of management, Wilson emphasized workload distributions based on calls for service and efficient management of personnel through bureaucratic design. Wilson also encouraged departments to gauge their success through measurable outcomes (numbers of arrests, citations, etc.) and rapid response to calls for service.

He was the first to require a college education for applicants in an effort to curb the rampant corruption. This is significant because as early as policing became recognized as a "profession" the leading law enforcement revolutionaries were already fighting organizationally engrained corruption. Bribe taking and gratuities for preferential treatment was the most common practices of this era. Many of the same low-level types of bad behavior still exist today.

Wilson also introduced the use of automobiles and two-way mobile radios for patrol work. His attention to the scientific processes of increasing the efficiency of policing led to many practices in place today. These advances, combined with the implementation of the telephone provided an emphasis on response and less on quality of services delivered.

Citizens were relegated from partners in fighting crime, to observers and anonymous reporters over the telephone. The beat cop knew more about navigation than neighborhoods, and knowing the name of officers was replaced by copying police unit numbers. Law enforcement wrapped itself in an isolationist bubble of glass and a steel police cruiser where communicating with the public was no longer of importance. Despite results from the Wickersham Commission Report and the National Institute on Police and Community Relations reports calling for improved police and community relations; law enforcement continued to focus more on scientific application than human interaction.

J. Edgar Hoover

Also influential during this time period was J. Edgar Hoover, director of the Federal Bureau of Investigations (FBI.) Hoover's leadership had a direct influence on local police agencies because of his portrayal of agents under his command as highly trained, educated, professional, and honest. In addition, he instituted the FBI's Top Ten Most Wanted List, controlled the Uniform Crime Report (UCR) system, and effectively communicated to citizens that his organization was involved in a "war on crime." Most local departments wanted to emulate the professional FBI agents and thus perpetuated the "crime fighter" image.

New Police Technologies

New technologies also had a significant influence on policing in the early to mid-twentieth century. Three technologies in particular have revolutionized policing: the two-way radio, the patrol car, and the telephone. As previously noted, policing in the nineteenth century was characterized as ineffective and inefficient, in part because officers could not be contacted on their beats. With the advent of the two-way radio, officers could be notified about calls for service and police supervisors could contact their officers directly. This change in technology had a significant impact on the provision of services to the public and the supervision of police personnel.

Likewise, the use of patrol cars in the 1930s greatly enhanced the mobility of police officers and significantly reduced their response time to calls for service from citizens. Finally, the use of the telephone allowed citizens to have direct contact with the police department. Citizens were encouraged to call the police for any type of situation and the police promised a rapid response.

These new technologies also had unintended consequences on policing, the effect of which was not fully understood until much later. For example, the patrol car served to isolate patrol officers from the community. Previously, when officers patrolled on foot, they had an opportunity to engage citizens in conversations and had a familiarity with the neighborhood that was lost once officers patrolled in cars. When officers drove through neighborhoods with their windows rolled up, citizens perceived officers as outsiders in their communities.

Police graft before this technology remained at local levels to include pay-offs to the beat officer as insurance the business owner's shop windows were not shattered during the night, or free food, drinks or clothing from the merchants along the cops' route. Although officers participated in illicit or illegal activities, they remained "sensitive" to the levels of corruption tolerance for their communities. After all, the officers were part of that small neighborhood and placing too much pressure on the residents and citizens would have jeopardized their easily gotten gains.

The implementation of the telephone, radio and automobile meant officers unfamiliar with a particular geography within their jurisdiction were capable of responding to a citizen's request for service. This not only subjected citizens to unknown officers, but presented tension for these communities when numerous officers began requesting gratuities from the same locations. The intimacy of the local cop, although accepting graft, was replaced with impersonal expectations and unaccountable nonstandard behavior. Additionally, because cops no longer had to personally take reports, officers were no longer tethered to the squad room or under constant supervision from the first-line supervisors. While scientific and institutional improvements were paramount during this era, so were new ways to fleece the system of public service.

Encouraging citizens to call the police for service and promising a rapid response dramatically increased the workload of officers. Citizens began to call police for minor problems and the police continued to respond. In addition, police were called to handle private matters that they had not been responsible for in the past. The interactions between citizens and police took on a more personal nature as police responded to citizens' homes rather than simply patrolling and engaging citizens on the street. A result of these new technologies "was a complex and contradictory change in police-citizen contacts. Whereas the patrol car isolated the police from the people on the streets, the telephone brought police officers into peoples' living rooms, kitchens, and bedrooms. There, officers became involved in the most intimate domestic problems"[20].

This era saw the most revolutionary paradigm shifts as it sought to change organizations characterized by inefficiency, corruption, and low personnel standards into "professional" departments. Police organizational structures during this time were centralized, specialized, and bureaucratic. Professional officers emphasized their functions of law enforcement and crime prevention through random motorized patrol and rapid response to calls for service.

In theory this was the industry's standard of expectation. In reality these changes were and still are slow to engrain themselves in the daily operating procedures across America. The paradigm clash between "social worker" versus "crime fighter" remains entrenched not just within public expectation, but within the official practices and policing's cultural expectancies. The demand for a return to community-oriented policing practices reached its apex during the 1950 - 1960's civil rights movements, and a nationally televised event that brought police violence directly into their living rooms.

Technology of Television

While technology introduced the Reform Era, it ultimately contributed to its end. The 1960's civil rights demonstrations and riots were regularly televised. The American public watched the brutality unleashed upon fellow Americans as police used everything from fire hoses to attacking K-9s against them. Regardless of the individuals' racial or societal ideology at the time, watching the televised images of public servants openly attacking others for the color of their skin served to reinforce that the purpose of police in America for serving as the arm of violence on behalf of the state's interests to ensure social compliance to the laws enacted by the state.

The 1968 Democratic National Convention hosted by the City of Chicago was marred by series of violent clashes between police and protesters. August 28, 1968 experienced the most intense violence as 10,000 protesters became involved in confrontations with Chicago Police Officers at Grant Park over an arrest being made. The confrontations continued and eventually were televised live as police engaged unarmed protesters in front of the Hilton Hotel. During the course of George McGovern's nomination speech, Connecticut Senator Abraham Ribicoff spoke of the "gestapo tactics" being used outside of the convention hall. Renowned television anchorman Dan Rather also became involved in a clash with police security inside the convention hall while covering the event. The event captured while Rather was reporting live documented his being punched in the stomach and then released to return to his broadcast.

Figure 4.1 – photograph of Chicago Police Officer responding to protesters at the 1968 Democratic National Convention. *Source*: A scene from *The Walker Report of the 1968 Chicago Democratic National Convention.*

These televised police brutality and the separation between police and the public on a daily basis created an atmosphere of dissatisfaction with the public safety services received. Coupled with rising crime and national discontent with police practices, a call came for a referendum integrating the community back into the practices of protecting their communities. Police as a partner was the mandate, and a community-oriented practice was the next evolutionary period; the era of Community Oriented Problem Solving Policing.

Community Oriented Policing and Problem Solving Era

As the 1960's began to fade, so did the nation's tolerance for the Reform (Professional) style of policing focusing on number of arrests and call response times. Social upheaval, racial unrest and community cries demanded an alternative approach to policing. The advancing body of research and justice administration literature questioned the status quo of cop work. These studies reiterated a need for exploring an alternative approach similar to the suggestions made by the earlier Wickersham Commission. Relying on incident-driven responses were quantifiably determined to be ineffective and an unwise expenditure of government's resources. It was time for change and the communities wanted to be included in the process.

A rush to change for the sake of change resulted in unrealistic planning, development and implementation. The promise of an innovative ideology for meeting the needs of law enforcement and community failed to reach critical mass, and the plan was scrapped. An effort to retool the paradigm of reconnecting with communities included a return of the old-school beat cop, and an introduction to problem-oriented policing. This led to a new and improved ideal branded Community Oriented Policing and Problem Solving. The remake included new police strategies equally emphasizing crime control and prevention.

An organizational approach de-emphasizing the traditional para-militaristic hierarchical command structure would allow street level officers the flexibility to become key decision makers in exploring alternative resolutions to traditional crime. Despite the centralized emphasis on community policing, the nation instead, focused enforcement efforts on the "War on Drugs" campaign during the 1980 - 90's. This battle led intensified policing directly against the communities. The progressively militarization of policing operations included street jumps and search warrant raids as the norm instead of researching alternative resolutions for neighborhood issues.

Moving the spectrum further from community emphasis were the events of and following September 11, 2001. While the law enforcement milieu attempted to attach COPS to homeland security, the divergent paradigms have failed to marry. The original ideology of Community Oriented Policing and Problem Solving fragmented into a variety of models.

COP Model

This popular model, Community Oriented Policing included a designated cadre of officers having the autonomy to identify problems, analyze them, offer solutions and implement programs to address the problem is a very proactive ideology. The reality is, it runs contrary to the historical reactionary role of police models. Most importantly, administrators did not willingly surrender institutional control to street-level decision makers, so it continues to falter.

The ideology of the COP model is identified with four themes; formality, alternative strategies, prevention focus, and organizational. These four areas form the backbone of the community policing paradigm shift from the traditional role of post-incident response. These four foundational principles failed to engrain the issues into the policing conscience. The best opportunity for the COP model to enmesh itself into policing was the massive amounts of federal funds made available through the Omnibus Crime Act of 1994. It provided for the hiring and training of new and current officers in the principles of COP. When the funding stopped, so did the momentum.

Counter-Terrorism Model

Since the launch of the COP model, research and evaluation of the programs have shown a positive trend in improving relationships between the community and police. It is believed that the same principles applied to create an effective COP program can be transitioned into a strategy by local law enforcement for detecting and deterring terrorism and Weapons of Mass Destruction (WMD.) The theoretical policy of community policing was already established and more effective than re-inventing the wheel.

The idea of adapting the COP model to Counter Terrorism (CT) initiatives seemed like a positive forward movement. The basic tenants of fostering community relationships, utilizing alternative methods of policing such as foot and bicycle patrols promoted the reciprocating relationship desired for decades.

This embedding of officers into communities was believed to build a pipeline of information about national security threats.

POP Model

A variation of the COP model is the Problem Oriented Policing (POP) concept that teaches officers to be selective in their targeting of problems. Once identifying that an actual issue exists, officers have the autonomy to develop analytical evaluations for best resolving the issues. Once approved, they are empowered to implement the solution.

POP officers do not respond to citizen complaints in a reactionary fashion. They are absolutely proactive in rooting out a community's social harms. They are also taught to evaluate the consequences of their work upon completion for ensuring that the original issue was resolved. The POP model remains active in current police applications.

CPTED Model

Crime Prevention Through Environmental Design (CPTED) is another community-based strategy born out of the COP Era. It attempts to curb crime through the use of resources like controlling natural access, providing natural surveillance and fostering territorial behavior. CPTED works between the community and police to increase observations of high-risk targets in a community for potential criminal activity. These same surveillance relationships can be focused on the prevention of terrorism and WMD incidents.

Other Adaptions for COP Model

A final effort for incorporating the COP principles into community involves the very neighborhoods served through citizen academies and educational programs. Utilizing the eyes and ears of a community will better enhance the first responder's role assigned to local law enforcement. True and sincere partnerships between police and communities may finally deliver the relationships desired.

What is the Next Era

The last decade has seen exponential improvements in technology benefitting law enforcement. While the remnants of community policing linger, the new era is upon policing. Still battling for title dominance are ideologies such as data-driven policing, predictive policing, intelligence-led policing and hotspot policing. Despite the title of the era, the age of big data is upon us, and police agencies are relying more on information to guide place-based policing efforts.

While beneficial to the agency and ultimately the community that enforcement efforts are becoming more laser-specific in combatting crime, it still neglects the detrimental effects to the officers. Each evolutionary era has presented new opportunities for the cop culture to slide counter-intuitive to the cultural ideals of the institution. The question is; how will the era of big data affect the cop culture? Or will it?

5

OCCUPATIONAL SOCIALIZATION

"It's like another family but without the bullshit."
(Nebraska Operator, 2009)

While the profession of policing continues to experience dramatic technological advances in equipment, forensics, mapping and data analysis, the "boots on the ground" are still filled by dedicated men and women. Though they may benefit professionally from the implementation of technology into their work atmosphere, they continue to be plagued by the detrimental effects of a secreted association. To study the cop culture's effects on the officer, agency, and the public, relevant literature is examined.

Providing an overview of information allows the data to fall into three major themes: occupational socialization, police culture, and organizational detection of problematic behavior. These categories are chosen to explain the powerful influence of becoming blue and the process of introducing individuals to the disjointed sectors within the seemingly environment of sameness that ushers officers into a system of acceptance for behaving badly.

Socialization shares similarities with other para-militaristic hierarchical professions, but law enforcement's authorization to use force on the citizenry, even the justification to use deadly force, makes it an occupation unique to any other American profession. This environment of uniqueness wrapped within an institutional ethos demanding "vanilla" adherence creates internal conflicts of purpose leading to an outcome for fitting in different from any other. Because the strength of influence during the assimilation process is so overwhelming, literature is included to show the challenges for holding officers accountable and deterring them from engaging in countercultural behavior.

Fitting In

Discovering information about law enforcement's occupational socialization is limited primarily due of the impenetrable culture. Using similar literature for supplementing data about organizations like law enforcement includes professions relying on chain of command hierarchies and position specializations, such as the military and health care professions.

The following researchers present studies specific to the process of "fitting in" for illustrating that as officers become more acculturated, they move further away from the central tenants of the organization. The socialization process includes definitive stages teaching officers the principles and practices of policing but simultaneously promotes a potential for a degeneration of moral and ethical behaviors. Because this process is grounded in bureaucracy, clearly drawn boundaries exist within which to operate. What happens when these lines are unrealistic for the mission of policing? Cops operate outside of those lines.

Bureaucratic Fraternal Order

The health care profession shares many similarities to law enforcement in various dimensions of operation, service to general public, rigorous training, certifications prior to independent field work and a rigid hierarchy ranging from the "candy striper" volunteer nursing assistant to the most skilled surgeon.

Looking at the health care profession,[1] four distinct stages of socialization generally relate to peer clustering and groupthink. This is similar to policing's socialization practices, and demonstrates the individual's progression through the stages of socialization and the experiencing at least one of four possible outcomes.

While the research[2] does not include the variable of job dissatisfaction, it is an important piece for policing due to high attrition rates. The element of quitting the service is addressed later in this study. In addition to the four socialization outcomes, there are also four thresholds in the socialization process. I relate each stage to the cop culture for understanding the parallel to the health care profession's fitting in process.

1 - *Anticipatory Socialization* – the first stage along the path to fitting in includes learning about the job prior to actually joining the agency. In law enforcement, this stage often involves the recruit developing unrealistic expectations created by media portrayals of police work. This begins even before the individual realistically considers a career in law enforcement. Childhood often involves the act of playing "cops and robbers." I personally spent much of my youth winning Super Bowls, Final Fours and capturing bad guys.

This is a lifetime experience of building an expectation of what the job should actually involve. It is also an opportunity to mentally rehearse the potential of working in that capacity. This stage may actually encourage some potential applicants against attempting the process, while solidifying the decision for others. Regardless the level of mental rehearsal or social preparation, the first day in the police academy destroys every preconceived notion. There is nothing to prepare you for the culture of policing, but the culture of policing.

2 – *Accommodation* - is the next stage when the reality of the job meets the individual's expectation as they attempt to become a participating

member of that culture. This stage in law enforcement usually occurs during the police academy. The conflict is presented immediately in the individual's career. The erroneous preconceived notions gained through the anticipatory socialization stages now contrast with the reality of police work. This is a natural social phenomenon requiring one or more individuals to adjust their thinking or behavior for the purpose of gaining equilibrium about their unfamiliar environment.

The act of accommodation is challenged due to the traditional traits of police cadets recruited for desired characteristics including the type "A" personalities, or the alpha dog mentality that makes submission or change for the sake of harmony a difficult task. This is a critical point of departure from the agency's ideology for individuals who seek the opportunity to serve, yet avoid the demand to submit themselves to a holistic culture of homogeneity.

The cadet academy is also an opportunity for instructors to "weed out" candidates who fail to accommodate for the purpose of adherence to the organizational standards. Accommodation is a continuation of processes throughout the entirety of an officer's career, and no society or institution may function effectively without it. This phase also prepares the individual for the following processes of assimilation into the informal subcultures existing within each area of disciple or assignment. The image presented to the recruit at this point, is still far removed from the reality awaiting graduation and assignment on the streets.

3 - *Role Management* - allows an employee the opportunity to begin resolving friction within his own work groups. The role management phase is an opportunity for the cadet to resolve conflicts between other people and groups placing demands on him. This is common as the para-militaristic nature of policing immediately divides officers into rank, departments, divisions, shifts, beat areas and partner assignments.

This institutional compartmentalization creates an environment for cliques and social tension. The clash between work-life and home-life begins demanding time away from families and personal activities. The nature of the work assignment serves as a motivating factor and is associated with the individual's need to reach self-actualization. This is common for most people finding themselves juggling more than one status pulling in various directions. This may occur once, such as the parent torn between work and a sick child at home, or over a career between a call to serve and a desire for a more normalized life.

4 – *Outcomes* – is the final stage for fitting in. This stage may result in the individual experiencing; general satisfaction, mutual influence, internal work motivation or job involvement. Once the individual reaches this level of actualization, they are considered fully socialized and moves towards becoming an independently productive and interactive member of the occupational culture. Upon this phase, the officer becomes exposed to opportunities for career advancement, illicit temptations and subcultural memberships through skill-set selection or organizational assignment.

An example of the Outcomes stage includes the officer's graduation from the academy and successfully passing through the field-training program. Once initially socialized, the officer begins working assignments independent of direct supervision. This is the most vulnerable time for the individual officer because they are primarily operating with autonomy. How they respond to the external forces available to them will depend upon which of the four possible outcomes have made the greatest impression upon them up to this point in their career.

Personal Effects of Cultural Conflict

The four phases of socialization help to prepare individuals enter into whichever profession they choose. The reality of entering into the cop culture is not fully understood regardless of how prepared someone may feel they are. Even officers with relatives in the world of policing, and may think they know what to expect once hired, are often shocked at the extremely different aspect awaiting them. The "role management" stage should be the beginning of an employee's discovering who they are within an organization. The reality is that this stage becomes the beginning of a time for turmoil with the officer, family and friends.

An example of this turmoil is the expression "police widow." It is widely used by cops describing the family abandoned during weekends, holidays and special occasions because of the demands of the assignment. The conflict for officers as described in the "role management" phase was examined in other studies[3][4] to show at least 40% of full-time police officer's families experience domestic violence. This is in contrast to the 10% of non-law enforcement families. The divorce rate among police officers is 60% higher than the national average, alcoholism is twice the national rate and police officers commit suicide three times more often than the civilian national average[5]. The personally detrimental effects of socialization are detailed in Chapters 12 and 13. This is not the adventure most signed up for, and the source of turmoil is easy to understand.

In summary, although conducted within the occupation of health care, the study[6] provides a way of understanding the changing perspectives of individuals entering into a new environment, and the requirements extending beyond the performance of new job tasks and skill sets. The project also indicates that the fitting in process does not always achieve the intended purpose. It does however offer a positive effect on the general satisfaction of the workers translating into decreased turnover and absenteeism.

The following studies[7] also help for understanding the negative effects of organizational isolationism. If an officer does not fit in, or "rocks the boat," more senior officers use a tactic of segregation and isolation as a tool to either force compliance or separation from service. Peer pressure is a powerfully informal tactic used by members of an organization to persuade individuals to adhere to the cultural expectancies.

Attitudes, Motivators and Satisfiers

There are several important investigations[8,9,10,11] focusing on the attitudes, motivators and satisfiers associated with fitting into the culture of policing. Occupational socialization has already been described as the process by which an individual learns the required behaviors and supportive attitudes necessary to participate as a member of an organization[12], but it bears reminding as it is the central theme. The studies include identifying intrinsic values as primary factors for entering law enforcement or military, but the decisions to remain with the organization vary between motivators[13] discussed below, and the quest for self-actualization.

The difficulty in obtaining an individual's self-assumed maximum potential may be what influences some to quit and others to resist the rigid structures of the organization. This is the point of tension between self-actualization and bureaucratic restriction. This state of conflict is a catalyst for the perceptual and personal changes occurring through the SOG socialization process. Those changes often solidify the officer's commitment to the homogenous state perpetuating the isolationist and anti-diversified fraternity. This tension influences those who stay on the job to commit to protecting the isolationist and anti-diversified fraternity of policing; even at the risk of becoming bad.

Marine's Motivational Method

The United States Marine Corps (USMC) directs a socialization process based on the factors of motivators. These motivational forces are usually intrinsic and categorized as either satisfiers or motivators[14]. Satisfiers are described as the elements of the profession resulting in either satisfaction or dissatisfaction over job tasks. The USMC recognizes that relying only on personal satisfaction may fail to mold a productive soldier. Many of the mission objectives of the USMC are not normally pleasant; therefore the Marine is not socialized to be motivated by personal satisfiers.

The second factor is motivators, and involves the occupation influencing the individual to become professionally productive.

During the socialization process, the Marine is taught that becoming a Marine is a main motivator, and that further motivation comes from accomplishing the mission as opposed to attaining self-recognition. Mission before self!

The USMC promotes the team and mission focus over self-actualization and personal satisfaction. The military's actual fitting in practices are similar to policing's despite the attachment of the process to a higher, overarching ideal. While military socialization practices are similar to those of law enforcement's, their focus of placing the organization before the individual is opposite of the policing's culture need for obtaining self-actualization[15].

The outcome of self-actualization is linked to the police officer's perception of the value or importance of the work conducted. A study[16] addressing officers' perception of work values and outcomes is similar to the "outcomes" stage[17]. Understanding the relationship between self-satisfaction, and why officers feel the desire to quit a career is critical for providing a better insight for changing the cop culture[18]. The following chapter examines the dynamics associated with experiencing occupational dissatisfaction, and despite the depth of fraternal bonds shared between these officers, leads them to leave the career.

6

WHY COPS QUIT

"...the guys should just quit. Then I realized that you can't. In a way you're trapped. It's a dishonor to quit."
(Arizona Operator, 2011)

Cops quit. That is the reality of the job. Understanding why people are so drawn to the profession, yet suddenly leave it remains a mystery. This chapter[1] examines why individuals enter the profession, endure the difficult assimilation processes, suffer the hazing, seek the social clustering, yet become so alienated leading to early separation. By definition of "separation", this includes voluntary, recommended and forced departures from employment. No matter how attached to the job, not everyone is cut out to serve the public.

In an effort to better understand the dynamics of attachment, loyalty and commitment to the job, a study surveyed officers to evaluate aspects of work ethic as it correlates to job satisfaction and retention. The outcome of self-actualization is closely aligned to the officer's perception of value or importance of the work conducted. The law enforcement profession experiences a high rate of attrition not associated with earned retirement, therefore it is critical to understand why individuals quit. The results looked at "intrinsic" values (pride in work, activity preference, and job involvement), "extrinsic" values (attitude toward earnings and social status), and "upward striving" values (desire to progress within the organization).

The effects of occupational assimilation are powerful and contribute to the individual officer's goal of obtaining self-actualization. The researchers looking at the selection of values as they relate to the job also use the same term. While readers may be most familiar with self-actualization as proposed by Abraham Maslow[2] in his hierarchy of needs, it is more accurately reflected to mean self-satisfaction. Maslow's formal usage involves mastering the preceding elements of physiological, safety, love/belonging, and esteem. Unfortunately, this is not the case with officers seeking to maximize their benefit and enjoyment of the position. This relates to the main difference between Marine socialization to believe that the act of becoming a Marine is the ultimate honor while cops seek satisfying themselves through select assignments, schedules, off-duty details and other temporal perks.

Encouragingly though, the results did show that officers care more about intrinsic values (duty, honor and service) than extrinsic values (monetary compensation, or public opinion). Additionally[3], officers value close friendships and peer clustering opportunities. The draw to the profession is the potential of working closely with your "Brothers." Males usually seek these bonds forged not through sharing personal intimacies, but uniting through action and adventure such as sports teams do.

It is this desire for developing friendships, which makes isolating[4] new officers from potential personal relationships such a convenient tactic used by supervising officers to ensure institutional assimilation. The rookie officer having just endured the intensity of a police academy training where they are officially taught and informally learn to depend only upon their fellow cadets, enters field work hungry for establishing those same relationships.

Seasoned officers serving as field training officers (FTO) and first line supervisors are aware of this bonding desire, and control the sociability of the rookie as a reward for conforming to the unwritten cultural behaviors for fitting into an established collection of officers. New officers failing to fit into the culture, despite working hard, are exposed to isolationism with the purpose of leading to termination or conformity. The acronym, "FNG" is not meant as a term of endearment, and is often used as a code to other officers to watch their conduct around the rookie. While their job performance may be satisfactory, their behavior remains suspect and may run contrary to the expected cultural behaviors. No, being labeled the "fucking new guy" is no compliment.

In the initial stages of a person's career, being purposely isolated from peers has a major influence on your behavior for exacting a desired behavioral outcome. In addition to this tactic, there are more formal aspects of influencing the occupational commitment as described in the next section.

Factors Affecting Commitment

Factors affecting job commitment[5] are associated with the term "organizational socialization" as it relates to the learning of the workplace's structural ecology. The term records[6] the fitting in process by looking at the academy cadets' job attitudes while progressing through a series of chronological socialization benchmarks; entry, introduction, encounter and metamorphosis.

Although most studies demonstrate the "fitting in" transformations extend for the duration of a vocation, the initial period[7] in an officer's career is the most influential in determining future attitudes and behaviors. The first benchmark, *"entry,"* is the successful completion of the application and hiring process, where wanting to be an officer transitions into actually becoming one and the stark realities of policing begins.

This is a key transformational point in the liminality process, and exerts great influence on the remainder of an individual's career. The cultural shock and realigning of unrealistic expectations versus the reality of what is to come is not necessarily a negatively influencing factor. This initial entry stage in the military's Boot camp begins the process of striping away who the recruit was, and preparing the person for the soldier they will become. This is a positive period of liminality because there is a definitive strategy for escorting the person through the period for ensuring a finished product. The focus on self-satisfaction in the cop culture may lead to a negative experience from the beginning and jeopardize the organizational attachment before the cadet completes their first week.

The second benchmark, *"introduction,"* is an indoctrination into the organization. The anticipation of being hired is over, and other cadets in the same situation surround the new officer. Immediately they are subject to strict discipline and behavioral commands from an academy staff of instructors. Failure to comply with orders result in physical punishment, demerits, and possible termination. The cadet quickly learns to depend only on classmates to avoid harsh treatment and disciplinary actions from the academy staff since all are punished for the mistakes of the few. This reliance upon other officers engrains the "no rat" rule that protects fellow cadets from punishment and discipline at the hands of authority figures and agency superiors.

This period of transformation holds an ironic twist because instead of engraining the spirit of public service through discipline and training, cadets learn to rely only upon each other to avoid harsh treatment and possible termination. The element of teamwork is not learned through drills and scenarios, but banding together to avoid punishment instead. This ethos remains with the cadet as they progress into their FTO period and then into independent field operations. The initial mistrust and unification against authority (academy instructors) continues as the officer rebels against the potential oversight of supervisors. Cops learn that by limiting the amount of work effort and therefore the [potential for making mistakes, they avoid drawing command's criticism. This is why the rookie officer's FTO instructs them to "forget that stuff they taught you at the academy, this is where you learn to be a cop." Making waves by making arrests, causes other officers on that rotation to look bad, and eventually gains the negative attention of the supervisor.

The third socialization benchmark; *"encounter"* begins after academy graduation as the rookie officer enters the Field Training Officer (FTO) training period. This apprenticeship introduces the rookie to the complex reality of policing where the expected attitudes and behaviors are learned. Beyond the purpose of showing the rookie the ropes, this is the opportunity for veteran officers to insure operational and attitudinal congruity from one generation of officers to the next.

As mentioned in the "introduction" benchmark, the cadet is now directly under the influence of and her immediate success is in the FTO's control. By showing the rookie the ropes, they do learn the policies, practices, reporting, geography, radio communications protocol and all of the other miscellaneous aspects particular to that assignment. More importantly, this is the FTO's opportunity to ensure yet another cadre of highly motivated "kick-ass wanna-be cops" learn that mediocrity is the standard. This is also the liminal transformational opportunity for introducing the rookie office to the influences of illicit and unethical behaviors. If the FTO practices bad behavior, the rookie officer will be expected to replicate that same activity for the sake of gaining approval and peer acceptance by their immediate supervisor. If not, they risk becoming labeled "FNG."

The final benchmark for successful socialization is *"metamorphosis"* and is closely associated with the concept of liminality[8]. In this period, the rookie adopts the perspective and attitude of veteran officers. Usually within 6 months of experience in patrol work they gain what is labeled the "final perspective" in the socialization process that mirrors the occupation's culture. The powerful adherence to cultural homogeneity is described as:

Consequently, the police culture can be viewed as molding the attitudes, with numbing regularity, of virtually all who enter[9].

Perceptions of Work-Ecology

In addition to identifying the socialization benchmarks, cop's attitudes are measured to determine how well they will get along with others in the workplace. The first attitudinal measurement addressed is "motivation," and is based on the "Expectancy Theory"[10]. It is useful in understanding individual behavior in organizational settings. The idea is that the potential for an individual to behave in a particular manner is based upon "the degree to which the person expects certain outcomes to result from the particular behavior (expectancy) times the attractiveness to him of the expected result (value)"[11]. This brings to mind the example of the officer who seems to never be able to detect and apprehend an impaired driving throughout the course of his regular duty assignment. Coincidently, the moment he begins an off-duty overtime traffic safety enforcement operation, the impaired drivers appear immediately.

The second attitudinal measurement addresses the "commitment" to an organization. It is understood as the willingness to put forth extra effort to help the organization succeed, loyalty and concern about the fate of the organization and willingness to recommend the organization as a place of work. "Needs satisfaction" is the final attitudinal measurement addressed and includes job characteristics such as security, opportunity to develop close friendships, feelings of worthwhile accomplishment, and authority. In addition to measuring these occupational attitudes, the study looks at the officer's performance rating once he begins working patrol duty on "the streets."

Demographic characteristics did not prove a strong relationship with job performance and occupational attitude. Most individual demographics creating a significant relationship with job performance appeared early in the career but were neutralized within several months of gaining experience on the streets. As an example, recruits with military backgrounds initially reported high levels of motivation, organizational commitment and needs satisfaction. Within the first few months of actual police experience, those levels dropped sharply to match the measures of the recruits with no military experience.

This is attributed to the decline in lowering expectations about what the job actually involved after graduating from the academy and adopting the veteran officers' apathetic attitude that hard work is not linked to a system of reward or recognition. Based on the sergeants' evaluation of the rookie officers during their initial exposure to actual police work, it was discovered that officers rating the lowest in attitude and motivational scores during the academy were actually rated higher by their sergeants in their performance on the streets. This inverted rating may be attributed to those officers having a more realistic expectation of the job than the recruits who were overly idealistic.

Furthermore, the recruits' level of satisfied needs increased upon academy graduation, along with their need to increase satisfaction. This is associated with their desire to begin conducting police work. When recruits were individually questioned about needs satisfaction, the self-actualization and social cluster elements were rated highest in the survey. These attitudes show the beginning of the organizational and individual isolationist behavioral patterns leading to the "us versus them" mentality.

Occupational social groups and individual needs will soon outweigh the recruits' desire to selflessly serve the public. The project[12] includes a quoted tip from a veteran officer passed down to academy graduates for generations. It was advice I personally received over twenty years ago upon police academy graduation as well. To quote the officer:

There's only two things you gotta know around here. First, forget everything you've learned in the academy because the street's where you'll learn to be a cop; and second, being first around here don't mean shit[13].

This investigation[14] shows the differences between the indoctrination to police work beginning with the anticipation of becoming an officer, the training to perform as an officer, and the realization of what it takes to be an officer. The combination of these stages produce the fully socialized officer who learns to acclimate to the culture by embracing mediocrity for the sake of avoiding isolation from peers. The mediocrity and isolation avoidance may also include the participation of unethical or illegal activities. Again, it becomes clearer to the observer once the dynamics of socialization are applied as a layer over the cop culture to understand the availability and near expectation for good officers to go bad.

Do Anything to "Fit In"

Understanding the significance of quitting a career is important because of the separation of loyalties from the agency and their high attrition rate. The focus on self-satisfaction versus mission-based motivators[15] may contribute to quitting, while the need for peer acceptance and social clustering[16] are critical factors.

Why an individual develops intentions to quit includes four elements of socialization tactics;

- Person change – in the context of work, it is the adjustments in a person's values, attitudes, career trajectory and even personality. The stronger the culture or institutionalization experience, the greater the change affect.

- Stress symptoms - physical and or psychological effects of anxiety experienced by newcomers. Factors increasing this element are role ambiguity and role conflict.
- Organizational identification – the extent to which a member of the agency defines himself in terms of the organization and what agency is perceived to represent.
- Self-appraised performance – associated more with self-actualization than cultural assimilation, but includes the individual's perception of self in that role.

A strong relationship exists between positive socialization tactics and the reduction of uncertainty and anxiety about remaining on the job. This creates a strong attachment to the job and the organization, as it relates to higher levels of job satisfaction, organizational commitment and identification, and the reduced intentions to quit.

Officers excluded from positive social clustering associate institutionalized isolationism with stress symptoms, job dissatisfaction, and intentions to quit. Isolationism is used by senior agency members for weeding out new employees who fail to adhere to the cultural norms, even the illegal ones. Officers willing to operate within a cultural expectancy outside of their ethical sphere to avoid institutional isolation from cohorts may compromise their moral character and become vulnerable to professional deviance.

The power of socialization and peer acceptance provides the fraternity of policing with a key strategy for maintaining the homogenous status of the profession. It is also an effective tool for limiting diversity. The thin blue line serves as a barrier to integrating the "others" into policing, and the following chapter demonstrates the efforts made to breach the barriers and bring change into policing.

7
ANTI-DIVERSITY IN THE RANKS

"I ain't no fag."
(Kansas Narcotics Operator, 2010)

Law enforcement services the entirety of every community in this nation. This includes every possible variation of race, gender and sexual preference. The profession has clung to the heterosexual white male ethos since the first professional policing organization was formed. Chapter 4 mentions August Vollmer's effort to promote an agenda of diversification, but the rapid technological advancements for policing during his era pushed the initiative aside.

Civil rights, women's rights and now gay rights movements have all attempted to breach the culture with minimal success. Why does law enforcement continue hiring primarily straight white males to fill the ranks? We will explore the facts about how fitting in focuses on the homogenetic state of law enforcement, and the requirements for demanding rigid conformity. This chapter also uncovers the antisocial behaviors creating a restricted access subculture that places further limitations on individual and institutional diversity.

No Place for "Others"

Several studies[1,2,3,4] examine the roles and exclusion of women, minorities, gays and lesbians from joining public service institutions like policing and the military. The dynamics of anti-diversity and the character of conventional institutional diversity are regarded as a phenomenon of the group homogeneity theory and are defined by the out-group hypothesis[5] with strong resemblance to characteristics of the SOG and cop culture.

To understand why some groups embrace diversity while others did not, a quasi-experimental design study[6] divides participants into well-defined groups and others into ill-defined groups. Information and activities are devised for each group and collects data about their behaviors. The "in-group" experiences more diversity due to the motivation for promoting individual characteristics and self-expression.

The "out-group" binds together against the "in-group" and is similar to the isolationist practices of the SOG subculture. This "taking of sides" is indicative of policing's subculture. The policing out-group (SOG) is exclusive and requires demanding subculturally informal processes that discourage or prohibits participation of women, minorities, gays, and lesbians. Additional research[7,8] tries uncovering the anti-diversity ethos dominant in the process of becoming blue.

This theory is actually very interesting and applies directly to the dynamic of exclusionary practices against minorities, females and the LGBT community. For the sake of appreciating the significance, I will carry through the explanation of the active differences between both groups.

The two "groups" are dependent variables used to describe an individual's connection to a larger association with people. The research identifies three elements believed to provide a reciprocating effect on both groups. The first explains that the in-group experiences less homogeneity due to a motivation for conveying individual characteristics and self-expression. Next, the out-group segregates itself as a justification against in-group diversification.

Finally, the variety of different people interacting with the in-group is greater than with the out-group; and therefore, it creates a more diversified environment than that of the SOG.

The descriptions of the "out-group homogeneity hypothesis" are consistent with the conflicting relationships between the law enforcement's traditional assignments and the SOG. The out-group obviously represents the SOG and their attempts to prevent integration from the "others." The last decades have seen more effort to embrace holistic diversification throughout the ranks of policing. Some improvements have been federally mandated such as affirmative action, while civil lawsuits and consent decrees have forced opened doors to agencies once adverse to anyone other than white males.

The influence of women, minorities, and homosexuals in the workplace was expected to breach the thin blue line, but as of yet the SOG milieu remains largely unfazed by legal or social demand. While the traditional assignments have experienced a more balanced combination of the representatively served population, the SOG continues to entrench itself with exclusionary practices intended to preserve the status quo.

Another prominent researcher arrived at the same conclusion about the diversification of policing institutions. The infusion of minorities and females[9] into the ranks of policing, mostly by affirmative action promised to break the traditional barriers. The degree to which diversity occurred did not affect occupational solidarity. A summary statement of the results for most police culture investigations said:

Traditional research in this area has suggested that the socialization process is so intense and the subculture so strong that individual characteristics are quickly overwhelmed[10].

Heterosexual Masculinity

The homogenetic state of the white male heterosexual is so dominant that studies investigate the possibility of ever diversifying the law enforcement milieu. Observations confirm that policing's culture actively protects the white male's masculine, heterosexual ethos[11]. The nature of policing that requires officers to respond to dangerous calls for service, and to depend upon each other for their safety and well-being is what inspires this dynamic and is regarded as "hegemonic masculinity."

The term hegemonic masculinity[12] is first defined in 1997 by Stanford University's Robert Connell as a "...masculinity associated with authority, aggressiveness, technical competence, and heterosexist desire for and domination over women as well as subordinated masculinities, including gay masculinities[13]." The term "masculinity" more commonly includes the various types and degrees of masculinity as evidenced by different cultures and sexualities. This modernization of the term did not enmesh itself within the policing milieu, and the sexist definition referring to heterosexual white males remains the cultural standard.

Despite the loosening of organizational restrictions created by court orders and lawsuits, the limited access fraternity of policing continues to resist the diversification invasion of "others" by clinging to the traditional racist and sexist spheres of influence exercised by the white heterosexual male officers.

The conservative nature[14] of most officers are similar to the military and includes a strong anti-homosexual attitude. This fraternal value system resists the implementation of hiring practices that openly recruits gays and lesbians. This resistance is based on behaviors perceived as feminine, being despised and not conducive to policing. Finally, a major source of resistance towards diversification is the homosexual lifestyles is that it was considered until recently as a deviant behavior. An ideologically opposed balance exists between perceived personal deviances and task of law enforcement's self-appointed role as moral entrepreneurs maintaining order over deviance.

Military Minorities Not Welcome

Group homogeneity and minority exclusion[15] show subcultural or out-groups existing within a larger and structurally established organization; the United States Military. Concerned with the obvious lack of representation of minority groups within the Special Operations Forces (SOF), Congress authorized an examination of the issues of why minorities do not join the SOF. They also sought solutions for increasing numbers to reflect the military's minority population.

Similar to cop culture, organizational structure has a strong effect on diversity. Perceptual barriers including attitudes or beliefs cause minorities to feel not welcomed or fit for SOF service. The military SOF are similar to the law enforcement SOG because both are small populations compared to the entire bodies. Also, both consist primarily of white males enduring the difficulties of entry level testing and specialized training.

Challenges to minority participation in the SOF include structural and perceptual barriers. Again, similar to law enforcement, these structural barriers include physical agility, application test scores, and academic requirements. Perceptual barriers include attitudes, manufactured cultures, and traditions causing minorities to believe they are not fit for SOF service.

Another key element to limiting the number of minorities is the current lack of role models. Minority candidates indicate that the lack of role models limits their interest in applying for duty. They claim the application and training processes were extremely difficult, but the absence of others with whom to identify made the prospect of successfully completing the process impossible.

Perceptions of Racism

The last major issue preventing minority participation in the SOF is the perceived racism within the specialized military units. The United States Navy SEALS, recognized as a white male dominated organization are not perceived as anti-minority or racist. At the other end of the spectrum, the United States Army Green Berets are associated with having racist attitudes limiting minority application. This perception whether actual or not may be an organizational tool used to exclude minority populations from even considering joining the forces.

The perception of racism has a historical connection to law enforcement beyond the fact that many military veterans migrate into policing following their active duty or during reserve service. The very origins of the profession have roots in racist purpose of mission with the slave patrols of the 1800's. The continuing social culture of policing as a white male dominated environment, and the restrictive effect of racial homogeneity in peer selections perpetuate this perception and reality.

The effects of social clustering[16,17,18] on agencies include high-level skill sets, demanding tasks and a hierarchical command structure provide as a tool for continuing subcultural segregation. By virtue of the group's desire to include only those of like sex, race and sexual orientation, the SOG promotes racism and sexism by exercising power over others wishing to join. The politics of racial and sexual exclusion not only affect public perception of the SOG, but policing as a whole. The powerful influence of the white, male heterosexual ethos remands policing into this current model of a restrictive work environment.

Culture Created by Assimilation

While race, gender and sexual orientation were the focus for these studies, all recognize the powerful influence of cultural perceptions. The researchers identify an institutional foundation capable of overwhelming individual characteristics through the socialization processes. The practice of becoming blue is prevalent in law enforcement, and an experiential change in perception is required to move diversity beyond the point of enculturation. Not only is the white-male centric fraternity entrenched in this population's mind, but it resonates in every minority's psyche. This unfortunate societal acceptance is what prevents women, minorities and gays from bothering to apply for positions with law enforcement. Application, testing, hiring, training and performance standards are founded in the historically heterosexual masculine institutional procedures. Cultural change remains in the gap between "others" not getting hired because they don't apply, and the straight white male getting accepted because they do.

In an attempt to understand the resistance to diversification, the following chapter examines the police culture created by assimilation and attempts to demystify the code of silence and the thin blue line. The formal and informal occupational socialization processes continue developing throughout the history of law enforcement to accommodate cop culture's status quo.

The formal processes centering on institutionalization confirm the difficulties of entering the profession. The informal processes centering on peer acceptance and social clustering demonstrate the difficulties of acceptance into the police culture. The strategies for professional entrance and social acceptance continue to evolve, but the culture of policing is very resistant to change. To understand the resistance to diversification, the following chapter examines the police culture created by assimilation. It will also attempt to demystify the code of silence and the thin blue line.

8
POLICE CULTURE

"Culture? I don't have a freakin clue about being cultured, but I know how to shoot the crap outta this sub-gun."
(Mississippi SWAT Operator, 2010)

Cop culture is described as combining themes of occupational activity, shared values, shared experiences, shared behaviors and shared efforts[1]. Common cultural characteristics are group cohesion, image of strength and authority, and territorial control. Many factors influence the cop culture, and the collective body's effects can be positive, negative or both on the individual. As part of this influence of culture, the officer experiences abstract concepts such as the thin blue line, the blue fraternity and a blue wall of silence affecting concrete behaviors.

Silent Codes and Blue Lines

To the idealistic applicant and cadet, the "line" separates the honest citizens from the victimizers of the public. To the fully socialized officer, the "line" separates them from the civilian population. To the SOG, the "line" is a barrier from civilian populations, criminals and officers (non-SOG) assigned to the traditional policing duties. To the civilian population, the "line" means nothing.

The "thin blue line" is the vanguard protecting the fraternity's behaviors, practices and activities from public exposure and accountability. Still, the fraternity of policing regardless of their concept of purpose, lives and dies to hold that line. The code of silence is an ideal that officers are socialized to comprehend and is what protects them while they conceptually fight to maintain the thin blue line.

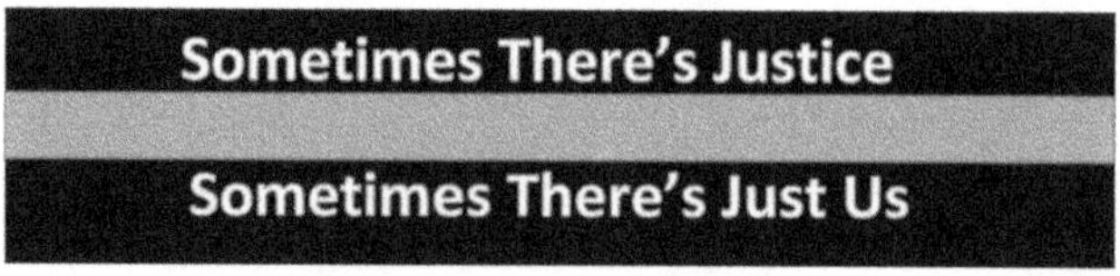

> Sometimes There's Justice
> Sometimes There's Just Us

Figure 8.1: Illustrates the Thin Blue Line and the isolationist ethos of the cop culture. *Source:* Created by Dr. Scott Silverii for *Cop Culture: Why Good Cops Go Bad*

A popular belief about the honor of the code of silence[2] is that officers are prohibited from reporting or testifying against fellow officers, the "No Rat" rule. In law enforcement the informant, snitch or rat is the lowest element within the policing operation. Associated with drug dealers and criminals willing to trade information for assistance in their own criminal prosecution, or for outright cash payments, the informant is despised. This institutional hatred for the "rat" is equally as intense for a fellow officer willing to turn on his "brother" by sharing information about illicit or illegal activities with the officer's supervisor.

This discourages an environment of accountability and permeates the culture of policing. Officers are reluctant to report misconduct by fellow officers, and may be punished by their peers for doing so. Exemplifying the strength of this code of silence was a study[3] of the Los Angeles Police Department (LAPD). The case looked at 90 LAPD officers who successfully sued the department. The officers had received disciplinary actions because of breaking the code of silence by reporting misconduct by other officers. This demonstrates how deep the institutional ethos of conformance to silence runs.

Code of Silence Protects Police Corruption

The relationship between police corruption and fitting into the police culture is strong. The altruistic selling point for silence is the engrained ideal first learned in the training academy that officers can only rely upon other officers. The "us versus them" paradigm begins there and increases in the depth of commitment to the practice as the stakes get higher and consequences become more serious than push-ups handed out as discipline from training instructors.

The code of silence not only protects cohorts, prevents researchers from gaining an outside perspective, but also shields the abnormal behavior each officer may choose to engage without ever worrying about questions from other officers.

Outsiders looking to explain cop corruption have created many elaborate theories of why it exists and how to stop it.

One of the first serious attempts to gain an understanding of the phenomena and is still referenced today, is the "Bad Apple" Theory of Herman Goldstein[4]. This theory surfaced during the 1970's community policing era and was an early attempt to understand the nature and extent of police corruption. The focus centered on "the problem officer" phenomenon and a Pollyanna view that only one or possibly a few officers were responsible for corrupt activities within an organization. Having gained popularity once proposed, it failed to explain how the isolated instances of corruption occurred in the first place and why some agencies were saddled with "rotten apples" but not others. This simplistic look at the actions of a few "bad" officers failed to examine the holistic picture facing the professional integrity challenge; the cop culture itself. Though discounted as conjecture because of the limitations of the study and the explanation, it still demonstrates a need for understanding and an avenue for exploring.

Discretion or Corruption

"It's not what you know, it's what you can prove."
(Alonzo Harris, played by Denzel Washington; Training Day (2001)

A primary concern for this work is that the terminologies gain an emphasis for one end of the descriptive spectrum over the other. The term "bad" is frequently used throughout the book but is operationalized to mean a vast expanse of understanding to cover police actions from an expectation for free tea at the burger joint to felonious criminal activities. Corruption is also a buzz word that immediately conjures images of characters from movies like the 1973 "Serpico" and the 2001 "Training Day."

Operationalizing the term "corruption" is difficult because of the unlimited applications associated with it and the appropriateness of context with which it is used. Similar to the term "bad," it depends on who is interpreting it. If an officer "fixes" a traffic ticket for a friend, is that corruption? If you get a ticket "fixed," is that officer corrupt and are you a co-conspirator? If the officer asks for a bribe of cash, sex or favor, is that corruption? Some lines are drawn more finely than others, so this is where once again it is critical to qualify the term "corruption." Any action taken where human interaction is involved is subject to allegations of corruption. Realistically, the only other option would be to handle the public like a robot-cop and use no sense of humanity at all. The interjection of humanity is called discretion.

The profession of law enforcement includes a majority of on-duty time that goes unsupervised. Officers are legally allowed a wide range of discretion in addressing situations they are called to investigate. Probably the most common occurrence and example are during the traffic stop. The officer regularly makes the determination to issue the violating motorist a citation, a written warning or a verbal warning. The officer also has the discretion to extend the scope of the investigatory traffic stop by checking the driver and passenger's criminal histories for active outstanding warrants for their arrest. Going further into the realm of discretion, the officer has the authority to detain the vehicle and summon a K-9 team to the scene of the initial traffic violation to sniff for the odor of illegal narcotics. Or the officer can do nothing, and just watch yet another speeding vehicle go by. This is a brief, but very typical example of officer discretion. Supervisors rarely question officers about the application of discretion, and the freedom to operate with a high level of autonomy provides a fertile ground for temptations leading to allegations of and actual corruption.

A research process attempts to take an in-depth look at corruption connected to occupational socialization. The value of this meta-analysis of police corruption demonstrates that the socialization process ensures a culture of isolationism as a staple of policing and remains entrenched to ensure autonomy between officer and citizen. The investigation into police corruption[5] failed to materialize, but did show the power of the code of silence and the restricted access allowed by officers.

Failing to penetrate the thin blue line, the researcher's final analysis admitted to relying only upon past studies, estimates and incomplete information. The process of indoctrinating police officers is a powerful tactic for organizational and individual self-preservation.

No police agency is completely free of corruption, and police officers, the "blue nights" entrusted and empowered to enforce the law can become some of the most aggressive criminals themselves[6].

Although unfortunate that this researcher choose to take this perspective by generalizing law enforcement into a category as corrupt, the issue particular to this project is demonstrating the power of the cultural expectation of silence. Being unable to gain access behind the blue line and able to breach the code of silence, this researcher also became a victim to the culture of isolationism.

The United States Department of Justice[7] (DOJ) reveals the culture of maintaining the code of silence is different among agencies. An instrument was developed to measure integrity among police officers by conducting structured interviews using hypothetical scenarios focusing on integrity instead of corruption.

This study measuring the culture of police integrity includes the definition of integrity as the "normative" inclination of police officers to resist the temptations to abuse the rights and privileges of their office. The reliance upon the term "normative" was not clarified as to whether the scale is based on the general civilian population or the law enforcement's perceptual predisposition.

While this attempt to examine cop culture was successful, it is the realization that interjecting terms such as "normative," that should readily apply to the entirety of the population, must be considered in the context of the culture with which it is applied. The cop culture is unique not only because of the function of the occupation, but equally in part to the potential for informal expectancies to lead once ethical officers to accept and then expect a normalizing of illicit or illegal activity as a perk of the position.

To avoid the difficulties experienced by asking officers about corruption, the DOJ only queries officers about integrity. The study attempted to circumvent the officer's concerns about civilians prying into their culture by only asking them to identify how seriously they view corruption, how willing are they to report it, and how willing they are to support the disciplinary actions taken because of the corrupt behavior.

The DOJ showed that the code of silence is practiced at most every agency, but the depths of commitment vary. A common thought is that most internal police problems are a result of a few officers. The idea that officers will autonomously investigate their fellow officers draws external criticism. Results from the measure of integrity survey shows that the more serious officers considered a particular violation, the more likely they were to report it.

The challenge also came with trying to define seriousness of violation. Actions such as covering up the receiving of gratuities, police alcohol related accidents (on and off duty), excessive use of force and supervisors providing preferential treatment for officers who provide private favors are not viewed as serious violations of behavior and would not be reported.

Equally significant as the measurement of integrity is the realization that environments of integrity differ greatly across police agencies. There are disparate levels of integrity throughout United States law enforcement agencies but the study did not provide a tool for measuring the degree of integrity. Although a different method was used than the corruption study, the project suffered the similar challenges as officers are reluctant to answer questions posed by outsiders. This is another example of the commitment to each other and the ideals for protecting each other's and their own self interests. While these civilian researchers toiled to design studies avoiding the code of silence, the next section describes efforts to directly target it.

Dishonoring the Code

Taking the culture head on, this project studied the inculcation for honoring the code of silence that significantly impacts the police profession in a negative manner. Through participant observations and institutional policy review, the report documents the code's presence in most law enforcement agencies to varying degrees. The code of silence is not written in police training manuals but is culturally expectant and honored within the institution of policing[8]. Additionally discovered is that the code of silence is passed down through the generations from veterans to rookie officers ensuring the continuation of the policing culture, and defines police culture to include the "us versus them" philosophy, along with the powerful feelings of loyalty and solidarity with fellow officers.

"...this sense of loyalty is displaced by the peer expectation of not reporting or lying about criminal behavior committed by fellow officers." [9]

Ultimately, the civilian researcher admits the inability to quantitatively report a level of confidence because the participants refuse to cross the thin blue line. Honoring the code of silence[10] has a significantly negative impact on cop culture and agency integrity. This explains why the sense of loyalty is displaced by the peer expectation of not reporting or lying about criminal behavior committed by fellow officers.

A former veteran police officer[11] documented the destructive nature of the code in an autobiography. The work summarizes the organizational infusion of the code and the negative impacts on the police culture as summarized in this statement:

As terrible as it is, there is no escaping the Code. It is as inevitable as your childhood disease and just as necessary. Each stinging battle with the Code will either be an inoculation of the spirit and an opportunity to grow stronger or a crippling injury to your integrity. Regardless of the outcome, there will be vivid images you can't erase from your memory. There will always be the mental and physical scars to remind you of your battles[12].

This misguided loyalty to another employee, who openly commits a criminal or procedural offense, relies upon an expectation of silence. This not only promotes the corrupt activities, but also destroys the silent witness's integrity. The code of silence protects the conceptual integrity of the thin blue line and supports an autonomous dark blue environment. It also voids an environment of accountability and leads to a culture of deviance and violence.

Deviance and Violence

"Certainly there is no hunting like the hunting of man, and those who have hunted armed men long enough and liked it, never really care for anything else thereafter."
(Ernest Hemingway, 1936)

How do officers become fascinated with the "hunting" of armed men? Is it an innate characteristic passed along through our primal genetic coding, or is it learning behavior reinforced by a profession encouraging the application of physical force against other people? I have found that liminality once again becomes an integral part of the process leading public servants into an environment that encourages the use of force upon the public it swore to serve.

It may be that slapping of the handcuffs on the first arrestee, or the first foot chase leading to a capture, or the first fistic encounter with a violent parolee who will go to any extreme to avoid going back to prison. Each time force of physical violence is applied, it ushers the officer further along the path of liminality and accepting the condition of "serving" the public also requires using power against it.

Perceptual changes leading to deviance and violence occur for officers while passing through the liminal thresholds. The experiential depth of cultural commitment spent behind the thin blue line promotes crossing through the thresholds until reaching a point of antisocial conduct. The more years on the job, the more exposed to violence, and the more engaged in deviant behaviors the officer becomes. This increases the opportunity for becoming disenfranchised with the organization's core ideology of duty, honor and service.

The following section describes the trajectory of evolutionary periods in the careers of law enforcement officers[13,14,15,16] and how the beginning a journey towards honest public service, may lead to professional deviance.

Policing and Alcohol Consumption

Would you believe attending a police academy causes you to drink alcohol? Data shows a causal relationship between attending a police academy and increased alcohol consumption[17]. The results from a longitudinal study uses a survey and structured interviews to examine police recruits for tracking increases in consumption patterns throughout their first twelve months in law enforcement. It also showed that as police training and experience increases, so does the risk of harm from consuming alcohol. This increase is caused by the indoctrination of recruits into a culture of alcohol consumption driven by peer socialization, desire for acceptance and social clustering networks.

Similar to a U.S. study, an Australian investigation[18] discovers the relationship between alcohol consumption and policing. Australian police self-reported that 48% of policemen and 40% of policewomen drank alcohol excessively. This is compared to a civilian population reporting 10% of men and 7% of women drinking to an excessive amount. Excessive alcohol consumption that begins with the desire for socialization and acceptance does not end with academy graduation. A survey of police sergeants[19] report that over 40% drank on workdays and binge drinking among the law enforcement profession occurs more frequently than the general population. Sex and age of the first-line supervisors were not influencing factors as both male and females reported a rate of 31% participating in binge drinking.

Police, compared to other occupations including transportation, health care, metal fabrication, hospitality and emergency services show officers reported higher consumption of alcohol rates than the other professions. The law enforcement's drinking subculture requires the consumption alcohol becomes as an element of fitting in. Drinking subcultures[20] are characterized by an environment stressing teamwork and peer pressure. Alcohol use is integrated into the job with a permissive attitude towards consumption. The nature of work leads to drinking off duty with peers to relax and debrief. The occupational identity is also associated with leisure time and activities involving alcohol consumption.

A classic ethnographic examination of over 20 years studied[21] the LAPD and discovered the drinking subculture characteristics. Although the permissive use of alcohol is not the only reason officers focus on the clustering aspects of socialization, the practice of drinking plays a role in solidifying close relationships between cops. The studies in this section show the profession of law enforcement does impact the individual officer's level of risk for alcohol problems. The process of induction and enculturation suggests a strong correlation to influencing the officer's alcohol consumption and further validates the unique environment within which police officers operate, both professionally and personally. Further, the act of consuming alcohol may serve as a gateway for more serious antisocial behaviors, leading good cops who may have never been predisposed to alcohol abuse to once again be ushered towards a path of becoming "bad."

Gangland Violence

The theory of legitimized police violence and peer acceptance is similar to the effects of groupthink[22] on the deterioration of moral judgment. It also dehumanizes others for gaining favorable opinion of those most like them. The components of groupthink are similar to the SOG subculture and are included to show the unique nature of "belonging." There is a safety in "sameness," and demonstrated in the earlier socialization studies, it is best for ensuring job longevity that the individual officer "not make waves."

Chapter 9 provides an in-depth examination of policing's state authorized use of violence, but this section serves as an example of the outcomes produced by a homogenous group binding together under the pretense organizational unity. Policing image regularly romanticizes about the cultural similarities to the gang-like culture in popular movies and television. This may explain why law enforcement promotes itself as the largest street gang in America and refers to itself as the Bad Boys.

Commitment to Deviance

To understand how an idealistic officer falls victim to the professional deviance promoted by groupthink, you must consider the influence of labeling[23]. Negative labeling leads individuals to become identified with that subculture. The identification with the label of abnormality creates a deep commitment to the actions and association of that group. Divergent careers and labeling processes may heavily influence career trajectories, and the disciplinary actions used to deter unusual behavior, may actually promote it.

The placement in an environment where deviance is the influencing force may lead to the development of deviance as a self-concept. This phenomenon is similar to the officers assigned to SOG. Although they serve in an elite unit of law enforcement, they are seen by non-SOG as "others." Because the SOG conducts legitimate policing functions using covert operations unknown to their fellow officers, they are perceived as "gray" cops existing too close to the unethical edge. The effects of associating with a stigma of deviance may lead to an irreversible investment into the label, thus strengthening the level of personal commitment to the career path, i.e. becoming bad.

A final source of structural commitment or the external influence is the difficulty of terminating the line of deviant action. The original target of this researcher's case profile[24] is a former outlaw motorcycle club (OMC) member describing the difficulty for getting out of the group, and shows many similarities to SOG. The subject explains that quitting an OMC often involves violent beatings, stabbings, shootings and the physical torture of removal by cutting off all club related tattoos.

Similar to this account of the difficulties for exiting the OMC's, my professional observations also show difficulty in terminating assignments into SOG except by poor performance reviews, disciplinary actions, termination or resignation. This makes leaving the SOG with honor a rare option and exposes the officer to a continuing irregular identity. The forced continuation within a culture of unethical or illegal behavior creates an atmosphere where affecting the liminal change of ideology becomes highly possible.

This section reviews illustrations of the influence of liminality and groupthink. Officers finding themselves in a suspended state of being, or a transitioning phase of being neither here nor there relative to the personal identity versus the collective persuasion of an identity unaligned with organizational ideals. Officers placed in a position of occupational transition are also susceptible to having their core beliefs shaped by subcultural associations. The power of ideological transitioning within the law enforcement community provides the foundation for understanding the detrimental personal effects of exposure to and becoming labeled as "bad."

Personal Effects: Social and Individual Fracturing

Cadets attending academy training unwittingly experience a transitioning or liminal state during the fitting in process. The liminality is made possible by the vulnerable status of officers as the enculturation process overwhelms conventional norms with tradition, identification with deviance and a fraternity based upon secrecy. This section of literature review examines the effects experienced by officers causing an institutional detachment and communal rebellion against traditional societal values. This is how the "us versus them" mentality takes shape.

Cops pride themselves in running towards danger while others flee, but what is the extent of the emotional and psychological toll suffered while they run? The SOG Operator prepares for physical demands of the assignment with regular and strenuous training, yet it is the undetected effects[25] causing the most personal and social harm.

The United States law enforcement profession employs over 800,000 municipal, county, state and federal officers. From these ranks emerge the SOG without clear or consistent qualifications for selection and whose professional standards vary between jurisdictions. What does it take to make a successful undercover agent? You may be surprised.

Making of an Undercover Agent

Since World War II, the United States government has worked to identify characteristics of an effective undercover agent for national and law enforcement interests. The duality of expectation begins when an officer is recruited based on performance measures to include good judgment and integrity, but then is taught to lie. The undercover agent must falsify his identity to misrepresent himself to others for the sake of detecting crime and gathering information. This same agent is also expected to return home at the end of their shift to resume a regular family life.

To examine the detrimental effects to SOG Operators in undercover capacities, a study[26] of 271 undercover agents demonstrate that chronic exposure to undercover work causes psychological symptoms. Also, those agents with cognitive traits such as extroversion and emotionality are prone to excessive drug and alcohol use. Undercover work becomes associated with an erosion of psychological, behavioral, and moral standards jeopardizing both health and police operations. There is a tremendous conflict of living a double life. This causes SOG undercover agents to experience elevated symptoms resembling those of psychiatric outpatients.

In addition to the psychological harm associated with undercover operations,[27] SOG Narcotics Operators were examined to reveal a disassociation from self-identity and unprompted reappearances of altered identities developed for conducting undercover operations. For example; upon entering an assignment into a Narcotics unit, the officer receives training in the practice of conducting undercover drug purchasing operations. The officer is instructed to begin constructing an undercover identity that shall be assumed during her role-playing in the course of actual drug purchasing operations.

The depth and complexity of the undercover identity might be as simple as using a false first name for initial introductions to a potential drug dealer who has become the target of your investigation. The assumed identity may also involve a completely new, yet fictitious life including official identification, residence and sometimes family. What might appear as innocuous fantasy or role-playing, when conducted under stressful or life-and-death situations exacts a heavy toll on the individual forced to slide in and out of character.

Despite the depth of commitment or the duration of the undercover operation requiring the falsification of the undercover agent's assumed identity, the toll is exacted upon the individual's psyche. Additional research shows that even the most ethical of officers may succumb to the powerful draw of the SOG sub-culture[28].

There are occupational maladjustment, psychiatric disturbances and personality changes associated with undercover work. Those at highest risk for suffering this effect are the elite units within law enforcement, who serve outside the traditional boundaries of policing. The acts of establishing deviant networks give rise to stress disturbances, corruption and perceptions of "self as unreal," along with paranoia and other troubles. This study expands the concept to determine the extent to which the alter-persona becomes part of who the agent really is. Dissociative Identity Disorder (DID) has been linked to undercover agents and was used as a criminal trial defense strategy in 1997 when a former Federal Bureau of Investigations undercover agent was arrested for attempted murder[29].

The DID phenomena was examined in a study of federal undercover agents participating in a three week training exercise to measure the strength of attachments to the false identities assumed by these agents. After just three weeks of role assumption, 61 percent of the participants acknowledged that their false identities appeared without calling it up in a nonoperational context. There are numerous actual experiences involving field operators who have experienced difficulty in subduing their fabricated identity, such as former FBI Agent Bennett cited in the study. The conclusion shows that predispositions to dissociative experiences have a greater influence on the reappearance of an alter-identity assumed during undercover work while in a non-operational setting.

The length of time spent in these operational assignments is also related to the similarly harmful effects to those in the cop culture working SOG duty. It is linked to higher rates of corruption, disciplinary infractions and social detachment. This time-in-assignment effect is related to the occupational socialization trajectory model influencing an officer's commitment to deviance as stages of liminality occur throughout the course of a career. While time-in-assignment is not the focus of this particular book, it does bear mentioning, and is again reiterated in the future studies recommendations.

Living on the societal and ethical fringe creates an antisocial effect[30,31] on the officers that may lead to deviant, subcultural allegiance to principles separate and apart from the organizational priorities. Studying[32] a municipal police department's undercover agents in the field of operation, the embedded participant observation shows a close affiliation with the criminal lifestyle and the exposure to the drug culture for determining if these relationship affected the SOG's beliefs, attitudes and behaviors.

A survey design was developed that included the undercover agents and patrol officers also as a comparison group. This unique element of simultaneously studying uniformed officers is critical to the purpose of the showing the disparity between the two cultures. While a patrol officer's performance is measured by anonymous activities such as writing tickets to motorists and making arrests, the undercover agent's performance is based on the ability to misrepresent herself for the purpose of establishing criminal networks leading to intelligence and arrests.

While traditional officers working assignments such as Uniform Patrol do experience great dangers of physical harm due to the nature of conducting numerous vehicular traffic stops on unknown persons, the undercover agent's ability to become intimately familiar with the target of their investigation causes stressors from undercover work manifesting itself as anxiety, loneliness, isolation, relationship problems and paranoia[33]. It is during that process that the agent's challenges begin. The agent seldom has the benefit of anonymity, as their goal is to establish a personal, albeit fabricated relationship with their intended target.

The results were similar to an earlier study[34] of the Honolulu Police Department to show that undercover agents experience stressors from undercover work that manifest themselves as detrimental to the individual officer and potentially the organization. Additional findings from this embedded attempt to understand and document the police culture shows that SOG Agents felt more nervousness and anxiety while performing law enforcement activities than did Patrol officers. More often, Patrol officers felt that working police assignments was detrimental to their health than did the SOG Agents. More SOG Agents expressed concerns over the stress of having to make split-second decisions that could have had serious consequences than Patrol officers. Each discipline noted dynamics effecting one over the other and the attempt to compare Agents to Patrol officers may not be as valid as originally intended. The civilian researcher[35] wisely admitted that no conclusions could be drawn based on the survey data.

Although this observational effort includes careful applications of social science methodologies, it once again proves the isolationist culture of cops. Attempting to measure the variables of fear and perceptions of other emotions in an occupation forced to suppress them was difficult to quantify. Finally, the researcher confirmed first hand that although the agents denied using drugs and alcohol during the survey, direct field observations contradicted their responses. This is a critical threat to the validity of all responses provided, and further reinforces the strength of the policing sub-culture's resistance to all on the other side of the blue line[36].

To discuss the psychological effects caused to undercover agents as a result of arresting drug dealers may seem like a foreign and unrealistic idea to anyone never having worked in an undercover capacity, there are dynamics unknown to those who have not. SOG

Narcotics Operators identify investigative targets based on information received or self-initiated activities such as street surveillances. Once a target is identified, the Operator begins compiling research about the target to include the criminal history, active arrest warrants, livelihood (legitimate or otherwise), his family, children, friends and associates. Sometimes, the Agent even listens to personal conversations of the target through court authorized telephone wire taps.

By learning as much as possible about the target, even watching him during regular surveillance, the Operator gains a degree of attachment (not affection) to the target. The target becomes a real person outside of their drug dealing activities, with parents, siblings, kids, etc. Your job, your duty as a SOG undercover agent is to remove him from those activities by purchasing illegal narcotics, affecting an arrest and search warrant for his person and property, and then invading his home and family with the SWAT unit to seize additional contraband.

Another element of conflict and identity disassociation for undercover agents may result through the course of becoming acquainted with the target as the Operator works to gain the trust of the drug dealer. The undercover agent enters another world to begin associations with other friends, targets, informants and innocent civilians caught in the mix of the underworld's illegal activities. Whether it means the undercover agent feels compassion, or hate for the target, or becomes seduced by the easy access to cash, sex, weapons or drugs, it is a realistic temptation that may prevent the Operators from disengaging in the behavior after the deal is done.

The cop culture is complex as it encompasses many disciplines, areas of specialization and individual interests. The undercover operation's subculture adds to this mixture a unique element of asking officers commissioned to serve as the public's moral entrepreneur to "make deals with the devil" in order to gain information, buy illegal drugs or apprehend dangerous felons. Recruiting "altar boys" for this type of work has not been successful in producing effective undercover agents, or stemming the deviant behavior of the SOG subculture. Although the undercover operations do not require a return to Francois Vidocq's claim that it "takes a thief to catch a thief," at a minimum, it certainly does require sheepdogs.

Don't be Sheep

"To protect the sheep you gotta catch the wolf, and it takes a wolf to catch a wolf." (Alonzo Harris, played by Denzel Washington; Training Day (2001))

Regardless of how tempted, stressed or strained an officer may feel inside, the cardinal rule is "Silence is golden." SOG are socialized to internalize stressful situations they face, and verbalizing these issues is a sign of weakness. The warrior ideal is promoted within the SOG subculture. A popular writer and speaker among this SOG warrior community is Lt Col Dave Grossman (retired), who promotes his work about the effects on officers who kill another person. His article describing policing's role in society inspires a phrase used by SOG to communicate one simple message; always be armed and always be prepared.

The phrase "don't be sheep" was heard while I conducted interviews and observations in different states. I use it personally to end correspondence to other SOG during my career. The phrase to most people would seem pointless, but to those understanding their position in society's margins, it is a powerful reminder of their place in this world. It is an analogy of where law enforcement stands within a society.

To law enforcement, peaceful and productive citizens are the sheep who never purposefully intend to harm another. Wolves, on the other hand are the violent chronic offenders preying on society. Sheepdogs are society's warriors standing in the gap when the wolves viciously attack the sheep. Sheepdogs remain in the margins until needed, but the mainstream flock of sheep never fully accepts them. The closing statement from this article is what encourages SOG to embrace their position in society for the sake of their sworn oaths.

.. and so the warrior must strive to confront denial in all aspects of his life, and prepare himself for the day when evil comes. If you are a warrior who is legally authorized to carry a weapon and you step outside without that weapon, then you become a sheep, pretending that the bad man will not come today. No one can be "on" 24/7, for a lifetime. Everyone needs down time. But if you are authorized to carry a weapon, and you walk outside without it, just take a deep breath, and say this to yourself... "Baa."[37]

The more engrained an officer becomes within the cop culture, the more entrenched they become in the warrior mindset. Survival at all costs dominates his focus, even if that comes at the expense of adhering to organizational policies and respecting the rights of the public. The warrior mindset, mixed with an absence of institutional accountability mechanisms overseeing operations are yet another combinations of variables providing the liminal pathway for good cops to go bad. Be it a sheepdog or the wolf, the culture of policing is embedded with violence. The next chapter examines the nature of violence and the requirement for applying it to ensure the needs of the state are met.

9

STATE SPONSORED VIOLENCE

"...I'm one of these guys who thinks cops can slap people around from time to time — if it's called for and if they don't get caught...."
(Jonah Goldberg, 2001)

The image of Darth Vader's Storm Troopers clad in a protective white shell with superior weaponry is one visual that surfaces at the notion that law enforcement's primary purpose is not to serve the public, but to suppress it. Absent the uniform and laser firing weapons, police do serve as the state's arm of violence to ensure social compliance with the laws and regulations enacted by the governing body. To clarify the terms force and violence, it is expressed to cover the range of actions available to officers from the mere threat of calling the police to applying lethal force and taking someone's life.

The relationship between policing's role in state sponsored violence and the application of that violence to legitimize an officer's credibility among peers while establishing the foundational tone for the organizational promotion for the use of force is dominant in the cop culture[1]. While the seeds of antisocial behavior are sown in the academy, the career attraction towards violence is found in policing's role of state sponsored violence[2]. When exploring the claim of justifiable use of force in American society you must ask; does the authority to seize or take a human life legitimize the policing profession, or further alienate it from the societal ideas?

The thin blue line and code of silence exist in cop culture to create a gulf between the civilian population and police to maintain autonomy as an act of power over the public[3]. This organizational separation from the public legitimizes the function of policing as an agent of control for the state. Secrecy allows the police to maintain a distance to deliberately mystify the public, thus creating an aura of command over the civilian population, and allows law enforcement agencies to act with impunity.

This social tension causes a natural fracturing between the public and the agency authorized to protect it. The police exist as a service occupation, yet exercise the power to discipline those whom it serves. It is this confliction of public servant / social authoritarian paradigm that contributes to the anti-social behaviors, and creates an environment of individual officer legitimacy through the application of force.

Whether this force of violence is innate or a learned behavior, the officers involved is introduced into this service society. The abnormal behaviors begin during the police academy's peer clustering experience that socializes the officer's imitative behavior patterns[4]. The socialized police officer's attraction to violence is entrenched in the relationship as their obligation to participate in it increases with their desire to become socialized. In a homogenous environment the encouragement for exercising force serves to bind the fraternal relationships.

The use of violence as a way for officers to earn peer credibility and provide justification for the fringe lifestyle is combined with a legislated use of force justifying their normative engagement[5].

Because officers are regularly accused of excessive use of force, police agencies use internal mechanisms to investigate complaints about officer misconduct. This mechanism may utilize a system or matrix (early warning system EWS) designed to identify behavior, characteristics, or independent information that an officer has over extended his appreciation for the use of force. A National Institute of Justice (NIJ) study[6] reports that agencies having an EWS in place show that officers referred into the system for counter-institutional or aggressive behavior were promoted at higher rates than those officers having never been identified as requiring intervention.

Research[7] also explains that police officers hold a sub-cultural affinity for the seductions of living on "the edge" as detailed in Chapter 11. This associational attraction may explain police officers' propensity to engage in the use of force against civilians, as well as the surprising phenomenon wherein police officers emulate the fringe behaviors of the OMC's "the other." Themes such as mental toughness; solidarity, independence, and edge control are common to both the police sub-culture and the world of outlaw bikers. Resistance to the control of the normative worldview of acceptable behaviors, secrecy, and a militaristic organizational structure characterize both groups and entrench them firmly with the margins of society. Although both sub-cultures are based on intimidation to demand compliance through image, action and behavior; only law enforcement is accepted as legitimate for social control.

The philosophical mission of law enforcement as the face of and foremost realization of formal social control is based on its ability and capacity to exercise force within the discretionary boundaries of the individual officer. Parameters for long-standing and continuing discussion of the legitimacy and authority for violence in society as expressed by police behavior and related consequences have been established[8]. The definitional understanding of police power states that the use of police violence is normalized, and claims, "It is possible, certainly not unthinkable, that at some future time policemen may be able to compel the desired outcome of any problem without ever resorting to physical force. But it appears that in the existing structure of communal life in our society such force is not wholly avoidable. This being the case, not only its avoidance, but its employment must be methodically normalized"[9].

Conflicting Roles

The police "role" in society is described as one being extremely difficult to change, and their capacity to use force is the core of that role. The role of exercising unquestionable force requires that someone in society has to play the role of "bully." The role of society's moral entrepreneur is one of unquestionable and indisputable authority as the police are not required to provide the general public with an explanation of their actions, nor secure public opinion or consent while exercising force to conduct their functions.

In a separate study exploring the public's perception of the police role as society's "bully"[10], the area of the public's greatest discomfort is the impunity with which police administer the use of force, especially lethal force. Policing is a unique provider profession that asks officers to deliver services to clients who both request their assistance (voluntary clients) and who do not want their attentions (involuntary clients). This complex relationship with the police is said to forge an iron fist inside a velvet glove paradigm when police take enforcement actions (iron fist) towards the involuntary "clients" and provide assistance (velvet glove) to the voluntary "clients."[11]

Another seminal study examines the relationship between policing's role in state sponsored violence and the application of that violence to cement an officer's credibility within an organization. It is the authority granted by the state to use force of any degree along the continuum of force from physical presence to deadly force that separates the occupation of policing from every other. Policies and regulations regarding the use of force by law enforcement are vague and purposefully left open to interpretation[12]. An observation is made that;

"The violent event is multivalent and the complexities are reflected in the control mechanisms, which are legal, administrative, and occupational in origin. Legal controls are weak, the substantive case law is inconsistent, and departmental regulations and policies on the use of force are variable"[13].

Leaving this area open to officer discretion is critical for the safety of the officer, who, if required to base every action of force on policy, would place himself in imminent fear of harm or death.

Currently there is no standard definition for the use of force exercised by law enforcement officers. The International Association of Chiefs of Police (IACP) is the world's oldest and largest nonprofit membership organization of police executives, and defines force as "that amount of effort required by police to compel compliance from an unwilling subject," and the IACP defines excessive use of force as "the application of an amount and/or frequency of force greater than that required to compel compliance from a willing or unwilling subject"[14]. Each agency is allowed the autonomy to establish their individual policies regarding officer use of force applications.

A police use of force review for the Bureau of Justice Statistics was conducted that states "...the legal test of excessive force...is whether the police officer reasonably believed that such force was necessary to accomplish a legitimate police purpose..."[15] However, there are no universally accepted definitions of "reasonable" and "necessary" because the terms are subjective. These terms along with the asserted vague use-of-force policies demonstrate the purposefully abstract concepts associated with very realistic circumstances based on the application of physical violence by the police. The NIJ published a national best-practice recommendation model[16] detailing the phases for the Use-of-Force Continuum. Most law enforcement agencies have policies guiding their use of force that loosely follow this guideline.

These policies describe an escalating series of actions an officer may take to resolve a situation. This continuum generally has many levels, and officers are instructed to respond with a level of force appropriate to the situation at hand. This recommendation also acknowledges that the officer may move from one part of the continuum to another in a matter of seconds depending on the level of threat presented.

Use-of-Force Continuum

- Officer Presence — No force is used. This is considered the best way to resolve a situation because the threat of civilian or officer injury is minimal. The mere presence of a law enforcement officer works to deter crime or diffuse a situation. The officers' attitudes are professional and nonthreatening, and compliance is directly the result of the civilian's consent.
- Verbalization — Force is not-physical. Officers issue calm, nonthreatening commands, such as "Let me see your identification and registration." Officers may increase their volume and shorten commands in an attempt to gain compliance. Short commands might include "Stop," or "Don't move." A common police academy training technique is verbal judo which enables the officer to calm confrontational people and redirect the behavior to diffuse potentially situations, perform professionally under all conditions and achieve the desired outcome in the encounter.
- Empty-Hand Control — Officers use bodily force to gain control of a situation. Using "soft" techniques which are control and compliance measures requiring no impact with the individual, but does involve the officer making physical contact. The officer uses techniques such as grabs, holds and joint locks to restrain an individual. Using "hard" techniques escalates the use-of-force option to a higher degree of physical violence imposed upon a non-compliant individual. The officers may use punches and kicks to restrain an individual.

- Less-Lethal Methods — Officers use less-lethal technologies to gain control of a situation. A variety of options exists to include;
- *Blunt impact* - Officers may use a baton or projectile to immobilize a combative person. *Chemical* - Officers may use chemical sprays or projectiles embedded with chemicals to restrain an individual (e.g., pepper spray). *Conducted Energy Devices (CEDs)* - Officers may use CEDs to immobilize an individual. CEDs discharge a high-voltage, low-amperage jolt of electricity at a distance (e.g. Taser device),
- Lethal Force — Officers use lethal weapons to gain control of a situation. This should only be used if a suspect poses a serious threat to the officer or another individual. Officers may use deadly weapons such as firearms to stop an individual's actions.

The NIJ describes the police's legitimized use of force as a means to control social order. Officers receive guidance from their individual agencies, but no universal set of law enforcement rules governs when officers should use force and how much. As an example of police using force against the public, is a report claiming that the police kill people at a rate that ranges from six to thirty times that at which they are shot. Those whom they shoot are not a random assortment of individuals, class members, ethnic groups, or perpetrators of crimes. Nor are those who are shot more likely to be armed and dangerous than to be unarmed and helpless[17].

A leading theorist in the field of police violence documents that "The police are violent, and their violence supports the social interests with which they are aligned."[18] He further illustrates how the direct relationships between judicial and legislative controls work to effect policies shaping the use of violence to achieve the end results of the state. To provide an avenue of expression through the application of state authorized and modestly regulated violence, police administrators have been ambiguous about post-use of force investigations for the purpose of allowing these rites of passage and acceptance into the policing fraternity. If the assertion[19] is true that the act of policing equals the application of violence, then the execution of that violence by the individual officer is critical for professional and peer acceptance.

A further contention is that the violent nature of individual officers is resultant upon the state's dependence upon force and the necessity for secrecy, loyalty and the internal orientation of the officer to be established through the exercise of applying violence.

"Because the sense of self of the officer is affirmed by exercises in violence, officers are motivated to define administrative rules as being arbitrary, capriciously applied, and the means by which higher administrators protect their own vested interests-'"cover their asses"[20].

Para-Policing Violence

A look at violence and the police role shows it encompasses various levels of institutionalization starting with the occupational socialization of the officer's peer validation. The frequency of executing violence is also linked with the officer's age, rank and assignment. In groups such as felony warrant apprehension teams and special weapons and tactics (SWAT) units, the officer is expected to encounter and display more aggression. Hesitation to do so is looked upon as failure and associations within the social cluster are threatened.

The proliferation of specially training police para-military units, commonly referred to as SWAT continue to increase[21]. Data shows that incidents of violent crime requiring an intensified activation of this resource are declining, yet the allocation of resources, training, finances and equipment are diverted into these units. Despite the disciplined propensity towards violence and destruction potential these units possess, American law enforcement is progressively moving towards further militarization[22]. The modern incarnation of the Special Weapons and Tactics (SWAT) unit began in 1967 at the LAPD for responding to and managing critical situations is detailed in Chapter 2.

The paradigm shift from "community officer" to the SOG Operator shows[23] that contrary to the country's request for a return to the neighborhood policing model, policing remains entrenched in a violent ideology. Law enforcement agencies entered into the tactical arena to claim their shares of federal funding, specialized training and surplus military combat gear ranging from BDU trousers to M-16 rifles to helicopters and APC (armored personnel carriers.) Although the demand for high-level response above the capabilities of Patrol and Detectives resources did not significantly increase, nearly every American city police department with at least one hundred officers claimed to have a SWAT unit. This increase marks a significant rise of SWAT units since the 1980s era of zero tolerance for crime[24].

The need to increase the potential resources for the execution of violence by a policing agency through SWAT has promoted an uncontrolled growth in the creation of these units. This proliferation for violence-mission based police units has also created an environment for unregulated training standards and operational practices. Unfortunately, the call for policing's toughest and most violent officers to join SWAT may have presented an environment for deviance that has attracted very aggressive officers. Because the use of force and the intimidation associated with SWAT, it is more common to staff a unit for status than to decommission them due to lack of need.

Although individual officers and units such as SWAT are highly trained, it is impossible to establish policy dictating every encounter scenario requiring officers to apply a degree of force. The attempt to do so would effectively constrain an officer's ability to protect himself and the public. The intentional open-ended interpretation for what is an appropriate level of force is meaningful and necessary for the state to maintain a posture of social control through physical deterrence[25].

Peer Validation

Demonstrating the relationship between the state's authorization of violence and the police role also shows a deeper interpretation particular to the occupational validation of the officer among his peers and the communal effect of the singular act of applying violence by that officer to the ideological conception of social acceptance. Whether it is through the indoctrination of death exposure, violent criminality, or a fraternal culture bound by the code of silence; stages of liminality or transitioning points in an individual officer's career are achieved through the experiencing of each threshold until the individual becomes "successfully" socialized.

This passage through the acculturation process creates an occupationally socialized officer who is advanced in the stages of separating himself from normative societal ideals. The officer's very participation in the acts of violence, both authorized and unauthorized begins to solidify his commitment to the social clustering phenomenon. There is a relational association between cops and organized groups living life within the fringes of society. This may be attributed to the "sheepdog" syndrome, or something more primal calling officers trapped within the doldrums of rigid conformance and standard operating procedures. Whichever the dynamic that draws cops towards the bad behavior, an association with labels of deviance are a product of operating absent of direct and informed supervision.

The professional and personal effects on the officer executing the state's violent acts upon its citizenry exacts a toll through the alienation from societal ideas. There are definitive characteristics associated with establishing a commitment towards a deviant career.[26] Another element critical to the deepening of deviance is the lack of what is referred to as "face-to-face interaction," or the absence of conventional ties to others. The officers begin to separate themselves from traditional support systems to include family, civilian friends, church and mainstream social activities. The separation is a result of the officers' use of violence against the community that makes it difficult for the officer to associate with the community, and the community to relate experientially to the officer.

This lack of grounding in the anchors of a civil society contributes to the officer's lack of access to conventional networks and promotes the deviant associations of those in a similar pattern. Because of the "us against them" paradigm, the fellow divergent networks consist of the other officers labeled likewise. This adversarial position towards civil society is created through the generational and informal education of the rookie officers that homogeneity is guaranteed, along with the duty of honoring the code. Official definitions[27] used to describe the police culture have multiple meanings to include the "us versus them" mentality that pits officers against society, criminals and agency officials. This adversarial socialization process begins at the police training academy as detailed in Chapter 5.

Once again, looking at the holistic act of policing, the bi-polar confliction of expectation exhibits yet another point of tension for police officers to address during the course of their duties. There are no official training manuals explaining this requirement of force, even the lowest level of force executed by mere "physical presence," but it is an expectation of the cop culture. The gaining of organizational autonomy by using violence reinforces the acts of deviance in the SOG, and indicates to the Operator that they are free from authority to operate as they chose. Is there any question why the cop culture isolates itself from administrative and public engagement?

Police are victim to the control of the state who wields the profession as the arm of violence against its own people to ensure compliance with social, political and regulatory agendas. Police are victim to their own culture of duality that lies between the arm of violence and a public service provider of aid to the community. Finally, police are their own victims as they succumb to the powerful effects of a cultural profession established for violence. As victims, they find themselves alienated from the citizenry they protect and who looks to them for protection. Therefore, they suffer in silence with nowhere to turn for their own protection.

10

POLICING THE POLICE

"Oh, I.A.(Internal Affairs) Fuck them. Kick one ass and they think they own you. One douche said to me, 'you have established a pattern of violent and destructive behavior.' Like that's a fucking insult?"
(Louisiana SOG, 2011)

Who polices the police; is a concern for the public about the effectiveness of self-regulation for activities and agencies. Many agencies utilize an Internal Affairs or Public Integrity Unit to internally investigate allegations of misconduct or criminal behaviors lodged against employees in that particular organization. There is an inherent mistrust in a system that offers to investigate itself using someone belonging to that very organization. Most agencies go to great efforts ensuring autonomy for internal affairs investigators, and although many are of the highest integrity, the employee still co-exists within the overarching culture of policing. While most agencies use mechanisms for addressing internal violations of policies and laws, this chapter addresses the challenges of monitoring and intervening in an officer's career before actions rise to a level of corruption or criminality.

The systems are generically referred to as an early warning system (EWS), and are also an internal process under the direction of the host law enforcement agency. Questions arise as to why an external oversight function is not assigned to promote public confidence in the process. The many challenges associated with an external administrative over watch include the fact that most law enforcement jurisdictions, such as Sheriff's Offices are independent political subdivisions operating autonomously. Most municipal police departments are legislatively authorized under the auspices of a city's charter or constitution. These cities are also independent political subdivisions. State police organizations also fall under the respective state constitutions that operate independently from federal control. The idea that one omniscient body monitors all law enforcement actions is not realistic or legally feasible.

Early Warning Systems

In 1981, the United States Commission on Civil Rights recommended all law enforcement agencies develop an EWS. This was only a recommendation, not legislatively mandated, and by 1999 only 27 percent of agencies serving populations of fifty thousand or more complied. There are many variations of the EWS operating throughout the country, but no federally mandated order for compliance. The basic premise of the EWS is a data based police management tool designed to identify officers whose behavior is problematic and to provide a form of intervention to correct that performance. Officers identified for EWS are usually those receiving repeated citizen complaints or engaging in inappropriate behavior.

The EWS consists of three basic phases: selection, intervention, and post-intervention monitoring[1]. The *selection* phase[2] is the point of entry for a system that is contrary to the tradition of law enforcement due to the culture of isolationism and silence. Internal issues are "addressed" by other officers, and are not "supposed" to be officially investigated. This creates a point of extreme tension between the organization and the individual officer introduced into an EWS by the selection phase. It is important that prior to an agency investigating an officer's personal life and actions, they first identify the most appropriate conditions associated with causing problematic behavior.

There are no uniform standards for determining what officers are referred to an EWS intervention, but among the agencies participating in the study include one or more of the following; citizen complaints, firearm discharge, use of force reports, civil litigation, resisting arrest incidents, high speed pursuits and vehicular damages.

Intervention occurs when the agency contacts the identified officer in regards to his problematic behavior. The majority of responding agencies (67 percent) reply that the intervention process includes a discussion with the officer's immediate supervisor. Only 45 percent of responding agencies indicate that a training course is included during the intervention. This critical phase of confronting the officer about the problematic history leading to an EWS referral is seldom documented and usually is a onetime conversation that serves as more of a warning than an investment into changing the irregular behavior.

The third phase, *post intervention monitoring*, includes a mixed bag of techniques used by the agencies employing an EWS. Nearly all (90 percent) reported following up on the initial meeting with the identified officer. An immediate supervisor usually conducts this monitoring, but is informal and goes undocumented. In addition to the surveys, three case studies are conducted with police departments in Miami-Dade County, New Orleans, and Minneapolis. An analysis of the data collected exhibits that male officers are overrepresented and do not differ in terms of race or ethnicity. An unexpected result shows that problem officers regularly referred into the EWS for bad behavior were promoted at higher rates than officers having never been in disciplinary trouble.

An example of this contradictory relationship is the case of the former NOPD officer Len Davis who was awarded the department's second highest honor, the Medal of Merit in 1993. One year later, Davis ordered the murder of New Orleans resident Kim Groves for filing a police brutality complaint with the NOPD's Internal Affairs section against his partner and him. Davis' order to kill Groves was captured on an FBI wiretap investigating Davis and other NOPD officers for drug trafficking. Tried and sentenced to death for her murder, he was once described as a "Robocop to some people...and an Officer Friendly to others."[3] Prior to Len Davis having received his Medal of Merit and death sentence, he had received 20 complaints against him and suspended 6 times between 1987 and 1992.

The study[4] shows a dramatic effect of the EWS intervention in reducing citizen complaints and other problematic behavior among those identified officers. In Minneapolis for example, the number of citizen complaints against officers participating in the agency's EWS program dropped by 67 percent within one year of the intervention. New Orleans Police Department shows a 62 percent decrease in citizen complaints within one year of the intervention, while the police department in Miami-Dade saw reductions in their use-of-force reports from 96 percent down to 50 percent in the same period.

The most realistic and critic observation made within the context of this study is that an EWS cannot foster a climate of answerability where a cultural commitment does not already exist. Another salient observation was that the EWS was not an alarm clock, a mechanical device programmed to sound an automatic alert. It is a complex, high maintenance administrative operation requiring close and constant human attention[5].

To achieve a level of competent human attention and intervention, most EWS focus on characteristics associated with problematic behavior, thus signaling the need for intervention[6]. These characteristics are divided into two categories: officer characteristics and job characteristics. The term "antisocial egocentricity" as measured by the Minnesota Multiphasic Personality Inventory is used with characteristics associated with frequent complaints against an officer from the public and hierarchical insubordination. The officer characteristic is associated with frequent complaints against an officer from the public and hierarchical insubordination. Additional personal characteristics associated with problematic behavior are excessive use of force, failing to exhibit self-discipline, and poor performance in training programs and testing. The professional characteristics for officers include not creating close relationships with positive role models in policing and that they exhibit risk for developing bad behavior. These personal and professional characteristics are more effective for identifying problematic behaviors when used with a database for capturing information about the individual officer and the development of patterns leading to problematic behavior[7].

These personal and professional characteristics are more effective for identifying problematic behaviors when used with a database for capturing information about the individual officer and the development of patterns leading to problematic behavior. The agency's organizational culture and situational factors such as assignment in high crime areas are taken into consideration, as they may affect an officer's behavior. Evaluating job environment, occupational socialization, and stressors are better indicators than personality characteristics for identifying the potential for problematic behavior. This study[8] also concluded that the fraternal socialization process is powerful. The desire to fit in is such a strong influence that once honest officers have little success in defending themselves from the inappropriate behaviors associated with deviance.

Early Intervention

Another process for detecting bad behavior is similar to the EWS, and is called the Early Intervention System (EIS)[9]. This system focuses on preventing problematic behavior linked to personal issues. The EIS attempts to be more proactive through predictive profiling as opposed to waiting for complaints against an officer. The EIS focuses on quality initial interventions with the officer by a better-trained first line supervisor and by expanding the resources available to assisting the officer.

A phenomenon labeled the "rotten apple theory" involves honest, moral officers exhibiting personality characteristics once thought of as desirable for recruitment and selection have the potential for engaging in inappropriate behavior if their agency socializes the officer into such behavior. The success of the EIS links the attention paid to the officer's personal needs, not only the unacceptable, professional behavior. This attention promotes an increase in agency accountability, integrity, and overall organizational health.

The EIS also focuses on the trained supervisor's observations of an officer's personality characteristics, as included in the following examples: an outgoing officer is suddenly quiet and withdrawn; the usual joking among officers suddenly takes on an edge with a note of hostility just below the surface; the quality of an officer's paperwork declines; begins avoiding responsibilities in small ways; going through a difficult divorce; or, their child is having serious problems.

While these alarms may appear to be intangible alarm triggers not traditionally of concern among an alpha male driven profession, they are necessary indicators for preemptively identifying and potentially prevent an officer from doing irrevocable harm to himself or his career. The organizational detection of problematic behavior through the EWS, employee assistance program, or any other variety of strategies used to seek out the "bad apples" in policing perpetuates a condition of tension between the state sponsored violence theory[10] and the institutional ideals of behavioral accountability. While these studies reveal promising efforts for establishing an atmosphere for accountability through intervention, there remains a void in literature for addressing the issue of anti-organizational actions by SOG Operators. The next section shall recap where we have progressed at this point of the book, and where we are set to go.

We have just taken a look at the difficulties policing the police. There are processes available for detecting organizational behaviors detrimental to the credible operations of policing, but as this chapter has shown, they are not mandated and subjective at best. The next chapter demonstrates the complexity of relational dynamics associated with law enforcement. Would you imagine cops and outlaw bikers cut from the same cloth?

11

COP CULTURE AND OMC

The Iron Pigs, Untouchables and the Reguladors support intimidating monikers and images as they roll through our nation's highways on customized V-twin motorcycles clad in weathered leather vests covered by patches illustrating their belonging to a subculture outside the standards of traditional community. A closer look at these renegades reveals they are not outlaws, but law enforcement. They are not working an undercover operation, but spending off-duty time in the company of other motorcycle enthusiasts who enjoy living outside the lines of standard police custom. Whether they are only imitating the desperado image or engaging in similar behavior, there is a connection between the cop culture and the OMC.

The emergence of a relationship between two subcultures embodying the trajectories of socialization and groupthink became obvious as I conducted research for this project. I include this chapter for demonstrating the similarities between two unrelated groups of individuals sharing characteristics developed through liminality in an environment of hegemonic masculinity. To demonstrate the phenomenon, I incorporate peer clustering supporting an isolationist environment where irrational actions and antisocial behaviors foster.

The similarities between the SOG, cop culture and law enforcement motorcycle clubs (LEMC), to the fringe organizations such as the OMC show a relational assimilation or acting out with deviant behaviors. The characteristics of both groups closely associate with risk taking, collective rationalization, an inherent immorality, threatening to the others, refraining from expressing alternative opinions, misguided belief that decisions are unanimous with the group, and filtering of information from the hierarchy contradicting group cohesion.

The LEMC are law enforcement officers (many SOG) joining together to create restricted access social clubs beyond the isolationist fraternity of policing. They consist of members sharing a passion for motorcycles, social events, alcohol, and portraying themselves as similar to the OMC. The common behaviors between two ideologically opposed groups are described[1] for confirming the connection between the LEMC and the OMC:

I compare outlaw bikers and police officers who band together in their off-duty hours in stylistically analogous motorcycle clubs – evocative of the same cultural themes and recreational activities as are ascribed to the 'outlaws'. The worldviews of both groups place a high premium on 'living large' and they also share a hedonistic perception on the meaning of leisure itself[2].

I also illustrate the depth of the shared personal characteristics between both groups through the lived experiences of former Bureau of Alcohol, Tobacco and Firearms (ATF) federal agent William Queen[3] and chronicle the confliction of allegiances between his ATF coworkers and the OMC "brothers" he infiltrated during a twenty-eight month undercover operation. He states of his experience:

Hard core gangsters would be going to jail today, but for years I'd been calling these gangsters my brothers. I was both proud of my work as an undercover agent and sad about the ramifications...for some of the men I'd grown close to[4].

The literature[5] and the real life experiences of SOG Operators[6] provide an opportunity to document groupthink as an element of becoming fully socialized once an Operator has successfully crossed the series of liminal benchmarks. The theory of legitimized police violence and peer acceptance[7] is similar to the perspective of policing's culture of cohesion emulating the gang culture outlook[8]. Although groupthink applies to many social situations influenced by hegemonic masculinity, the examples of occupations and groups with similar subcultures listed earlier in the work differ from the SOG and OMC comparison due to several factors.

More specifically, the influence of violence, purposefully outward appearances of danger and intimidation, and the regular association with known criminal felons separate these two subcultures from stockbrokers and schoolteacher for example. The violence temperament is embodied in the deviance of the OMC, who display an intimidating outward appearance and a crudely hedonistic public behavior distinguishing themselves from traditional societal ideals for perpetuating the fringe lifestyle. Law enforcement imitates this posturing by promoting itself as the largest gang in the world.

Figure 11.1: T-shirt item marketing membership in America's largest street gang. *Source:* Tees4cops online http://www.tees4cops.com/

Figure 11.2: LEMC members escort hearse for fallen police officer. *Source:* Reprinted with permission from The Courier and Daily Comet

The suggestion that LEMC are similar to OMC in behaviors, traditions, beliefs, and socioeconomic demographics should seem impossible, but research and observation show differently. The two cultures are similar. Librett, a retired police officer from New York after twenty years, now a professor of criminal justice documents this connection. The depth of his research and professional experience laid the foundation for my comparative analysis between the similar subcultures as it focuses on the cohesive nature of each group.

The OMC originated following World War II with the return of military veterans to the United States who became disillusioned with the new society awaiting them. A California-based motorcycle club, the Pissed Off Bastards of Bloomington (POBOB) engaged in a highly publicized confrontation in Hollister, California in 1947. Taking over the small town for three days, the event was immortalized in the 1953 movie starring Marlon Brando, *"The Wild One."* This club of mostly World War II veterans separated, and in 1948 became the Hells Angels. The name and Death Head image were adopted for a bomber squadron during World War I and II. True to their military roots the

OMC maintains a militaristic hierarchy and uses patches like military insignia carrying various significant meanings.

Similarly, the SOG began developing criteria for undercover agents after World War II because of the changes in crime and national security threats. Their missions were secreted and included a separation from an established core of law enforcement. The SWAT element in this study was first created in 1967, and consisted of returning military war veterans. Their group relied upon militaristic principles, weapons and tactics.

Both groups are highly and purposefully visible to project an aura of dominance and superiority, not unlike the military offensives they once participated in to shock the senses and overwhelm their enemy through intimidation. The similarities of both cultures are indistinguishable,[9] as stated in the findings:

They are characterized by hierarchical command structures, initiation rites and socialization processes, oaths of loyalty, codes of silence, a uniform mode of dress, and outwardly symbolic accoutrements of rank and achievement[10].

The cohesive LEMC is similar to the OMC as both promote a deviant milieu of countercultural ideologies. This work displays the similarities on multiple levels to include surface and general appearance, anti-institutional posturing, racial and sexual attitudinal practices, and socioeconomic similarities.

The career commitments made by LEMC lead to an affinity for the "edge" lifestyle similar to that of the hedonistic lifestyle of the OMC. The riskier the activity, the more enmeshed within the subculture. Librett[11] reports that the thirst for pushing the "edge" and risking it all for a chance to feel the power of survival and conquest may be what connects and labels the two countercultural institutions as deviant.

The Bureau of Alcohol, Tobacco and Firearms (ATF) retired Special Agent William Queen lived the experiences observed by Librett and detailed by Ulmer's[12] labeling of deviance. As an undercover Operator, he was also at times a victim of groupthink[13] while enmeshing himself deep within the alpha-male driven fraternities of the SOG and OMC. The melding of attitudes, behaviors, and beliefs led to an association with the deviant label, and Queen[14] began to distance himself from the bureaucracy of the ATF and associate with the love of his OMC "brothers." He wrote about his feelings:

Over the years, testifying against my former Mongrel brothers became a kind of personal purgatory[15].

He served twenty-eight months of deep undercover operations while riding motorcycles with a violent OMC, the Mongrels of Southern California. Despite his high ethical character, he struggled with his sense of duty and acceptance by both sets of "peers." The influence of socialization and groupthink are closely related and linked by the element of hegemonic masculinity. Queen[16] further illustrated the conflict between his duties and his associational loyalty by this statement:

God, I wished I could be a regular cop like Zack. It was all black and white to him... I'd not only witnessed it and lived it – I had felt it... We could take them down...prosecute them for...rape and homicide. The thing we could never attack was the love these guys felt for their brothers; in many cases it was a love stronger than for their blood relations[17].

I provide practical illustrations for the effects of liminality, occupational socialization and groupthink in my comparative analysis. The two subcultures are different in purpose and mission statement for demonstrating the strength of these three elements. The comparative analysis provides the following description and visual representation of those similarities. The purposefully hedonistic portrayals of fringe type behaviors led me to examine the two subcultural worldviews. There is evidence demonstrating the fringe organizations are more closely aligned than mere imitation. Based on Librett's documentation, Queen's lived account, and my professional experiences with both subcultures, a comparative analysis illustrates a strong relational association and imitative linkages between the two edge fraternities.

Basic observations show both subcultures consist of primarily white males as full members. Females are not allowed to hold full memberships and may serve as a club "Supporter," wearing only insignia designating that role. While there may be no official restriction against minorities, neither club hosts many if any. Usually, minorities form their own clubs and refrain from membership application based on the same reasons discussed in Chapter 7's "Military Minorities Not Welcomed" sub-section.

Both OMC and LEMC share membership demographics to include similar race and gender, high school, GED educated or drop outs. Members were raised in middle to lower socioeconomic statuses. Many have military backgrounds and desire belonging and close personal relationships through heterosexual bonding. The ideology of "brotherhood" to males united outside familial structures carry an unnatural allegiance of loyalty, service and sacrifice to one another. Both clubs fringe lifestyle are counter to the normative ideals of civilized society, and are outwardly demonstrated by an affinity for tattoos, weapons and physical violence or intimidation. While the OMC first established the outlaw image, the copied appearance by the LEMC goes deeper than leather vests and patches.

A news event from Chicago exemplifies the depth of substantive association between the two subcultures. In 2005 a group of Melrose Park Police (Illinois) formed a LEMC. They not only imitated the dress, brand of motorcycle ridden, and behaviors of the OMC, but they actually approached one of the clubs identified by the FBI as a "Big Four" to wear leather vest patches displaying their support of the Outlaws OMC. Their club name, the Reapers and emblem were similar to another OMC, the Grim Reapers who are associated with drug distribution, violence, rape and home invasions. I am including key phrase excerpts from the 2013 news article to demonstrate the currency of this dynamic relationship between the two subcultures.

CBS Chicago News on February 19, 2013:

...but when Melrose Park Police Sgt. N.M. founded the Reapers motorcycle club in 2005 he "actually reached out to the Outlaws, a motorcycle club that's been labeled a criminal enterprise by the Justice Department, to essentially ask permission to ride so there wouldn't be any altercations," said BGA Investigator A.S.

The Reapers also wore patches saying support the Outlaws. Not a good idea says an ATF agent who infiltrated criminal biker clubs. "That signifies that they're affiliated with or aligned with the Outlaws," said the agent.

Then there's the Reapers name and logo similar to the Grim Reapers, involved in everything from "drug distribution to violent beatings, home invasions, rapes and bombings," said the ATF agent.

...Melrose Park cops joined the Reapers despite all the controversial images. A problem for D.B., former president of the Illinois Association of Police Chiefs. "If I raise my hand and I say to the public I swear to uphold the United States constitution, the laws of the community in which I live, and then I turn around and go out and I affiliate myself with an organization that is openly against what I held up my hand and swore to you. "How can you do that?" said D.B.

D.B. says a bar fight in Villa Park underscores the conflict. A Villa Park Police report describes the battery of an off-duty Villa Park fireman allegedly hit and injured by a group of Reapers including Melrose Park Cops.

The Reapers told ... they were not affiliated with the Outlaws, but wore the patches for protection.[18]

This story exemplifies the context of this chapter on so many levels to include the obvious relationship between the two subcultures. This is the first instance I have observed where law enforcement goes so far as wearing an all-important designation patch on their official club "colors" labeling that their club supports an outlaw motorcycle club. Another example from this account demonstrates the similarity of intimidating club names and violent imagery chosen for outward display. Police officers purposefully selected a grim reaper image and name from an OMC criminalistically associated with drugs, violent and sexual assault.

The barroom brawl the Reapers LEMC engaged in with other public servants copies the culture of physical violence demonstrated by the OMC. The quote from the sergeant, and still a current law enforcement officer, that they wore the Outlaws' patch for "protection" stands alone in a field of data collected specific to justifications for imitating the OMC. This LEMC effectively became recognized as affiliates for the Outlaws in a term called, "patched over." This is a practice for smaller clubs who desire the protection and permission to ride within the "jurisdiction" of one of the Big Four's territories.

Finally, an observation that I make later in this book is that senior law enforcement executives either have no idea that these subcultures exist, they allow the participation as fellow fraternity brothers, or they claim ignorance or institutional tolerance to their fringe existence. The sergeant stated the club began in 2005, when they first approached the Outlaws for patch permission. The news report following the fight with neighboring firefighters occurred in 2013. The 2011 population for the Village of Melrose Park is just over 25,000, and makes the idea of a criminally-associated LEMC in operation for 8 years without senior executive knowledge most unlikely. This case study provides a valuable illustration for the following section involving a comparison table for demonstrating the many similarities between the two clubs.

A chart comparing characteristics between the two groups allows me to develop a visual representation of the depth of commonalities. The chart titled, Table 11.3: *The OMC v. LEMC Characteristic Comparison Chart* provides an initial observation and an introduction to future examination. It lists the unique characteristics of the OMC and LEMC in singular columns, and then the similarities shared by both are combined in the final column. The similarities exceed the differences and show the nature of associational imitation going deeper than an imitative surface appearance.

Outlaw Motorcycle Club	Law Enforcement Motorcycle Club	Both Clubs
Life of crime	Oath to uphold law	Band together "off" duty. Freedom from doldrums, seeks adventure
1% Patch	1* Patch	Power to influence social controls.
Legitimizing illicit money making operations into legitimate business (commercialize merchandising)	Emulate the "others" Give appearance of outlaw lifestyle in dress, actions and behaviors. Deviant behavior bumps up to criminality.	Enjoys living on societal "Edge" Mental & physical toughness, dominant, alpha male. Militaristic organizational structures. Alcohol, violence, tattoos and weapons culture.
		"Biker" worldview includes dominant male & submissive/servant female. Badge bunnies & Biker mommas
		Code of Silence
		Meaning & symbolism assigned to patches, pins, ribbons, emblems & motto
		Infiltration of minorities
		Minimal naturalistic research conducted. Both demand privacy & resist external forces. Total unity, group cohesion, brotherhood, mystical aura of power and violence.
		Probationary periods, rewarding of Colors; rocker patch- Agency Shield
		Socialization process involves total immersion into culture. Sacrifices of personal privacy to organizational control.
		F.T.W. (Fuck The World) mentality

Table 11.3 – "The OMC v. LEMC Characteristics Comparison Chart"– demonstrates the uniquely different and the surprisingly similar characteristics of each subculture. *Source:* Original figure produced by Dr. Scott Silverii for doctoral dissertation; *A Darker Shade of Blue; From Public Servant to Professional Deviant*, 2011)

Directed by the results of the *OMC v. LEMC Characteristic Comparison Chart,* I conducted additional research to compare the academic and experiential understandings of these two groups to their own perceptual ideologies that influence the creation of organizational images. The FBI identifies four OMC as the "Big Four"[19] based on membership, criminal influence and detrimental social influence. The Big Four are identified as the Hells Angels, the Banditos, the Pagans, and the Outlaws. The FBI's National Gang Threat Assessment[20] describes the OMC's activities:

...posing a threat to public safety in local communities in which these gangs operate because of their wide-ranging criminal activity, propensity to use violence, and ability to counter law enforcement efforts. OMGs are highly structured criminal organizations whose members engage in criminal activities such as violent crime, weapons trafficking, and drug trafficking. OMGs maintain a strong centralized leadership that implements rules regulating membership, conduct, and criminal activity. As of June 2008 state and local law enforcement agencies estimate that 280 and 520 OMGs are operating within the United States[21].

The LEMC, mostly SOG, band together during off duty hours and limit participation based on occupational assignment clusters and the adoration of motorcycles. Although not criminalistic by creation, LEMC emulate the OMC so that deciphering who is who becomes difficult. I selected four LEMC to compare to the OMC by conducting an internet query by typing "law enforcement motorcycle clubs" into a search engine. The results list over forty clubs on the World Wide Web. Before opening any of the LEMC websites for content, I printed the screen page containing links to the LEMC's webpages and blindly selected four random clubs.

Once the four LEMC were chosen, I examined all eight websites (four OMC and four LEMC) for content and context. I created a comparison table based on my observations and began to code the images on each motorcycle site. These codes are used to populate the chart of all eight clubs demonstrating similarities.

The OMC websites selected were from clubs known by the FBI as the "Big Four":

- Pagan's Motorcycle Club http://www.jailedpagans.com/
- Bandidos Motorcycle Club http://www.bandidosmc.com/
- Hells Angels Motorcycle Club http://www.hells-angels.com/
- Outlaws Motorcycle Club http://www.outlawsmc.com/.

The four LEMC websites selected include:

- Iron Pigs Motorcycle Club - http://www.ironpigs.com/Homemain.htm,
- Untouchables MC - http://www.untouchablesmcnj.com/,
- Iron Brotherhood MC - http://www.ironbrotherhoodmc.com/, and
- Wheelmen MC - http://wheelmenlemc.com/.

MC Website	Pagans OMC	Hells Angels OMC	Outlaws OMC	Bandidos OMC	Untouchables LEMC	Wheelmen LEMC	Iron Pigs LEMC	Iron Brotherhood LEMC
Club Patch	1	1	1	1	1	1	1	1
"MC" Symbol	1	1	1	1	1	1	1	1
1% Symbol	1		1	1				
1* Symbol					1	1	1	1
Trademark Warnings		1	1	1	1		1	1
Motto / Creed	1	1	1	1		1	1	1
Highly Stylized Site	1	1	1	1		1	1	1
Heavy Metal Music	1		1	1		1		1
History Page		1	1		1	1	1	1
Our Colors Page		1	1	1	1	1	1	1
Memorial Page		1	1	1	1			
In-Jail Page	1	1		1				
Merchandise Page	1			1	1			
Chapters Page		1	1		1		1	1
Links Page	1	1		1				1
Guestbook Page		1	1	1				1
Members Page								1
Photographs Page	1	1	1	1	1	1	1	1
Events Page		1		1		1		1

Table 11.4: *The Motorcycle Club Website Survey* documents results from each site surveyed and lists the similarities between the subcultures.

While examining the websites, I saw both subcultures relish secrecy and anonymity, yet post their respective websites on the internet for public consumption. This may serve as another "in your face" tactic from a technological perspective, as all sites contained threatening logos, photographs, and symbolism. Skulls, club colors, and demonic images dominated the artistry. The majority of sites offered sign in sections and contact options for recruitment or fundraising. Pictures posted of events, riders, parties and various activities were near impossible to distinguish between the OMC and LEMC, and the "edge" lifestyle is obviously portrayed by both.

Despite the countercultural deviance practiced through participation in these clubs, the vast majority had the wherewithal to protect their site's images through registered trademarks and copyrighting licenses. Clubs use these restrictions to market merchandise to further support their activities. The most noticeable element of each site was how interchangeable all were with each other.

Whether by design or coincidence, the *Motorcycle Club Website Survey* illustrates the differences between these contrasting social organizations are negligible and purposefully portray deviant lifestyles outside the acceptable realm of the public. Both subcultures intentionally categorize themselves as the "others" and appear to enjoy operating within society's margins.

The examination confirms my professional experiences and the work of Librett[22] particular to LEMC distancing themselves from the policing norms to devolve into a deviant subculture of disengagement from the institutional organization of law enforcement. The desire to live on the "edge" and within the margins of society is a powerful draw to officers escaping the daily regimented operating procedures that direct policing activities.

This comparative analysis of the OMC and LEMC provides a unique look at the separation officers may find themselves from the core institutional ideals. In an occupation where perception becomes reality, the imitative attraction to the OMC through dress, behavior, and ideology threatens the core institution of law enforcement. The example illustrates the possibility of any combination of unlike groups finding similarities when engaged in a subculture defined by the detrimental homogenetic entitlement.

Both Clubs
Life of crime
Oath to uphold law
Band together "off" duty. Freedom from doldrums, seeks adventure
1% Patch
1* Patch
Power to influence social controls.
Legitimizing illicit money making operations into legitimate business (commercialize merchandizing)
Emulate the "others"
Give appearance of outlaw lifestyle in dress, actions and behaviors.
Deviant behavior bumps up to criminality.
Enjoys living on societal "Edge"
Mental & physical toughness, dominant, alpha male.
Militaristic organizational structures.
Alcohol, violence, tattoos and weapons culture.
"Biker" worldview includes dominant male & submissive/servant female. Badge bunnies & Biker mommas
Code of Silence
Meaning & symbolism assigned to patches, pins, ribbons, emblems & motto
Infiltration of minorities
Minimal naturalistic research conducted. Both demand privacy & resist external forces. Total unity, group cohesion, brotherhood, mystical aura of power and violence.
Probationary periods, rewarding of Colors; rocker patch- Agency Shield
Socialization process involves total immersion into culture. Sacrifices of personal privacy to organizational control.
F.T.W. (Fuck The World) mentality

12

DRIVING DRUNK BEHIND THE BADGE

In 2009, the National Highway Traffic Safety Administration [NHTSA] documented 10,839 alcohol related deaths in the United States. Thousands more were left disabled as a result of impaired and drunk drivers. Alcohol-related fatalities nationwide accounted for over one-third of all vehicular fatalities in 2009. Statistics show a life is lost every 50 minutes in this country by an impaired driver[1]. This equates to approximately 30 lives lost each day[2].

In an attempt to reduce the number of impaired drivers on the nation's roadways, DUI check points and campaigns are conducted. Campaigns like Stay alive, don't drink and drive; Over the limit – under arrest; and Drive Sober or get Pulled Over. Campaign slogans like these are used by law enforcement agencies nationwide in an attempt to draw attention to drunk and impaired drivers, while also deterring motorists from driving under the influence. So how can the number of officers arrested and charged with DWI, DUI, or driving impaired be explained?

Do some officers feel entitled to drink and drive? Does the code protect them? What role does the culture play in perpetuating such behavior? How can officers witness the devastation of alcohol and bad decisions (i.e., fatalities, ruined careers, health issues, and the erosion of families) and still choose to drink and drive? Or is it just a case of "do as I say, not as I do?"

Take the case of a Seymour Indiana school resource officer (SRO). This SRO was charged in July2011, with operating a motor vehicle while intoxicated. As if that were not bad enough, at the time of his arrest he was hauling a Drug Awareness Resistance Education (D.A.R.E.) trailer[3]. It should come as no surprise that officers and agencies everywhere will take a hit on a story like this, but what message is such irresponsible behavior sending? Are departments more concerned with appearances or accountability?

The answer seems to be with appearances, at least for the first couple of DUI's received. How do officers and department's view habitual offenses? How can some officers rack up DUI after DUI with no apparent consequences? One such example is an Anaheim California police officer who racked up three DUI arrests in a single year, yet remained on the department payroll since the first DUI in 2008. Following much publicity, this officer eventually resigned in March of 2010[4].

Another example is an Aurora Colorado police officer that received two DUI's in a year and was initially suspended for 160 hours[5]. This officer was warned that any subsequent DUI arrests and convictions would result in immediate termination. However, after the second DUI, the officer was terminated and then reinstated by members of the Civil Service Commission. The Commission believed officers should be held to a higher standard[6]. However, this officer was not held accountable for either of his drunken driving arrests.

What about departments with numerous officers facing DUI charges? In 2009, 10 Memphis officers were arrested for DUI[7]. Prior to these 10 DUI arrests, Memphis Police Department policy regarding such activity indicated immediate termination for charges of DUI.

Since these 10 DUI's, Memphis officers now receive a "second-chance." Current departmental policy indicates officers facing DUI charges will receive a minimum 15-day suspension, are required to sign a statement announcing any subsequent DUI's will result in immediate termination, and officers must undergo mandatory counseling[8]. Does this send the wrong message about the accountability of police officers? Does this seem reasonable?

Documented cases of police officers arrested and charged with DUI nationwide since 2000, have reached well over 275[9]. Yet, these only account for the cases in which officers were not given a free pass to drink and drive. The real concern remains with officers who receive free passes to drink and drive, DUI's going unreported, and officers covering for each other. Do officers arrested and charged with drunk or impaired driving receive similar outcomes to average citizens arrested for similar offenses, or do officers receive preferential treatment?

Seattle P-I Investigations explained, "Cops confronted with a drunken-driving arrest fare better than the average citizen."[10] A seven-year investigation conducted by Seattle P-I uncovered a disturbing trend of cops driving drunk in Washington State. Five of the officers investigated never faced prosecution. Six more officers were never required to surrender their state-issued driver's licenses, due to missed filing deadlines at the state licensing office. The missed deadlines were the result of fellow officers not getting the proper documentation to the state licensing office in time. One officer even asked another officer to extend a "professional courtesy," and still another asked, "How could we take care of this."[11]

Seattle P-I's Investigations discovered impaired officers in Washington State accounted for 14 vehicular accidents while in agency vehicles. Yet, many of the impaired officers received no more than two-day suspensions, lost vacation days, or in-house reprimands[12]. Reasons ranged from the lack of uniformity in laws regarding impaired and drunk driving laws, inconsistencies in the severity of discipline received, the good old boy mentality, and a lack of personal and departmental accountability. Discrepancies in uniformity are noted between agencies, arrests, disciplinary records, and geographical location of the incident within the state and the nation. When is officer discretion appropriate or inappropriate in making a final determination regarding a fellow officer's DUI? Will the Code prevail or will justice be served? Or does this give way to further preferential treatment for officers? What about zero tolerance laws?

Zero Tolerance

What role does "zero tolerance" play in the role of DUI, DWI, or impaired driving? Zero tolerance laws focus on underage drivers, who account for the majority of alcohol-related fatalities. According to the Illinois Secretary of State, Jesse White, zero tolerance laws apply to drivers under the age of 21, who have alcohol in their systems while operating a vehicle. These drivers will relinquish their driving privileges. "They can also be charged with DUI if they have any trace of other drugs or have a blood-alcohol content (BAC) of .08 or above, or in excess of .05 with additional evidence proving impairment."[13] Shouldn't zero tolerance laws also apply to adults who should know better? What about cops?

Guild President for Seattle police officers, Rich O'Neil, believed officers were treated much harsher than the general public. O'Neil explained that officers were not only susceptible to court fines, but to lost wages, due in part to suspension for charges of DUI and mandatory court appearances as a result of DUI charges[14]. Are you kidding me?

So "drive hammered get nailed" is true? Unfortunately, "drive hammered, get nailed" only seems to be the case for a handful of officers who are arrested and charged with DUI. A mindset exists that as long as there was no accident or injuries, there was no DUI. One of the most disturbing trends associated with officers being arrested for DUI, rests on the lack of personal and departmental accountability.

A recent case from Southern Illinois involved an off-duty detective who was reportedly found passed out behind the wheel in the middle of the road. Passerby's notified police who conducted a welfare check. Once on the scene, officers were eventually able to wake the detective who stated he "... was fighting a cold and had taken large doses of Nyquil, Tylenol Cold, and a nasal spray."[15] No field sobriety tests were conducted. Officers showing up on the scene took the word of this officer, who was passed out in the middle of a busy road at 5:00 am. As if this wasn't bad enough, he was in possession of his duty weapon. That sounds reasonable, right? Wrong! This was another prime example of preferential treatment taking precedent over accountability.

Just to recap: you find a man, later identified as a police detective passed out in the middle of the road. Once awakened, he explained he had consumed a large dose of Nyquil, Tylenol Cold, and nasal spray. Yet officers on the scene did not conduct a field sobriety test, rather they took his word for it. Even at face value, Nyquil contains alcohol, so taking large doses would equate to increased levels of alcohol in the system and at a minimum, an impaired driver.

How does this happen? Well, according to a reporter[16] for the Belleville News Democrat, because "Neither department has a policy stating what officers should do if they find someone passed out behind the wheel on over-the-counter (OTC) medication. The chiefs say they leave those situations up to the officers' discretion because there are so many variables." What? Illinois DUI law includes impaired operation of a motor vehicle by means of alcohol, drugs, or other intoxicants. And since when is it appropriate for the police take the word of an impaired individual? Why are these individuals not being held accountable for what they consume and their actions, especially when they choose to drive impaired?

Wait, this story gets better. Once officers realized this was a fellow officer, they contacted his Department. The on-duty sergeant dispatched an officer to the detective's location to give him a ride home. Ultimately, the sergeant was criticized for using "poor judgment." So, now the sergeant and not the detective used "poor judgment." Officer discretion in this case only seems to be used to protect officers from wrongdoing. What about the discretion displayed by the sergeant? She was merely trying to get her officer home safe. If this officer was not under the influence and was safe to drive, then why could he not drive himself home? And why was he passed out in the middle of the road? The sergeant was pulled onto the carpet and accused of using poor judgment even though she broke no laws or department policies. The blame was shifted from the actual guilty party. It seems as though the elusive and secretive police culture wants to conceal the real issue. The behavior by both department administrators was appalling. Officers that really want to know why there is so much public distrust towards them and their profession only need look in the mirror and at the officers they work with.

Society is tired of being misled and lied to by the police. The general public would most likely have more respect and possibly be more forgiving, if officers were held to the same standards set forth by the law they uphold. After the initial article came out, numerous comments filled the newspaper website, many of which were filled with disbelief and disgust at the double standard. An anonymous source from the Belleville News Democrat stated: If you were so zonked on meds in the wee hours that you passed out behind the wheel in the middle of the highway armed with a handgun, would you expect a kindly police officer to give you a ride home? Only in your dreams."[17]

Your problem is that you are just part of the great unwashed, a Joe Average. You aren't one of the Brothers or Sisters in Blue. They get a wink, a nod, a free pass and a taxpayer-funded ride home. Since when do the police take the word of an impaired driver? Why are officers not held accountable for what they consume, especially when they choose to drive impaired? Nyquil's label clearly states "do not operate heavy machinery" and "do not exceed the recommended dose. "Illinois DUI law clearly covers this issue. Thus being said, what "variables" are we talking about? According to David J. Hansen Ph.D., "Laws against driving under the influence of alcohol (DUI) or driving while intoxicated (DWI) do not distinguish between blood alcohol content (BAC) that comes from drinking alcoholic beverages, [or] from medications." In addition to using large amounts of Nyquil, this detective claims to be sick, yet he is out driving around at 5 o'clock in the morning until he is found passed out in the middle of a major roadway. He was also in possession of his duty weapon, and no one sees an issue here.

Facebook postings make it appear as if this off duty detective was out drinking with family and friends in a nearby town and was probably on his way home when the incident occurred. The fact remains that this detective admitted to consuming over-the-counter medications, which are clearly labeled as containing alcohol. However, since no field sobriety tests were conducted, it will never be certain exactly what was consumed, or in what quantity. Again, it seems as though this elusive and secretive culture is trying to conceal the real issue. The real issue remains that officers not being held accountable for their bad judgment.

Several local officers were asked for their opinions regarding this case. All of them said the detective was obviously under the influence of alcohol and that the direct actions by both administrators only contribute to distrust of the occupation as a whole. In addition, several citizens were also asked for their opinions about this case. They were all appalled. Several asked, "How dumb do they [the police] think we are? Do cops want to know why there is so much public distrust? Because people are tired of being misled and lied to by the police. Cases in which officers are not held accountable and those in leadership positions allow such indiscretions and illegal activities to be swept under the rug, only contribute to the breakdown in public trust and the growth of distrust between the police and the communities they serve. How do agencies and officers manage to keep these stories under the radar? Zerubavel explained;

"The intensity of silence is thus affected not only by the number of people who conspire to maintain it but also by the length of time they manage to do so."[18]

How long will officers and administrators continue to have these unspoken conversations? At what point will officers be held accountable for their actions? At what point will fellow officers and administrators quit covering up such behavior? Extending professional courtesies, providing free passes, looking the other way, and not holding officers accountable only exacerbate issues of favoritism and decreased public trust in law enforcement personnel. Additionally, ignoring misbehavior by officers can also lead to missing the signs and symptoms of possible emotional problems, mental illness, alcohol abuse, and alcoholism.

Take the case of a former Sunset Hills Missouri Officer. On the night of March 21, 2009, this officer left a local bar/restaurant with a blood-alcohol concentration (BAC) twice the legal limit. Her decision to drink and drive not only resulted in her traumatic brain injury, but also in the wrong-way crash, which resulted in the death of four college students from India. This officer was charged with four counts of involuntary manslaughter and one count of second-degree assault[19]. The charges resulted in an 8-year prison sentence.

The leniency in sentencing this officer angered not only the families of the victims' but also the prosecuting attorney and the public. Many believed harsher ruling was warranted, given that this was an officer of the law and most believe she should have known better[20]. The officer's attorney asked for leniency because she was an officer, somehow extending her immunity from the heinous crime she committed. This case was somewhat unique, in the fact that very few female officers are ever arrested or charged with DUI, but also that this officer's decision to drink and drive resulted in the loss of four innocent lives.

Is accountability determined in correlation to the loss of life? What about habitual police offenders? Are DUI's received by law enforcement personnel merely the result of bad decisions? Or possibly a mindset – "it can't happen to me." Furthermore, if it does happen, maybe the badge will allow a professional courtesy. Professional courtesies should not be extended in the case of impaired or drunk driving arrests, regardless of who is behind the wheel! Is this problem really about bad decisions or do underlying issues exist, which need to be addressed? Individuals dealing with suicidal thoughts and ideation often partake in risk taking types of behavior. This could be a call for help or an easy way out. How many on-duty accidents are not accidents at all? After all, aren't officers killed in the line-of-duty forever remembered as heroes?

Increased risk taking includes behaviors such as speeding, not wearing a seatbelt, not wearing a vest, or responding without adequate backup. This can include any risky behavior that places officers at increased risk of death or serious injury. Driving under the influence may actually be a cry for help, a cry, which sadly comes too late for many? Numerous conspiracies of silence exist within the police culture. This culture conceals those things officers and administrators don't want to discuss. However, their silence often speaks louder than words. The problem, according to Zerubavel;

"...for a conspiracy of silence to actually end, there ultimately needs to be no more conspirators left to keep it alive" [21]

In order to stop providing the public and media outlets with ammunition, the bad behavior of law enforcement officers must stop. The time is now to demand accountability, while assisting the wounded among your ranks.

Police DUI

Ask any officer how to reduce the number of DWI's or impaired drivers on the nation's roadways and most will respond, "Don't drive impaired." Yet, the evidence provided earlier in this chapter suggests otherwise. There is often a mindset among officers that getting caught drinking and driving cannot or won't happen to them. Some officers believe that simply flashing their badge will result in a free pass. This mindset exists because it has happened, more than once. Oftentimes, the embarrassment of having one's name and picture plastered in the newspaper or on the local news would be enough of a deterrent to keep an individual from attempting to drink and drive. However, this is often an afterthought.

Have you ever been given a free pass to drink and drive or a pass to drive impaired? Or was the officer who gave a free pass another officer? An officer on the receiving end of a free pass may have thanked the good Lord their career wasn't ruined, or that they didn't face public humiliation, or even more, that they didn't cause an accident or kill someone. However, what likely was experienced after the initial relief subsided was a feeling of entitlement. After all, you are one of the good guys. At the same time, if you were the officer giving out the free pass, this whole situation was probably a compilation of mixed emotions. You may have wondered whether or not the right decision was made. For example, will this officer expect preferential treatment in the future? Or what if, after giving out that free pass this officer hit a family of five head on and was the only survivor? The "what ifs" could go on forever, but what if this was your family? What if those killed included a new teenage driver, newlyweds on their honeymoon, or first time parents? Would you be able to face that officer again? Could you face yourself?

Think hard about the consequences of a free pass. Remember, nothing is free. Would the average citizen receive a break for drunk or impaired driving? Not chance. In fact, officers across the country are rewarded for keeping drunk and impaired drivers off the nation's roadways. What would Mothers Against Drunk Drivers (MADD) say about the number of drunk and impaired police officers on the nation's roadways? A population many believe should be held to a higher standard, a population who should have no excuse.

Deeper Issues Facing LEO's

Police work is a career that often chooses its suitors. The fit is unmistakable, like a hand sliding into well-formed glove. Ask an officer early in their career about their work, and most will glow. Most officers are proud of their career choice. Most recruits get into police work for the right reasons, to uphold the law and keep communities safe. Unfortunately, as careers progress some become less enthused about their career choice.

Police work is commendable, but long hours, less than stellar pay, and danger might make some reconsider their career choice. In fact, police work was considered the 10th deadliest job nationwide for 2011.The rise in law enforcement deaths caused police work to raise from being considered the 12th deadliest ranking profession in 2008, to the 10th deadliest ranking profession in just three years[22].At some point during an officer's career, feelings of disappointment may surface. Many officers are out busting their asses each and every day, only to be underpaid and unappreciated. Who wouldn't begin to question their career choice? Officers are subject to name calling by criminals and thugs who are just pissed off they got caught. They are spat at, hit, lied to, assaulted, and even killed just for doing their job.

However, officers can feel just as unappreciated and beat up by administrators, family, and communities. Left unaddressed, these feelings may contribute to stress, burnout, fatigue, depression, and even suicide. The answer is not just to appreciate officers more, but rather to begin conversations early in their careers, explaining to them the risk factors associated with police work. Officers need to be provided with information about all the dangers of the job. Informing them about these dangers may help reduce the negative impacts of stress and burnout, due to job and family demands. The culture must stop marginalizing the number of officers who choose to drive impaired. In addition, agencies must hold officers accountable for bad decisions and questionable behavior. Attention must also be given as to whether or not bad decisions and questionable behavior are the result of deeper seeded issues.

NOTE:

The material for this chapter was extracted without contextual modification from *Behind the Badge: Broken in Blue*; Chapter 3, courtesy of Dr. Olivia N. Johnson. *Source:* Published by Blue Wall of Silence©, Copyright© Olivia N. Johnson, ISBN: 978-1-105-54298-5.

13

SILENT SUFFERING

Materials for the three themes of this chapter; Part 1-Stress, Part 2-Depression and Part 3-Suicide were extracted without contextual modification courtesy of Dr. Olivia N. Johnson.

Source: Reference cites for each part are listed at the end of each theme.

PART I

STRESS

Do you give more of yourself than you have to offer? Are you feeling rundown, neglected, or taken for granted? Well, you are not alone because many officers report feeling this way at some point in their careers. Oftentimes, this give/take relationship feels more like "you give" and "they take," resulting in hurt feelings and disappointment. The problem with constantly feeling unappreciated and taken for granted is that it can lead to burnout.[1]

So why does this matter? It matters, because officers suffering from burnout are less productive, they are at greater risk for injury and illness, and often have more negative public encounters.[2] These are telltale signs that your caregivers are stressed out and have no more to give. Burnout in essence, increases departmental and individual liability; it wears on the body and mind, and it can contribute to declining mental health.

Officer burnout must be dealt with proactively. Reactively addressing officer burnout not only exacerbates the issue, but can contribute to issues in the home (e.g., relationship issues, breakdowns in communication, resentment, self-medication with drugs and/or alcohol, and even violence.)³ That being said, it is very important to remember that the two leading contributors to law enforcement suicide are relationship issues and substance abuse. It is easy to see how overextending one's self each and every day can lead to burnout, but it doesn't have to.

Do not allow others to control your happiness or your emotions. It is just a fact of life that others will take advantage of you and oftentimes, without even realizing it. You may be guilty of this as well and that is okay. It is just time to make sense of these things so you don't constantly repeat them. Learn to identify what is contributing to your burnout (i.e., what are you complaining about all the time?). It is also important to realize that just because you are feeling unappreciated or taken for granted, does not mean that you are. This may just be your perception. However, your needs are not being met in some way, and in order to bring back the balance, this issue(s) has to be resolved.

How do we get back the balance? We regain balance by recognizing what causes our stress, how stress affects each of us personally, and how to reduce stress in our lives. By making a conscience effort to address our stressors every day, we significantly decrease our chances for burnout.

Stress manifests itself in many ways. Be able to identify how it manifests itself in you and be able to recognize it early. Once you are able to actively recognize your stressors, make a game plan to begin reducing your stress. Make a plan that includes being able to escape, and one, which does not allow you to leave. For example: if you are getting ready to leave work, go for a run, go to the gym, or go home and regroup. If however, you are mandated to work overtime and are unable to leave, make a plan for reducing your stress right where you are. This could include deep breathing, positive self-talk, taking a few minutes to revive yourself, or even making a quick call to vent to someone.

We have to realize that we cannot always escape from our stress.

Sometimes it follows us. However, we can feel empowered knowing that we are prepared to head it off before it has a chance to lead to imbalance and burnout.

Source: Stress and Burnout: Take Back Your Power, posted February 26, 2013 in Law Enforcement Today, by Dr. Olivia Johnson.

PART II
DEPRESSION

"Diseases of the soul are more dangerous and more numerous than those of the body."
~Cicero

The National Institute of Mental Health[1] estimated at any given time, one-quarter of American adults (over 18) experienced at least one psychological disorder. In fact, research suggests the United States is on the verge of becoming the global leader of mental disorders.[2] One of the most common and concerning mental disorders in the U.S. is depression.

Depression is "a medical illness that involves the mind and body... it affects how you feel, think, and behave."[3] Described by bouts of sadness, numbness, sleep disturbances, weight loss or gain, altered moods, feelings of emptiness, irritability, fatigue, worthlessness, anxiety, hopelessness, helplessness, and an overall loss of interest in once pleasurable activities; this often debilitating illness is categorized by levels of severity ranging from mild to severe.

Nearly 35 million Americans will suffer from some type of depression in their lifetime[4], with depression as the leading cause of disability and suicide worldwide.[5] Nationwide, 60-90% of individuals completing suicide are diagnosed with depression.[6] Based on the World Health Organization's "Disability Adjusted Life Year" scale, projections indicate by 2020, depression will be the second leading cause of death for all ages and sexes worldwide. The scale equates "life lost to premature mortality" and "years of productive life lost due to disability."[7] DePaulo & Horvitz suggested:

One of the most disabling aspects of depression is that often you don't know that you have it at all. That doesn't happen with most other painful diseases that are usually quick to announce their presence and location. But depression can sneak up so insidiously that you literally don't know what it is, sometimes until years later.[8]

Depression sufferers should remain optimistic, as depression is highly treatable. However, less than one-third of depressed individuals ever seek treatment.[9] The large numbers of individuals refusing to seek treatment is a direct result of stigmatization of mental health issues.[10] "Atypical manifestations of depression often mask the underlying disease."[11] Self-medication contributes to difficulties in a proper diagnosis and treatment of depression.

Depression alone does not have a single origin, but rather, has been linked to an assortment of causes (i.e., genetic predispositions, learned behaviors, biochemical changes, prescription drugs, a life changing event, psychological issues, and can be present in conjunction with other Illnesses.)[12]

Besides the multiple origins of depression; certain occupations are at greater risk for acquiring this debilitating illness. According to Christopher Willard, Psy.D. Tufts University, Clinical Psychologist, occupations experiencing the worst of society (i.e., police officers, judges, and lawyers) are at increased risk for depression, due in part, to the repetitive and negative nature of the job and changes in world perspectives.[13] Diamond explained there was "no reason to expect law enforcement officer possess any special immunity from this disease [clinical depression], or its fatal consequence."[14]

Direct Effect on Law Enforcement

Certain jobs, like law enforcement ... have the paradoxical effect of the fact that to be good at them, a pessimism bias is adaptive...that becomes problematic in other areas of life. Law enforcement is also an unfortunate combination unpredictable, boring, sometimes dangerous, and often without room for much autonomy, and often interactions with people at their worst (either perpetrators of crimes, or people who have just been victimized by crimes) all of which are known contributors to unhappiness.[15]

Occupational hazards for law enforcement personnel are far reaching. The appearance of physical ailments, injuries, and accidents are much easier to detect. However, occupational hazards resulting from trauma, exposure to death and violence, and grotesque forms of death, often result in emotional and psychological injuries - much more difficult to identify. Mental functioning and decline are influenced by extended exposure to stress and trauma.[16]

As a result of trauma and exposure, law enforcement personnel also experience "... repetitive adrenaline dumps in the body where the fight-or-flight response is triggered."[17] This automatic response is the body's internal defense against real or perceived threats of harm.[18] Nevertheless, frequent releases of these stress hormones (i.e., adrenaline, nor-adrenaline, and cortisol) contribute to numerous physical, emotional, and psychological ailments, including depression.

Initially, adrenaline produces a natural painkilling effect, resulting in feelings of almost super-human strength, power, and ability. Subsequently, numerous adrenaline dumps can be catastrophic. As alluded to by Wasilewski & Olson[19] (e.g., Einstein's Theory of Relativity and Newton's Law of Gravity), "what goes up must come down" (p. 3). Individuals are left dealing with the adrenaline high and ultimate crash. Adrenaline dumps occur hundreds, maybe thousands of times in the average law enforcement career. Residual affects resulting from these ups and downs leave dangerous chemical deposits in the body, contributing to illness, susceptibility to injury, increased pain, stress, and burnout.

Prevention limits exposure, while brining attention to such occupational hazards. [20] There are three key factors provided for the prevention of stress and burnout (i.e., recognize, reverse, and resilience), which can and do contribute to depression and other mental disorders.

- Recognize: signs and symptoms of stress and burnout
- Reverse: understand the effects of stress and burnout and seek assistance
- Resilience: being accountable for your personal health and well-being.

Depression is a debilitating illness, affecting millions of Americans every year. The largest detriment for individuals seeking treatment for depression is stigmatization. In addition, manifestations of atypical symptoms replicating other illnesses and self-medication with drugs and alcohol make diagnosing depression difficult. However, those suffering from depression should remain optimistic; as this devastating illness is highly treatable. The debilitating effects of depression are far reaching and can affect anyone at anytime in life.

Occupations, which experience "the worst in people and circumstances," such as law enforcement, seem to have higher than normal rates of depression. The nature of police work places officers in danger of many occupational hazards, including physical injury, depression, stress, and burnout. Law enforcement personnel possess no extraordinary resistance to depression or the effects of this deadly disease. Acknowledging and understanding the occupational hazards faced by law enforcement personnel will better prepare them for the immediate and residual effects of stress, trauma, and burnout on their bodies and their minds.

Source: Occupational Hazard: Depression on the Force (2011). The Journal of Law Enforcement, Vol. 1, No. 2, ISSN: 2161-0231 by Dr. Olivia Johnson

PART III

SUICIDE

"When there's an elephant in the room introduce him." (Randy Pausch - The Last Lecture)

Officers remain aware of the dangers involved in their work, in terms of losing their lives to an assailant, being killed during a vehicle pursuit or traffic accident, or to a lack of care and concern for their own well-being. Though these are all tragic ends to often bright careers, what remains even more tragic is the lack of training and education on a topic claiming more lives each year – officer suicide. According to the American Foundation for Suicide Prevention[1] of all suicide deaths approximately 90% of these individuals suffered from a psychiatric illness which was diagnosable and treatable. —The intensity of silence is thus affected not only by the number of people who conspire to maintain it but also by the length of time they manage to do so.[2]

There is no time like the present in which to introduce the elephant in the department, possibly in your department. The elephant's name – *Officer Suicide*. The sooner we name the elephant, the sooner we can tame it. We can no longer afford to hide behind the badge or the ever-popular —Code of Silence when dealing with this sensitive and deadly topic. Time spent avoiding the topic and debating over numbers does not save lives, and I am sure we all agree that one suicide is one too many.

Let's put aside our differences about whether suicide is the first or second leading cause of death for law enforcement officers. Let us stop hiding behind the badge and start preparing officers for the demons they will face. After all, Jamison explained:

[M]ethods of suicide are far from being just a sideshow of freakish death; they give testament, instead, to the desperation and determination of the suicidal mind. They evoke horror, certainly, but they also give us a glimpse into otherwise unimaginable misery.[3]

The unimaginable misery witnessed by individuals ultimately contemplating suicide must be recognized for what it is "… a final gathering of unknown motives, complex psychologies, and uncertain circumstance…"[4] Suicide in and of itself is not unique; rather suicide is about the individuality of the act and the circumstances surrounding the ultimate decision to end one's own existence. We cannot bring back those who have chosen to end their existence. We can and must work diligently to save those who currently suffer and will suffer from such unimaginable miseries before they seal their own fate.

Imagine for a moment that you are that desperate officer who is suffering silently from an unimaginable set of circumstances. You just found out your spouse is having an affair and intends to leave you and take your children. Coupled with the fact you will now be alone for the holidays and were just passed up for a promotion to sergeant. Going to work seems unimaginable in light of these circumstances and inattentiveness leads to rookie mistakes. The major chip on your shoulder has resulted in several citizen complaints, as well as a cold shoulder from your crew.

Sure, no one knows exactly what you are going through, but how could they, if your strategy is jumping down their throats every time they ask the question: is everything OK? More time is spent at work to avoid family issues. When off-duty, time is spent at the local bar with a fellow officer drinking and sobbing over your current situation. In the meantime, you have been written up twice this week for coming in late and your appearance has much to be desired. The shift sergeant hinted that there appears to be remnants of alcohol on your breath after a late night bender and has asked another officer to provide you an escort home.

Arriving home to an empty house, feelings of pure desperation leave you spiraling deeper and deeper out of control. With Isolation taking its toll, the excessive drinking only fuels the flames. Focus on anything is nearly impossible. The little focus and energy remaining is centered on the affair your wife is having and the dirtball destroying your family. Risking life and limb to keep those you serve and love safe are a testament of your dedication to them and the profession. How dare he do this to you and your family?

You eventually collect yourself enough to get ready for work, but the pain and frustration become more apparent as the Chief calls you in for a talk. In light of your recent actions and flying off the handle at the Chief, you land a three day suspension. Unable to explain to the Chief what is going on; after all, he could care less. Right?

Does this sound familiar? Have you been in a similar situation? Are fellow officers facing these difficult situations? Sure it may not be exactly the same but what about money problems, drug and alcohol abuse, terminal illness, death of a loved one; do you share these concerns with your peers? Seemingly everyday issues arise without notice, coupled with relationship issues or problems at work can seem unimaginable, even hopeless.

So where can you turn? And why does it seem so difficult to resolve your personal issues? You spend anywhere from eight to 12 hours a day helping others resolve their problems. Could it stem from a feeling that you always get your way, and when you don't get your way you do not know how to act or react? Compliance is demanded of everyone and anything less is unacceptable. So what happens at home when a power struggle exists between you and your teenager who believes he or she is old enough to date, stay out past curfew, or take the family car without permission? And let's not forget your spouse or significant others. What happens when there is a disagreement over something trivial and neither side will budge?

Has your spouse ever been non-compliant to your demands? Do you solve issues of non-compliance by talking or do you revert to intimidation and force? After all, it is reported that police families experience incidents of domestic violence at a rate of 2 to 4 times that of the general population.[5]

Officers are problem-solvers by nature, but underestimating the availability of tools and resources in the way of training and education, coupled with an overestimation of the emotional well-being of officers could be deadly. So, why are officers so afraid to seek assistance? The fear of seeking assistance often stems from a fear of disclosure, a fear of rejection and a fear of losing the law enforcement identity.[6] Officers are provided numerous tools and resources to protect their lives and the lives of those they swore to serve and protect. No one would fathom putting an officer on the street without the proper tools and training (i.e., academy training, weapon, vest, car, radio, etc.), all of which make the officer's job simpler, more effective, and most of all safer. Not only would it be irresponsible, but negligent to fail to provide the tools necessary for officers to effectively do their job, in-turn, increasing the risk of officers and departments being sued. "Instructors have a moral and legal obligation to constantly research methods to enhance training and, ultimately, the survival of their students."[7] We cannot research, nor train on what we do not acknowledge to be a legitimate issue facing law enforcement.

Suicide remains a leading cause of officer death and without the proper tools, training, and education; departments are left dealing with liability issues when a negligent failure to train is apparent. Such negligence could not be more apparent than in the lack of available training and education on the topic of police suicide awareness (PSA). According to Robert Douglas, Director of the National Police Suicide Foundation, less than 2% of all police departments nationwide provide any type of police suicide awareness [PSA] training.[8] The lack of training only reiterates to officers there is no problem, forcing officers to deal with difficult issues in maladaptive ways.[9] Furthermore, agencies lose valuable governmental funding for PSA types of training and risk being sued by the families of officers who ended their own existence due to a lack of proper and appropriate training.

In order to break the silence we must introduce the elephant in the department [name it], but we must introduce him publicly [tame it]. "Acknowledging the elephant's presence in private is unlikely to end a conspiracy of silence."[10] An officer suicide plays a particularly significant role in the lives of the officers left behind. The unexpected death of an officer leaves many unanswered questions, ultimately forcing surviving officers to ponder their own mortality.[11] This is due in part to the significance officers and administrators place on law enforcement culture and the ability of all members to maintain silence. The secretive culture entangles its members in a web of silence, initially shielding them from the daily devastation the officers witness, ultimately leading to a mutual understanding that officers keep their mouths shut and learn to deal with personal issues personally.

Symbolic silence is evident on the part of law enforcement personnel to mutually deny the truth about officer suicide within its rank; the idea that if we do not talk about the elephant in the department, it does not exist. Denial often evolves out of the need to elude pain.[12] A mere acknowledgement of something painful jeopardizes one's own well-being, resulting in the activation of internal mechanisms used to keep such painful and disturbing knowledge from penetrating into the consciousness.

Denial is not only apparent within the department but also the communities being policed. The general public remains largely unaware of the daily devastation and horrific incidents witnessed by law enforcement.[13] Silence and denial provide dangerous, possibly deadly facades for law enforcement to hide behind. "[V]isible to anyone willing to simply keep one's eyes open ... if anyone fails to notice it, it can only be as a result of deliberate avoidance, since otherwise it would be quite impossible *not* to notice it ...to ignore an elephant is to ignore the obvious."[14]

The truth remains we have skirted around this topic long enough. The elephant has grown too large to continue to conceal or ignore. We can no longer deny the fact that officers are taking their own lives. We must ACT - (A)cknowledge, (C)ommunicate, and (T)rain officers on the hazards of the job. Officers and administrators must acknowledge suicide as a leading cause of death for law enforcement officers. In doing so, we not only alert officers to potential occupational hazards earlier in their careers, we open the lines of two-way communication for law enforcement personnel to start talking about difficult issues. More importantly, we demonstrate through intentional action we are concerned with officers overall safety and well-being.

Source: Police Suicide; Name It, Tame It: the Elephant in the Department (2011). The Journal of Law Enforcement, Vol. 1, No. 1, ISSN: 2161-0231 by Dr. Olivia Johnson.

Source: Additional material for this chapter was extracted without contextual modification from *Behind the Badge: Broken in Blue*; Chapter 5, courtesy of Olivia N. Johnson, DM. *Source:* Published by Blue Wall of Silence©, Copyright© Olivia N. Johnson, ISBN: 978-1-105-54298-5.

14

INVESTIGATIVE STRATEGIES

Research Design and Methodology

Before starting any serious research or investigation, you must decide which angle to explore, or what lens to use for looking at cop culture. There is a worldview referred to as "constructivism" which simply means a way for understanding the world in which we live and work[1]. This perspective also relies on the participants' (SOG Operators) views of the situation. The process of qualitative research is largely inductive with the inquirer generating meaning from the data collected in the field. I am using this worldview to interpret and understand the dynamics of law enforcement's socialization process.

This was the best choice of perspective since my passion for policing has driven me to investigate the cop culture. I want to completely understand the dynamics involved in socialization, sacrifice and what makes good cops go bad. The story telling aspect of qualitative study also allows me to interpret what I see in the field based on my personal experiences, studies and observations. This is a great way to study something you are interested in, and help it come to life through your own eyes for the world to share.

Role of Researcher

I have the unique experience of serving in the SOG during the course of more than twenty-years in law enforcement. My SOG experience includes sixteen years in SWAT and twelve concurrent years in a multijurisdictional narcotics task force. After leaving the position for promotion to a division commander and then accepting a position as a city Chief of Police, I am able to both understand the subculture while being separated from it.

Access into the fraternity is critical and something I mentioned to you earlier. Civilian academic scientists have tried, and failed to gain the trust and openness from officers. The code of silence prevents us from sharing and them from learning. Having earned their trust, I gain immediate access to officers throughout this country. The trust established within the SOG community allows me an opportunity into the autonomous activities covertly conducted by the SOG.

While I may have been tempted to shade the findings to glorify the "blue," I rely on research techniques to validate the findings and ensure reliability in documenting the facts. This is very similar to a chain-of-command for fact checking. Ultimately, it is more important for reporting the truth than another mythical tale of police lore. The officers deserve better and the culture requires a revolution for change.

Qualitative Design

There are many opportunities available under the umbrella of qualitative methods for conducting in-depth studies of policing. Although there are challenges to the researcher, such as entrée; the flexibility of methods associated with qualitative research provides alternative options. There exists a broad description for explaining qualitative research as a multi-method, naturalistic strategy to examine its subject matter[2]. This multi-method is described as "the combination of multiple methods, empirical materials, perspectives and observers in a single study is best understood, then as a strategy that adds rigor, breadth, and depth to any investigation."[3]

Another perspective describing qualitative research claims the process is rooted in the form of meanings and interpretations, which are transitory and situational.[4] The objective of qualitative research is to comprehend the significance of the meanings and interpretations by examining the subjects and environment in natural settings. Qualitative research is classically defined as the focus on methodological nature, and "complexity of the end products and its nature of the naturalistic inquiry."[5] This study is for understanding the social or human problem as research builds the complex, holistic pictures, analyzes words, reports detailed views of informants, and conducted the study in natural setting.[6]

Ethnography

In order to conduct this investigation into cop culture, I use a technique called "ethnography" that includes describing and interpreting a cultural or social group or system[7]. Since the genre of policing has many avenues for discovery, the SOG becomes the focal point, or my "unit of analysis as a means to better understand the cop culture. The interesting part of using ethnography is it allows me to describe, and then interpret the "shared and learned patterns of values, behaviors, beliefs and language of a culture-sharing group[8]," i.e. cops.

Looking at the SOG's behavior, language and the way they interact with one another helps to demystify the secretive services of policing. Over two years' worth of watching and talking with them helps me to see the spontaneous lived realities occurring in their lives in both their personal and professional experiences. The ethnography's narrative form represents the complexity of social interactions within and beyond a formalized organizational structure.

This strategy also depends heavily on the observation of human interaction and the patterns emerging from those observations to establish meaning of the SOG Operators' lives and experiences. The ethnography allows for the description of the symbolism and institutional traditions enmeshed in the subculture influencing the potential state of liminal transition for the officers. The value of using this inquiry process is the periods of prolonged observation of the group in the day-to-day lives of the people, and one-on-one interviews with individuals or the group. The structure of ethnography serves as a valuable framework for conducting the examination to consist of:

- Introduction: problem and questions
- Research procedures: ethnography, data collection, analysis, outcomes
- Description of culture
- Analysis of cultural themes
- Interpretation, lessons learned, questions raised

It was important that I engaged in active participation through social and environmental immersion to ensure the nuances of the culture are captured through internal (emic) reflections and external (etic) observations. I also attempted to gain the insider's perspective, while balancing their preconceived notions of what may be occurring versus what actually is occurring. This allows me to close the distance between an outsider's interpretation (the etic perspective) of social order and the real meaning of life experience to those under study (the emic perspective). In order to achieve such a goal, I became both "an actor and a subject who's learned definitions can be themselves to be analyzed"[9]

In the participant observations where I worked directly with people under study, the ethical issues are embedded in all aspects of the communication in the field. It is always stressed the ethical considerations involved with ethnographic work to include; doing no harm to people or the community under study, respect for the rights of the people, for integrity of the data, and for people's way of life[10]. It is critical that I did not impose my will upon the subjects or environment, and must understand that the role is not to judge but to learn. As an ethnographer, I was a collector of artifacts and physical trace evidence, which unveil stories, rituals and myths in a process to uncover cultural themes. In order to serve as an ethnographic researcher to discover these themes, I engaged "...in extensive work in the field, gathering information through observations, interviews, artifacts and materials."[11]

The principles of ethnography have been established through years of rigorous standards and best practices for methodologies used in various supporting research designs in conjunction with ethnographic research. Those strategies identified as being useful not only in the overarching field of ethnographic research, but specific to the study of policing are; grounded theory, survey methodology, consensual qualitative research, and sociocultural observation. This list is not exhaustive, but does relate major supporting methodologies to the field of law enforcement research.

The value of ethnography is that it allows for the identification of grand themes and ideological conclusions. These processes may be based on the generalizable theories accessed from various locations to provide ideological baselines for comparative analysis in localized case studies. It is this flexibility that allows policy research to recommend changes either nationally, or internationally. The interviews and observations include opportunities from literally every corner of the United States, and coupled with a literature review purposefully accessing global data includes policing studies to ensure broad-base applicability.

Methods

Similar to any type of intense investigation, you must be methodical in collecting evidence. There are proven techniques used in the social sciences for gathering your evidence about culture.[12] Collecting evidence also includes analyzing and interpreting what the information tells the researcher. These methods involve forms of data collection, analysis, and interpretation. The qualitative research design includes the use of open-ended questions, interview, observation, and audio-visual data. From the collection of information; codes and themes are identified for description, analysis and interpretation of the materials. Participant observations, semi-structured interviews and the auto-ethnography were used to translate the approach into practice.

Data

Data collected during interviews and participant observations did not include Operators identifications for the purpose of protecting them from detection. Additionally, the idea was to create a cultural portrait of the SOG's world and not focus on any one individual statement or story. Since this is not my personal story, personal recollections have also been sanitized for guarding against the detection of identities. My original research design included a pictorial ethnographic account of the symbolism associated with cop culture and the SOG through tattooing. Operators who willingly displayed their inked artwork also refused to have anything photographed. The adherence to the code of silence, desire for anonymity and fear of institutional accountability through identification prohibited every opportunity for documenting this cultural phenomenon.

Semi-Structured Interviews

The semi-structured interviews include informed consent and the asking of permission to audio record and / or videotape the interview. The subjects were not willing to participate if their identity was potentially exposed, and their requests were honored. The sources of the semi-structured interviews occur in different states with a mixture of SWAT and Narcotics Operators. Twelve current and two retired Operators are included in this section. Interviews are conducted with SWAT Operators in Louisiana, Texas, Florida, and Virginia, while Narcotics Operators came from Arizona, Virginia, and Louisiana (retired) and Alabama (retired).

Limited recordings are taken for reference materials only and multitudes of detailed field notes were written to document their experiences. Upon completion of the subject interviews, the recorded data was personally transcribed to ensure accuracy of the information. This data is not incorporated verbatim into the body of this project to protect against unintentional identity exposure.

The four accounts of salient personal experiences required to illustrate specific examples involve the use of code names assigned to ensure anonymity. The SOG Operators asked to participate in the semi-structured interviews were chosen based on the population selection criteria and their depth of experiences involving line of duty activity and undercover and/or SWAT operational experience. Interviews of retired SOG Operators were conducted as semi-structured interviews and include no participant observations. These participants were initially identified through a convenience sampling by approaching subjects who I share a personal acquaintance. Snowball sampling is used to identify additional subjects to interview. This tactic involves asking subjects you know to introduce you to others you have yet to meet.

Criteria for Semi-Structured Interview Participants

The criteria for identifying the semi-structured interview population are based on my personal experiences in the policing milieu. There are seven criteria listed below with explanations of each criterion preceding them. Since they are unique to my research, I provide justification for their inclusion.

- *Criterion 1.* Law enforcement academy graduate.

Justification: Criteria number one is significant because graduating from the law enforcement academy becomes the gateway into the policing universe.

- *Criterion 2.* One full year of service in a traditional policing role, such as detention center, patrol, or detective prior to SOG assignment.

Justification: It is used for demonstrating the socialization trajectory that the SOG Operators are grounded in the experiences of traditional policing roles prior to their assignment into SOG. The pre SOG, during SOG and post SOG analysis also requires the base of experience in the traditional policing roles to serve as a comparison of occupational experiences.

- *Criterion 3*. Officer was selected for SOG assignment as result of an agency application announcement and a screening process to include panel interview, weapons qualifications and a physical fitness assessment.

Justification: The third criterion is included to ensure a standard of professionalism and accomplishment is achieved prior to the SOG selection process.

- *Criterion 4*. SOG Operator has served as a full time Narcotics Agent for a minimum of two years, or
- *Criterion 5*. SOG Operator has served either full time or collateral duty with SWAT for two years.

Justification: Standards four and five require two years served in SOG to ensure the Operator has had ample experience in the culture prior to evaluating their experiences. Normatively, it takes at least one year of experience through mentoring and supervised field training before an officer is independently productive in the assignment. Most SWAT Operators serve a collateral or part-time duty assignment, and the time-in-assignment requirement compensates for the lack of full time status.

- *Criterion 6*. Relative to retired officers, the period of separation is not relevant, but the same time-in-assignment requirements for active duty service remains consistent. Retired will refer to those SOG Operators who either officially retired from active service, who resigned voluntarily, whose service was terminated by the agency without their consent or whose service did the agency and SOG Operators mutually end.

Justification: The sixth criterion details Operators no longer employed by law enforcement, but still possess the experiences of SOG assignment.

- *Criterion 7.* SOG Operators shall not be excluded from this study based on sex or race.

Justification: The final criterion is included to ensure that although SOG is predominantly a white male population, the minority or sex of a willing participant will not exclude them from this examination.

Participant Observations

Twenty participant observations are conducted to provide the opportunities for documenting thick, rich details of the SOG environment. Participant observations also occur in different states with a mixture of SWAT and Narcotics Operators. One hundred eighty-six Operators were observed during a period from January 2009 to August 2011.

I observe SWAT Operators at Louisiana training sessions, in California at a National Sheriff's Office conference, in Colorado at an International Association of Chiefs of Police conference, in Florida after conference hours at a bowling alley, in Mississippi during a pre-raid briefing, and in Virginia at a training session.

I observe Narcotics Operators in Pennsylvania at a Lifesaver's conference, in Missouri at a Governor's Highway Safety Association conference, in Louisiana at an officer's funeral, in Virginia at a national MADD conference, in Nebraska during a post workshop supper, in Louisiana during an undercover purchase of illegal narcotics briefing, and in North Carolina following an undercover surveillance operation.

I examine SOG Operators under observation for identifying patterns of speech, interaction, and relationships. Participant observation is described as a fluid strategy for gaining access into segments of society that would not allow entrée except through the application of deception on behalf of the researcher[13]. Although not useful for quantitative studies, this style of recording human activities provides a mechanism for researchers to enmesh themselves in the everyday lived experiences of their subjects.

The goal of participant observation is to move beyond the classification of an analytical tourist and experience the novel social reality[14]

I am aware through personal experience and research that officers will not usually volunteer information for fear of breaching their code of silence. This strategy allows me to move freely between observational opportunities and document detailed field notes for detecting patterns of behavior and conversations.

Auto-ethnography

Auto-ethnography[15] is "a narrative study of an individual's personal experience found in single or multiple episodes"[16] It is categorized as a type of narrative research with growing purpose and popularity. Most shared events for this study involve criminal cases with individuals arrested and undercover operations targeting drug violators. I change the names of jurisdictions, agencies, agents and anyone involved other than me to protect the confidentiality of those SOG Operators still engaged in active covert operations.

I enmesh lived experiences throughout the findings and discussion of the data in the descriptive, analysis and interpretative sections of this project. To illustrate examples of SOG subcultural and professional experiences, I include my first day on the job as an officer, first SWAT training, first day assigned to the narcotics unit, first undercover purchasing operation of illegal narcotics, first SWAT activation, and last SWAT activation as part of the cultural portrait. In addition, I incorporate my last undercover purchasing operation of illegal narcotics, narcotics and violent crime training conference, an OMC confrontation at narcotics conference swimming pool, reflection of SWAT career, and career as an undercover narcotics agent.

Sampling

The population of Operators consists of professional officers employed or retired by federal, state, county/parish, and municipal law enforcement agencies. I did not select the population of SOG Operators, but it is a result of subjects attending trainings, debriefings, conferences, or social events unorganized by me.

Data Analysis

Consistent with strategies[17] for presenting ethnographic analysis of qualitative data, information is indexed and coded. This leads to the creation of themes for extracting specific details and accounts of rich lived experiences of those officers under direct observation. I identify patterns and themes from the experiences shared by the subjects to assist in achieving a comprehensive understanding of the data. I decipher the categorical and chronological organization of data for detecting themes in the coded information to ensure an accurate understanding of the major categories while implementing the processes of research design.[18]

The first step involves organizing the data. This includes personally transcribing all recorded statements to ensure accuracy and familiarity, then typing out all field notes. Next, the data is sorted into various categories or types to include semi-structured interview data and observational data. Data secured from retired SOG officers is categorized separately from current SOG members. The third step is to gain a comprehensive understanding of the material by reading through the data in its typed form. The overarching review provides the complete meaning of the tone and main themes and ideas associated with the depth of the shared information.

The fourth step involves the detailed analysis and coding of major sections of the data prior to categorizing the information into specific themes based on meaning and significance. The final process of analyzing the data requires a systematic procedure for digesting and evaluating textual data for discovering the models of behavior shown to demonstrate consistent patterns.

Coding

The process of coding identifies major categories within the data to begin extrapolating those sections of research falling into the areas of common patterns. Coding is a process of organizing collected materials into "big chunks" of text before bringing meaning to the information[19]. The gathered data is segmented into sentences or paragraphs, and then labels are applied to those categories with a term best describing the actual language.

A mixture of inductive and deductive coding combines the best of each strategy. The inductive coding process allows for a determination of categories as the data develop and unexpected results emerge from the interviews and observations. It also serves as a safeguard against my bias as a former SOG and current researcher from overlooking valuable categories. The deductive method establishes codes that were predetermined based on the project's theoretical perspective and actual experiences in the SOG.

Themes

Upon completion of filling the coding categories with contextual data, I established themes to represent these broad descriptive statements. The technique of building themes begins after the detailed information is assigned to coding categories[20]. These patterns develop into theories or generalizations suggesting an end for qualitative studies. Themes may reflect the evolution of frequency of terms used to illustrate or describe a topic[21]. This reemerging and frequency of use also assists in establishing reliability for the data and research project.

Validation Strategies

Several social science "best practices" are used for promoting the authenticity of data secured during the semi-structured interviews and participant observations.[22] The first technique is to triangulate the various data sources to determine congruity of the major themes and patterns of behavior. This is accomplished by regularly reviewing the sources of information to identify commonalities of theoretical perspective. After collecting information from the semi-structured interviews and observations, a comparison is conducted based on what is experienced along with the literature reviewed to ensure consistency. The second technique incorporates rich, thick descriptions allowing the reader to experience this isolationist culture from an insider's perspective.

A third strategy is utilized by acknowledging my personal biases as addressed in the section titled "Role of Researcher." I examine the sample universe by documenting data regardless if it supports or refutes the central themes of this project. This allows me to experience the different views that did not agree with the majority of information collected but important to collect for documenting all perspectives and experiences. The final process is spending prolonged time in the field. I spent more than two decades in the field of law enforcement, and while not in the researcher's capacity, the depth of observation provides a foundation for evaluating the information given to me during the data collection process.

Reliability

Qualitative research presents limited options for examining the stability or consistency of responses. A strategy for examining the stability and consistency of responses is the process of coding interviews to identify the major themes and inconsistencies of data provided by the various subject participants[23]. I initiated the coding of transcripts and detailed notes of interviews not recorded. A team of stakeholders were assembled who are working in the criminal justice profession and who had graduate degrees. These stakeholders of the research project subsequently reviewed and coded the same information to determine consistency of interpretation, major theme identification, and discrepancies.

Description, Analysis and Interpretation

Once the process of coding and then placing the data into one of the three major themes was complete, I utilize a strategy[24] for analyzing the data. The three-phase process allows for a continual reviewing of the data to ensure a precise study of the volume of secured information over multiple times to capture an accurate and richly descriptive presentation of the restricted access SOG subculture.

The first step in the manner of presenting the collection of data is the description. This phase asks the question, "What is going on?" Data is presented in thick, rich detail as told to me and based on my observations and interviews; it is memorialized in written form. Research warns that there is no "pure" description[25], and the attempts to relate every spoken word by the interview subjects still lack the scientific rigor of quantitative analysis. This requires a concerted effort on my part to insure the identification of potential biases and diligently work to filter their accounts from my own perceptions.

The descriptive phase is an effort to provide a breadth of detail without losing the purpose of the research. A reader always want reassurance that there is a point to the lengthy descriptions[26], and researchers must weigh what they think is essential with what is actually relevant to the account. The researcher is encouraged to base his descriptions on "sufficiency" of data specific to what should be eliminated or included. My accounts are reviewed by cohorts (stakeholder team identified in Reliability section) unfamiliar with the research to ensure information included is focused on the objective of this project.

Using the description, analysis and interpretation method suggests that during the descriptive phase of data presentation, the accounts are best served as implicit analysis or interpretation before leading to more explicit analysis and interpretation. I chose to use two strategies recommended to guide the preparation of the descriptive materials. The first technique described is the "Plot and Characters," and it is used when individuals or sociological roles are central to the description. The researcher introduces the characters, and the story is put into motion while the researcher's role varies from narrator to participant. The second technique is the "Groups in Interaction." This is helpful when presenting various groups operating within the same space. Creating distinct groups assists in distinguishing the social clusters under examination.

The next phase of presenting the data is the analysis of the detailed descriptions. The section of analysis addresses the question, "How things work?" by identifying essential features of interrelationships among them. This is more formally defines analysis as the "... systematic procedures followed in order to identify essential features and relationships consonant with the descriptors noted above"[27].

By submitting my data to rigorous analysis, I offer a method for achieving credibility of information by presenting the more orderly and less speculative side of data transformation. Similar to the descriptive strategies, this practice is developed for those addressing the analytical presentation of the materials. Relying on standardized techniques for analysis[28], I first employ the practice of "Flesh out Whatever Analytic Framework Guided the Data Collection." It is similar to the narrative technique and is best for content analysis and analysis of social settings. The next analytical technique used is the "Contextualize in a Broader Analytical Framework." This draws connections with external authorities by using recognized bodies of theory in a specialized field, recognized classics, or tradition of known literature. I chose to connect my analysis to the traditional literature in the fields of sociology and anthropology.

The final phase for transforming data is the technique of interpreting the data for presentation. This phase addresses the essential questions of meaning and content. It asks, "What is to be made of it all?" Interpretation shall designate the point where the researcher "... transcends factual data and cautiously analyses and begins to probe into what is to be made of them"[29]. Also recommended is that researchers should err on the side of too much description and too little interpretation to ensure the focal point remains on the topic of research and not the researcher's opinion.

To interpret the analyzed data collected during the observation and interview processes I use two additional techniques referred to as the "Turn to Theory." This method is used for linking the limited scope of research with larger issues. My association with the classical anthropological theory of liminality is conducive with this strategy for interpretation.

The final technique is the "Connect With Personal Experience." Inspired by Clifford Geertz's "I-witnessing," this involves the personalization of interpretation as I address in my auto-ethnography.

This chapter is heavy with social science language, but like any quality investigation it is important to ensure that every rock is flipped. This is what distinguishes valid research from the cop tell-all. To the reader who is thinking I didn't sign up for class, rest assured it gets back to discussions of cop culture. To the student of cultural studies, you will see the value of this descriptive information in the event you choose to replicate or critique this study. To either reader, this chapter is necessary for providing assurance that the most rigid application of research methods were employed to protect the integrity of the material and honor the nature of the subject matter. Thanks to the structure of the project, the next chapter reveals the results of this multi-year, cross country examination of cop culture.

15

JUST THE FACTS

Studying culture, cops or crime requires basically the same skill sets and procedures. You have a question that requires answers. Maybe it's a "Who dunit?" or an issue of "why or why not?" Either way, there is a challenge or it is there for the inquirer to solve. Of course we know that our question is, "Why do good cops go bad?" We have worked our way through gathering the facts, conducting the surveillances, and interviewing the participants and witnesses. Now is the time to lay out what this investigative process has shown us.

This chapter relies on the process of "coding" to decipher the information and make conclusions based on the volume of information collected through interviews and observations. To properly code large amounts of information, the data is digested through several stages starting from a free-form collection of all notes and documents. This bulk is categorized by large portions of the total data set. Identifying recurring words phrases or concepts helps to refine the categories into themes. Drilling down into the themes to examine very specific recurring patterns, abnormalities or continuation of words or actions, the creation of concepts begin to emerge. From these concepts, conclusions, observations and recommendations can be offered. This section presents the result of the coding process.

After years of investigating the SOG and cop culture, I am able to conclude that the process of liminality is supported by the evidence. It is through the observations, interviews, sharing of lived experiences in the SOG, and from the experiences of cops across this nation that the dynamics of the subculture are shown to actually exist. Since the evidence confirms the liminal stages of becoming blue, the next step is to examine the depths leading to professional deviance. The discussion centers on the interpretive issues relating to liminality and the trajectory of socialization phases that may lead to professional deviance. I divide the descriptive data into three major themes that are detailed in this and the next two chapters; the trajectory of socialization, hating the others, and the final shades of blue. This categorical division assists in transforming the bulk of raw qualitative data into refined concepts available for describing, analyzing and interpreting.

Transforming Data; Description

The descriptive phase emerges from coding the data and the emergent themes. This section is a cultural portrait of the SOG incorporating the emic perspectives of the group, as well as my (etic) views of the collective culture. The first concept is the *"Trajectory of Socialization"* and contains the narrative accounts of data representing the code "homogeneity" which is further divided into the subcategories; race, sex, chronological age and physical appearance.

The subcategory of physical appearance is further separated into categories representing coded data specific to style of clothing, hairstyles, tattoos and language. The next codes involve alcohol involvement, physical contact, and occupational socialization / becoming blue.

The second theme emerging from the coded data is titled *"Hating Others"* and incorporates the coded categories of attraction to violence, degradation of women, and the anti-diversity / anti-homosexuality. The final theme entitled the *"Final Shades of Blue"* consists of the codes; deviant and antisocial behavior, apathy for traditional policing, and ideological transformation. The value of presenting a portrait as opposed to a singular example of the cop culture is this tactic is representative of the larger body of law enforcement, instead of just a few.

Trajectory of Socialization

During the process of coding data, the major theme of trajectory of socialization emerges. Learning the environment within which an officer works is a dynamic experience. The law enforcement profession uses hierarchical rank structures attained through promotional opportunities. The achievement structure of the organization creates a linear trajectory throughout the course of an officer's career. The socialization aspect is the learning of traditions, customs, and the expectant behaviors conducive to operating within the policing environment. Together, the trajectory of socialization follows the path an officer takes during their career. The journey toward occupational socialization travels along a continuum beginning with cadet phase at the police academy and progressing through liminal transitions during an officer's career.

This career pathway is supported by the codes associated with 1) homogeneity, 2) alcohol involvement, 3) physical contact, and 4) occupational socialization / becoming blue. The process of socialization is closely associated with the stages of liminal transitions officers experience throughout the course of their careers as they move from shades of light to dark blue.

Homogeneity

I use the term homogeneity to describe the parallels of individual members in the policing culture and am similar to a statement about the "numbing regularity" of becoming socialized[1]. Despite the individual's personality, professional background, or prior life experiences, the ultimate goal of the journey is to achieve socialization - becoming blue.

Across the country, stories of the numbing regularity are recorded through the observations and interviews of SOG as patterns emerge with the specific categories of race, sex, physical appearance, and language (cop talk). Literature reviewed and my personal observations identify the effects of peer clustering and a pack mentality by individuals once taking their position behind the thin blue line. Details describe the powerful effects of stratified social bunching and the desire to conform to the cultural norm for the purpose of institutional survival by "not making waves."[2] A narcotics agent from Arizona who discusses struggles with maintaining his integrity states,

"I know I have a choice, but you cannot afford to swim upstream too often. Better to go with the flow.

To emphasize the cultural effect of homogeneity, I describe the demographics of the study's Operators. The characterizations come from 200 law enforcement participants. Within that group, 193 were males and 7 females. Of those 193 males, 179 were white, 11 black, and 3 Hispanic. Five of the 7 females were white, and the remaining 2 are black. This is listed to show how similar Operators are as they dominate the SOG with males that are white.

Race

The element of race is consistent with literature[3] documenting the lack of minorities in policing, especially the SOG. An observation recorded in Philadelphia shows that of the 10 officers, 9 are white and 1 is black. I note that the 1 black male did not distinguish himself as different, and I add a researcher's note that all appeared "blue." The descriptor "blue" refers to their characteristics being so strong in appearance, physical mannerisms and speech, that race by color is not a factor. In the homogenous environment of policing, although the white race is present more than any other race, the personal characteristics of physical appearance in body build, hair style, clothing, tattoos, language used, close physical contact with other SOG, and the mannerisms are used by all officers to transcend the color of skin.

In regards to the white race being the majority, the group lists 93% are white officers; 5.5% are black, and 1.5% are Hispanic. The 2010 United States Census claims the percentage of population claiming to be white was 72%, while 12% claim to be black or African-American. Persons claiming Hispanic or Latino decent report 16%.

Obviously, those entering the SOG community do not mirror society's racial composition. During an observation of a Louisiana SWAT training there are 13 white Operators and 1 black Operator. Although the interaction between these men became raucous at times, racist comments are not noted. The only observations where comments about black people occurred came from the sole black operator. He states,

"Crack dealers always wanting to shoot Uncle Tom first. With all these fucking crackers around, why they gotta take it out on a brother?"

Minority women were an even rarer occurrence. Of the 200 officers observed, there were only 2 black females. One is in a North Carolina narcotics unit and the other is in a Nebraska narcotics unit. Neither claims to have much experience in the SOG and though both make comments about suspicions that their selections are based on race, the North Carolina black Operator expresses it was to "color it up."

The 3 Hispanic males are observed during SWAT trainings, presentations and a briefing (Colorado, Virginia and Florida), but none of the 3 interact with their cohorts. I observed they each look very young, act timidly within their respective groups, and refuse to participate in an interview.

Sex

Similar to the dominance of the white SOG in law enforcement's milieu is the sex of SOG Operators. Male SOG represents 97% of the Operator's population. The 2010 United States Census reports a male population of 49.27%. None of the 7 SOG females are SWAT Operators, but work in narcotics units. The SOG is a male dominated culture despite attempts by federal mandates to integrate policing. Some of the strategies employed through affirmative action and consent decrees[4] are initially successful, but quickly lose the effect on policing's environment. Despite well-intended efforts or mandates, the results default to the hegemonic masculinity[5]. Two SWAT trainings observed in different jurisdictions in Louisiana consisted of only men. Male officers also dominate the funeral I attend for an officer killed in a motorcycle crash.

In another observation, a Louisiana narcotics unit pre-undercover purchase briefing had 7 men gathered to provide security for the single female narcotics agent assigned to purchase narcotics from a drug dealer. These examples express the minority standing for females in the SOG and are consistent with studies of females hired as police officers[6]. The SOG's subcultural solidarity has no significant effect on breaking the gender barriers.

Age

Studies[7] show the law enforcement hiring process taking long periods from vacancy to announcement, testing and appointment. Because of the length of hiring, attending college and serving military duty before beginning a policing career, the average starting age is approximately 25. Many states also allow for retirement after 20 and 25 years of service, and make the mid-40 year old age range common for attrition by retirement. In a culture of youth, seniority is measured by years of service and not chronological age.

While watching SWAT training, I am acquainted with some of the Operators, so the interaction with them turns to extended bouts of hazing. The main topic of harassment involves reasons why I am no longer active in SWAT. Most comments center on being too old for the strenuous tasks associated with SWAT. Although I know the kidding is in jest, it is also obvious that the majority of the males are in their mid-30s at the oldest.

While in Kansas City observing a group of male officers after a conference presentation, I watch as the 6 men who range in age from 25 to 55 years, sit in a lounge discussing police work. The oldest in the group identified as Carl (name changed) diplomatically confronts the SOG Operator in the group, Bob (name changed), over disparaging comments made about traditional policing operations. When the group decides to leave the lounge for supper, a verbal exchange occurs between Bob and Carl. We exit the lounge; the elder officer in the gray slacks (Carl, about 55 years old) decides to return to his room. After Carl exits the elevator, Bob says to the other Operators, "Well, fuck that old mother fucker then." I thought this was inappropriate and commented that maybe he was tired. Then Bob replies, "Yes. Old ass and tired." This interaction is common and part of the larger patterns observed during the interviews and observations.

Physical Appearance

While some "markers" of cultural inclusion such as age, race and gender are not naturally altered; other identifying characteristics are learned and imitated only after assimilation. The distinctive merit badge sash of a Boy Scout, the Freemasonry image of the square and compasses, or the iconic red and white patch of the Hells Angels' "death head" needs no explanation to members or observers to understand the unique culture. Law enforcement has similar attachments to images of inclusion, but they are not that well known to the public. In addition to speaking with officers, observations also show commonalities and consistencies in their uniform of dress, grooming, and language.

Style of Clothing and Accessories

In the majority of SOG encounters there are specific items and articles of clothing worn by the participants that serve as "markers" that could be used to identify an SOG operator. One of the most distinguishing "markers" includes the tactical folding knife accessory held in the front pant pocket by the sturdy metal clip. Officers, especially SOG carry these knives at all times whether on or off duty. In September 2011 while attending a special church service honoring law enforcement officers called a Blue Mass, I stood in a pew behind two Louisiana State Troopers to notice the same style knife clipped to the interior rear of their leather motorcycle boots.

A more contemporary "marker" is the popularity of a certain police clothing manufacturer; 5.11© Tactical Clothing. The wearing of the 5.11© police clothing line of products ranging from khaki cargo pants, watches, polo shirts with radio microphone tabs and ink pen holders to the supply of eyewear, socks, shoes, undershirts, tactical boots and even underwear are common among individual officers and agencies.

Although the brand is popular among all officers, the on duty wearing of these items is associated with the tactical SOG assignments. During all 5 SWAT training observations, Operators dressed in similar tactical dress uniforms (TDU) identified with law enforcement special operations type clothing.

In Pennsylvania, California, Virginia, Florida, and Missouri the males in the observation groups are dressed with similar clothing in slacks or the khaki colored tactical style 5.11© police cargo pants (popular for deep pockets on each thigh, reinforced knees and additional pockets for securing gear, ammo or miscellaneous equipment.) Each wore a polo style short sleeve shirt, and most have police logos stitched onto their polo style shirts with their agencies badge or emblem embroidered on the chest. Within all of these disparate gatherings of SOG, no one stood out among the others.

The briefings held by narcotics agents should have provided opportunities to observe SOG in a variety of clothing types. The pattern of similarity remains consistent as all are seen in casual attire with comparable style blue jeans and tee shirts with different logos on the front. They also all have tactical vests with ballistic capabilities and police patches for identification placed on the outer shell. This reinforces their unified association despite the slight differences in denim jean colors and shirts. Some did distinguish themselves by wearing baseball caps in the typical style of the bill turned backwards.

In another example, the funeral I attended for the police officer killed in March 2011 provides a visual illustration of the split between SOG and non-SOG. I was aware that the deceased officer belonged to a law enforcement motorcycle club (LEMC), and that group, the "Brothers In Blue" asked to participate in the funeral procession. I note about 50 motorcycles at the funeral services, and standing around the motorcycles were police officers dressed in motorcycle attire. These officers are clad in tattered jeans, t-shirts, headbands, bandanas, and leather vests with menacing patches and symbols representing the LEMC "Brothers In Blue."

Figure 15.1: LEMC members escort hearse for fallen police officer. *Source: Source:* Reprinted with permission from The Courier and Daily Comet

Figure 15.2: Uniformed Police Honor Guard and LEMC members wearing respective "colors" during casket transport for fallen police officer. *Source: Source:* Reprinted with permission from The Courier and Daily Comet

The LEMC officers are "flying their colors" to show respect for the loss of the officer, and it is similar to what every officer was doing who arrived in dress blues. Before the services begin, I watch how the various groups of officers segregate themselves by uniform and LEMC attire. As the memorial service begins, I stand at the rear of the chapel to observe, provide support to my officers and await my cue for presenting this officer's family with an American flag.

There is great symbolism in police burials, such as the twenty-one gun salute, bugle blowing "Taps," the rider-less horseless with boots turned backwards, the black mourning band worn over the shield, the "Last Call Radio Transmission" and the presentation of the flag to the surviving family. The ceremony associated with memorializing the death of an officer engrains a level of reverence from society for the passing of someone "special." The public displays of appreciation and tradition also serves as reassurance for surviving officers that despite the low pay, long hours, hostile conditions, or the detrimental effects associated with serving the public; that they will at the time of their death be missed. Religious services surrounding police memorials are often used to demonstrate liminality[8]. It explains how segregated social ideologies seem to coalesce into a unified body for the purpose of reverence. I observe that not even the emotions attached to attending an officer's funeral blurred the lines between officers in dress blue uniforms and LEMC.

Figure 15.3: Chief Scott Silverii presenting an American flag to the officer's surviving family. *Source: Source:* Reprinted with permission from The Courier and Daily Comet

Finally, during an interview of a SWAT Operator from Texas I asked if he thought there was a level of comfort from everyone looking and dressing similar. He responds, "I'm not crazy about cloning, but you gotta keep it tight." Whether it was SOG in training, operational, educational, or social environments, all SOG dress similar in style and the functionality in garments further reinforces the pattern of "markers."

Hair Style

Institutional policy may direct the issue of hairstyle more than personal preference, but it is a reoccurring observation made of this para-militaristic profession. Most police agency grooming policies mandate that the male officer's hair shall not touch the collar of his shirt, clean shaven face with no beard, and all mustaches must be trimmed neat and not extend below the mouth.

While these guidelines leave some room for individuality, the majority of SOG encountered chose to sport a style of haircut referred to as a high and tight or crew cut. This involves the hair at the base and above ears; shaven or closely shaven to the scalp and the hair left incrementally longer as it progresses to the crown of the skull. The hair on top of the head is either spiked up, or combed to one side or the other, and all have a similarly short and manageable hairstyle.

The narcotics agents, who usually have latitude with grooming regulations, still chose to wear the same basic hairstyles. A minority of narcotics agents sport goatees and an earring in the left ear lobe. In the last twenty years, I saw a variety of changes in the grooming styles worn by SOG. When I began, the SOG wore long hair and thick beards to mimic a popular look of the late 1970's and mid-1980's. During the late 1990's through the early 2000's, I saw the hairstyles change to a shorter style to remain consistent with societal trends. During my last undercover operation in 2002, I sported a shaved head and a giant goatee that covered most of my jaw line. Prior to shaving my head, I grew hair below my shoulders and sported a combination of beards, goatees, and other menacing facial hair combinations.

Police Organizations and Culture

Figure 15.4: Author during SOG assignment exhibiting non-traditional police appearance. *Source*: Original photograph property of Dr. Scott Silverii

Tattoos

The most traditional of all markers separating one culture from another is some form of permanent identification on the body itself, the tattoo. As stated by one Florida SWAT Operator:

"It's funny I never had a tattoo until joining this shit. First thing you got to do. Give you the template and address to the shop. Hurts like hell but got to get it or they kick the crap out of you. My wife, ex-wife, hated the thing and after a while I didn't give a crap."

While hairstyles are only as pertinent as the last barbershop visit, the presence of tattoos is a permanent commitment in the SOG. This

Operator's recounting of his first ink session reminds me of my own desire to have a tattoo. Seen as a rite of passage, I wanted the experience of going into a tattoo shop to earn my wings in the subculture. I wanted just one permanent commitment to the culture that had consumed me; the SOG. Having now lost count of my many tattoos, the final one was in honor of leaving SWAT and those brothers killed in the line of SOG duty.

In Kansas City, Missouri, sitting in a 54th Street restaurant and bar, I observe 4 SOG lift their pants legs, shirt sleeves, and drop their collars to display various tattoos representing SOG brotherhood, dedication to their children, country and themselves. While attending two SWAT trainings in separate jurisdictions I observe Operators with visible tattoos. In most interview and observational opportunities, I am told about and shown tattoos on the SOG Operators.

Tattooing was the subject of a federal hearing in Los Angeles relative to the gang-like culture and the demarcation of deputies belonging to white male dominated "social clubs" within the Los Angeles Sheriff's Office (LASO). An excerpt describing the purpose of the federal hearing reads:

"He is still proud of his tattoo. The somber image of Death's hooded skull and scythe tattooed onto the inside of the deputy's left ankle in 1989 initiated him into a select fraternity called the Grim Reapers. Then a street cop at the Lennox station, this deputy has risen to a key position in the Los Angeles County Sheriff's Department - along with other members of his "club." The groups - with macho monikers like the Pirates, Vikings, Rattlesnakes and Cavemen - have long been a subculture in the country's largest Sheriff's Department and, in some cases, an inside track to acceptance in the ranks. Senior officers say they began with the creation of the Little Devils at the East Los Angeles station in 1971, and membership continued to swell in the 1980s at overwhelmingly white sheriff's stations that were islands in black and Latino immigrant communities"[9]

Membership tattooing continues in practice since this California report. From the observations, there is a pattern of tattoo designs common within the SOG milieu. These patterns consist of an American flag or a patriotic combination of American colors and symbols inked into their skin to show the eternal love for country and bond to the SOG. Also observed in multiple states were designs including a police badge, or sheriff's star, image of SWAT Operators in action, weapons such as long guns, and skulls with various accompanying designs.

The most common image is an eagle with its wings spread. In the right talon, the eagle is holding a submachine gun; in the left talon is a lightning bolt. In between the submachine gun and the lightning bolt is a dagger. A tactical SWAT saying is, "Speed, Surprise and Violence of Action." The assembly of these items held by an American Bald Eagle would seem to symbolize those principles. This image is not the "official or sanctioned" image of SWAT, yet it appears on Operators as tattoos in almost all of the states.

Figure 15.5: "Unofficial," but highly recognized as the image of SWAT. *Source:* Used with permission from Center Mass, Inc. online; http://centermassinc.com

Language
The language of the SOG is a unique dialect of official police radio codes (10 codes), local slangs, training terminology, and legal jargon all woven together by threads of profanity. I ask a Virginia SWAT Operator about relating to his SOG peers the same as when he was in a non-SOG assignment. The SWAT Operator answers,

"10-50. Fuck no!!! You gotta watch your cock around the suits. They always looked to crack it off in your sweet ass."

In his reply, he encapsulates official police radio communications, masculine jargon, anti-institutional disdain for supervisors, and references to homosexual prison rape. Of course he smiles as he comfortably delivered this statement.

During an observation in Kansas City, the cop talk was evident. While waiting for supper we sat in a lounge getting to know each other. I notice that prior to anyone introducing himself as having SOG experience, the conversation was civil with not a curse word used. Once the four SOG huddle together, they began throwing expletives. During a Louisiana SWAT training some Operators use profanity like a comfortable second language.

Although the training sessions are demanding and purposefully stressful, the harassing language is never directed to another person in a provoking manner. Narcotics Agents in North Carolina engage in conversations that are often personal including talk of sex with other Operators' family members. No one appears outwardly angered by the verbal abuse.

In contrast to the earlier observations of Operators using cursive and harassing language, I observe a group of Narcotics Agents where I hear none. The danger inherent to operations involving the undercover purchase of illegal narcotics creates an environment of determined focus. The briefing in Louisiana includes no verbal hazing or ridicule of each other. Another observation of this group is during the operational briefing when very specific individual assignments are distributed, no one is called by name or nickname. This is consistent with group unification and the hegemonic masculinity's surrender of identity for social clustering.

The emerging pattern of cop talk lies at the base of SOG communications and seems to escalate under stressful situations or while recounting those situations. Other than the single observation of the Louisiana narcotics briefing mentioned above, it is a blend of street level law jargon and prison yard gangster chatter. Whether it occurs in the form of sex, age, race, dress or behavior and language, the SOG establishes organizational power through homogeneity. The power of homogeneity is apparent. It is at times a security blanket to the Operator for reassurance and acceptance into an institutional subculture often contrary to the public ideals of the organization. Other times it creates moral and ethical conflict between who the public servant wants to be and the professional deviant he became.

Alcohol Involvement

The use of alcohol becomes part of the everyday life of SOG Operators. I witness and experience the confluence of alcohol within the cop culture. Alcoholism is documented at levels twice the national rate for police officers[10]. Forty-eight percent of policeman and 40% of policewomen drink excessively, compared to civilians at 10% of men and 7% of women drinking excessive amounts of alcohol. From the observations, other patterns emerge. These are similar to the dynamics discussed in detail in Chapter 12.

A SOG in Kansas City asks a group to explain how police officers could enforce the impaired driving laws when cops are the worst violators. All SOG in the group admit to coming on duty either drunk or hung over. One of the SOG, who has experience as a narcotic agent, tells the others how he used to drive his unmarked police vehicle home from the bars. He would activate his blue lights so other officers would not stop him since he was so intoxicated. He said it became a game and he would serve as the DD (designated driver) for nights out drinking.

In the account of my final undercover purchase of narcotics, I use alcohol as a tactic during the actual role-playing that leads to the purchases of illegal drugs. In this undercover assignment, I sparingly drank beer throughout the night while in the bar, and although not intoxicated, I act as if I were. This role-playing of intoxication helps ease the drug dealers' tensions about selling narcotics to a total stranger. Once I complete the purchase of the drugs from three women in the dark parking lot, I use the ruse of being intoxicated as an excuse to avoid engaging in sex with them.

During this same night after working undercover, my SOG team of Agents and I engaged in an eventful post-operation tradition:

After more beers, shots of whiskey, offers for wild sexual experiences and arm wrestling matches, it was time for the bar to close. I led my crew into a neighboring state to begin the regular celebration. Working undercover, you are always on duty and looking for the next dope buying opportunity. Duty could wait. That night, like many others, we drank extremely too much tequila, danced too poorly with ugly women, and threatened to kick too many redneck asses. I woke after just a few hours of sleep and reported back to the off-sight narcotics office to prepare for the next day's mission of working undercover. I felt like a knife had plunged deep into my head, chest, and back as my years of conducting operations and age had left me not so quick to recover after a night of "working" undercover, but it was the job I swore to do.

A pattern of alcohol use is consistent, and these excerpts from interviews and observations demonstrate the presence of alcohol in the SOG. A SWAT Operator from Mississippi describes his team's nights out as,

"Just acting like assholes who shit don't stink. Kings of the fucking world. Drinking and fucking around like some freaking spring break movie."

Meanwhile a retired SOG from Louisiana says,

"Long hair, beard to my dick and all the beer and pussy in the world. No

hassles with your brothers. Those fuckers would buy us beer before, during and after work. We would stop at the bars on night patrols and get tanked. These probes would shit themselves because they knew they would get busted. The vets told them. Do it or walk out. Too much ego I guess. They drank up. Then we would leave their asses in the dark and pop rounds over their heads. How in the hell did we not get killed. End of the day, it made you tough. We were all brothers then."

In Arizona, a SOG associates alcohol consumption with off duty social activities and as a factor in cheating on his wife. He states,

"I've come home blasted drunk from work, nights with the boys, softball games, you name it. I've also got caught with my pants down a few times if you know what I mean? I'm not that kind of person, but the shit this job puts you through almost makes you feel like you have no control of your life."

This SOG also made peer socialization comments earlier about "not swimming upstream", and they are similar to the results conveying this indoctrination into a culture of alcohol consumption is driven by peer socialization, desire for acceptance and social clustering development[11]. Research is also consistent with the observations relative to social clustering, peer acceptance and groupthink.

The cultural synergy leads SOG Operators to blend for acceptance even if it requires uncharacteristic antisocial behavior such as chronic alcohol consumption. This is yet another emerging code supporting the trajectory of socialization theme, as SOG enmeshes the drinking of alcohol with personal and professional activities.

Physical Contact

Street survival instructors teach police officers from the beginning of the academy that anyone coming within three feet of their personal space is an assault on their position. Physical contact and close proximity are not common with the culture of traditional law enforcement, but observations of SOG demonstrate something different. Just watch an officer as they either interact with the public or remain alone. They naturally fortify their position and personal space by holding both hands at waist level. Their hands often touch and remain ready to defend themselves or access the force options carried on their belt. This is practiced even in non-adversarial settings. Another personal defense trigger is that their elbow over the side of the duty rig where their firearm is located regularly taps the holster in an involuntary weapon retention maneuver. SOG do not wear traditional uniforms, and tend to lose those personal space defense mechanisms. This attributes to the close personal contacts often engaged in between them.

Oddly, it was the refusal to engage in close contact that demonstrated to me on one occasion that I was not accepted into the subculture by some SOG and that I have crossed the line to becoming a "suit." While attending a funeral for an officer, I spotted a longtime SOG dressed in full LEMC attire to include the tattered clothes, bandana, and a leather motorcycle vest full of patches with emblems, logos, and language. We went back over 20 years although in different agencies. Clothed in my Class A dress uniform, I approach him and shake his hand. I lean in to hug him as SOG often does; he instead steps back and addresses me as Chief. The other SOG around him looked at me without acknowledging my presence. We were in two very different worlds and the physical contact usually shared between SOG brothers was not mine to participate in that day.

Literature does not detail physical contact between SOG, but in my experiences and observations, they are more likely to engage in physical contact than officers that are more traditional. This may be attributed to the need for small group reliance, as opposed to traditional assignments often requiring operational autonomy. Because of the operational need to maintain noise discipline during silent covert maneuvers, Operators communicate using hand signals and touching their partner. The combination of tactical communications, operating in close quarter tactics, touching to alert your partner while maintaining silent, and the bond of this fraternal subculture creates an environment for close physical contact.

Literature discusses the need for social clustering[12] and peer acceptance[13] among males, and this is demonstrated through physical contact. Close contact among SOG Operators was vivid in my recollection, so I made a point of greeting these participants with hugging and hard patting as they approach. This level of greeting is symbolic of the deep bond between individuals experiencing similar ideological believes, though possibly through a shared experience of the fragmentation from traditional institutional values.

During a SWAT observation in Virginia, touching is a normal level of physical contact between these men. From the handshakes and hugs to greet one another to the punching and grabbing throughout the training session, it was obvious that physical contact in the form of playful striking and wrestling is the dominant interaction among the group.

Another example of close contact occurs in a social setting while in Philadelphia teaching law enforcement officers. A small group of officers came to talk with me between sessions. Although all are cordial, no one makes personal introductions or shakes hands. One officer references his SOG experience during the talk and another officer responds that he too was SOG. Once identified, the two SOG physically relocate within the circle of officers to stand together and make a close personal introduction quietly as to not disturb the larger group.

The act of social clustering among homogenous groups occurs while observing a group of officers in Colorado. There were 10 male officers standing in a group discussing training sessions, places to eat and other mundane topics. During the conversation, 3 of the men identify themselves as SOG. The initial gathering of these men involves no handshaking or physical contact. The 3 men readjust their positions within the circle and formally introduce each other with handshakes. The independent actions of the other 7 seem typical of officers used to working routine, autonomous police assignments. Compared to the other 7 non-SOG, who do not as much as pat each other on the back; these 3 SOG regularly make physical contact with each other in a friendly manner to include patting on the shoulder and back and grabbing the forearm or triceps.

Close personal contact occurs in 18 of the 20 observations. SOG Operators relocate to each other when in mixed company with either civilians or non-SOG. The relocating does not disrupt the group or the conversations, but appears to be an attempt to establish comfort rather than dominance over the environment.

SOG gravitating towards each other in public settings exemplifies a benchmark for the trajectory of socialization. Although officers begin the police training academy void of loyalties or associations with others, the desire to develop close relationships and cluster among peers soon over takes their individuality. Through the transformative process of becoming blue, SOG Operators develop the relational bonds of brotherhood, and the desire to cluster with those most similar. This groupthink[14] or pack mentality is an evolutionary step in the trajectory of socialization's process of becoming blue.

Occupational Socialization / Becoming Blue

The duality of conflict in becoming blue exists between loyalties to the subcultural fraternity or the institutional ideals of duty, honor, and service. The process of separating from the law enforcement institution intensifies the process of socialization. My investigation shows the gang like clustering characteristics of the SOG. During an interview with a Florida SWAT Operator, he detailed the expectations of acceptance into the SOG. I ask a follow up question: "Like a club?" and he immediately snaps back:

"More like a gang. You got rules and if you don't follow they kick your ass out. You run your face and you get blackballed. You learn the rules fast. It's great if you fit in, it sucks if you don't."

His accounts reflect my own experience and illustrate the difference between assignment into SOG and acceptance by SOG.

The negative impact of organizational isolationism for creating dissatisfaction and termination of employment are explained in literature[15]. I ask a retired Louisiana SOG about the toughest part in working with non-SOG. His reply is a typical effect of the isolationist tactic;

"I feel like I'm on a deserted island but I see everyone. No one sees me and probably don't give a rats ass who I am."

SOG who become a darker shade blue continues through liminal phases as they progress along the trajectory of socialization. An undercover narcotics agent in Arizona shares his struggles over maintaining the integrity he desires versus getting pulled into a lifestyle he wants to avoid:

"I'm not like some of these cats who just do it for the rush, or the pain. They live to chase women and tell war stories after each night of partying. Hell, I find myself at the center of these stories, and I'm like, this ain't the me I want to be."

He exemplifies the strain of subcultural socialization when he states:

"Just the peer pressure ... is crazy. Worse than any college frat I saw. I used to think if it's that bad then the guys should just quit. Then I realized that you can't. In a way you're trapped. It's a dishonor to quit."

The three SOG all use powerful expressions (ex: like a gang, on a deserted island, ain't the me I want to be) that illustrate the internal difficulties of SOG socialization. SOG learn that exclusive membership to this subculture comes at a price. The unity of SOG creates an atmosphere of surrender of individuality and dependence upon each other. Operators cannot call upon the staff of the regular police to assist in most covert operations. During my period of SWAT command, I shared this isolationist ideology by creating a unit motto: "If not us, who?" This stresses the realization of the commitment of the Operators, and that once SWAT activates; it was our responsibility to resolve the crisis. We adopted and trained with a mindset that literally there was no one else coming to help us if we struggled in the mission. It provided a motivational push that sharpened our focus and resolve, but also deepened the isolationist divide. We printed metal dog tags with this motto and wore them under our uniforms.

A Colorado SOG Operator captures the isolationist credo of organizational disenfranchisement:

"Once they (SOG) trust you, everything is possible and you are always in. You never rat. Never! It doesn't matter what you see or do. No one talks. This is the way things should be."

Throughout the trajectory of socialization, SOG Operators become entrenched in the ideals of the subculture. A series of liminal transitions further remove them from the traditional organizational values of duty, honor, and service. The findings demonstrate the intensity of belonging and the allegiance to the SOG. Samplings from data include an observation of California officers, Dave, and his partner Earl (names changed). These officers attempt to convince me they were fulltime SOG. I know they were lying based on the inconsistencies of their stories. These two officers are practicing the blue code of silence; one lies and the other swears to it. Although not Operators, these two officers are socialized to believe that SOG status provided them credibility.

The occupational process of becoming blue is so strong that this Operator's response to quitting the unit prompts a preference for death over leaving. A Louisiana SWAT Operator was asked why he just did not quit SWAT. He replies:

"Serious? Dude you don't fucking quit. I wanted that shit my whole stupid life. On the ground motherfucker, SWAT in the house. That's better than crack. All the hell I went through to get in, and to get out because of that bitch? She can go. You work at McDonalds and you make fries every day. I'd eat a bullet."

A Nebraska SOG Operator sums up the fraternity over family ideal by saying,

"It's like another family but without the bullshit."

Another example of the strength of connection to the isolationist ideals develops at a Louisiana SOG funeral where the officers are flying their colors (LEMC patches) to show respect for the loss of the officer.

A Mississippi SOG Operator says,

"You know how it is. You wait your ass off to get hired and then they stick you in the jail to rot with those fuckers for about a year. If you're lucky you break into the academy. I waited about a year and a half till it broke. I said hell yea I wanna go."

Finally, a Virginia SOG Operator comments on the value of becoming socialized and isolated as "blue" by saying:

"We are like a family who watches each other's back. Most of those fuckers (non-SOG) don't run when you call for help."

The trajectory of socialization is a complex process and includes many stages of liminal transitions occurring before full acculturation. During this process, the Operators develop an identity influenced by the fringe lifestyle of their peers. Part of this identity includes the expectation of entitlements associated with the assignment. Characteristics present themselves as organizational autonomy, disassociation with traditional uniformed police.

Other characteristics include the mystique of SOG operations fanaticized by media portrayals, close association with living on the edge and risk taking, and the self-identification as existing outside the law. This attitudinal persona creates a loyalty to the SOG and a divide from others who threaten the existence, and hating the others to protect the fraternity comes easily.

This chapter was an eye-opener after having enmeshed myself in the cop culture for so many years. Yet as I traveled, speaking with the many officers and listening to their personal accounts, they all seemed so familiar. I realize just how strong and universally applicable the socialization process is. Probably 95% of these officers have never or will ever know each other, but they all share common characteristics, traits and behaviors. They are not the result of genetic in-coding or nationalized training. How they assimilate is a result of semi-similar basic academies. Who they are is a result of the informal practices of institutional ecologies. Why they are is a result of fitting in as they become blue. No matter where they are; cops are cops.

16

HATING OTHERS

Others Need Not Apply

In 2012, I was asked to co-chair an exploratory roundtable discussion about police relations with the lesbian, gay, bisexual, and transgender (LGBT) community and fellow officers at an international law enforcement conference with the national president of PFLAG (Parents, Families, Friends of Lesbians & Gays.) Besides myself and others responsible for logistics, there were maybe 2 Chiefs of Police who attended. Was it institutional apathy, fear of a stigma for attending, lack of awareness on the topic, or maybe it was just an inconvenient time slot allotted this session? This chapter will demonstrate that it was not the time slot preventing attendance, though I wish maybe it might have been.

The hegemonic masculinity (old boys club) creates a protective nature for the preservation of ideals associated with the fringe lifestyle. Outsiders, others, and alternatives are identified as threats to the congruity of the small groups given the latitude to carry out their missions without direct hierarchical supervision. Within that fringe comes the disdain for conformity, respecting of others and a propensity for physical force during the execution of their duties. The study shows the antisocial lifestyles associated with the actualization of a socialized SOG that does not avoid the intensity of hating others for maintaining their status.

Attraction to Violence

This section details the promotion of the use of force as necessary for conducting certain missions, as a mechanism to gain social acceptance, and exclude others. The Operators express no regrets for injuries inflicted and justify their actions of strategically applied violence. I share the following story from my autoethnographic record to demonstrate a potentially deadly situation I was in while conducting an undercover drug deal with a possible OMC member.

I was assigned to the cover team tasked with monitoring and ensuring the safety of rookie undercover agents targeting a possible biker-run barroom in the middle of literally, "nowhere." They were too fresh, too clean, too academy grad stiff. No one bit and the night began losing the promise for buying illegal narcotics. Late into the night, I signaled for the agents to leave the bar and clear away from the area.

The "hooks" left as instructed and it was just a few of us left in the place. There had been plenty of alcohol, lies, and promises, but no offers for buying illegal drugs. The rookie agents left a chilling effect on the entire rat hole. But they were now gone, and the feel changed immediately. It was darker, smaller, and deadly quiet.

I found myself alone in a small one-stall bathroom with a giant man holding a steel-blade Buck knife and a plastic cigarette wrapper full of methamphetamine. It was an odd situation to find myself. My long-time partner and fellow SWAT Operator had walked outside of the barroom and unknowingly locked the door behind him at closing time. I was walking slowly behind and heard the bartender call out. This guy stood over six feet six inches, with shoulder length hair and a long, gnarly beard. He was a target of our undercover mission and identified as a possible member of an OMC.

Because of his intimidating build and disposition, I avoided eye contact during the night other than ordering alcohol. I did not want him to mistake me as being confrontational, but only that I was there to party and buy drugs. Once the place emptied, he asked me to follow him and we walked into that small bathroom. There, he pulled that long, sharp Buck knife from the tattered leather sheath on his side.

I forced myself to remain calm while my heart pounded wildly. My mind began rehearsing the SWAT close quarter combat strikes and kicks I anticipated using if he attacked me. I knew the confrontation was going to be violent, but I strangely looked forward to it as that stall seemed more like a coffin than a toilet. He shoved the knife in front of my face with the point filled by caked up methamphetamine powder and demanded that I taste it.

It was no friendly gesture of sharing his supply. He smelled the other two undercovers and put the halt to anyone doing business with them. With me, he was not so sure. The years taught me plenty to do, and not to do. Living the character you create is key and stress tends to crack that facade. Not me. There was no bend or break in who I portrayed, because there was so much of whom I am in that character's role.

The encounter became heated, and I braced for his assault. Then, I noticed a hesitation in his decision about fighting, so I began inciting him for establishing dominance. My tactic worked, and he dumped the dope into a plastic baggie and handed it to me. I tried walking calmly towards the exit door, praying that it was unlocked and that he did not change his mind. It was too late. I busted into the sticky night air and greeted my partner. His "where the hell you been" look told me he realized his mistake. I left quietly because I knew his fate had been sealed.

This account is typical of the attraction to violence that permeates the SOG. The execution of violence[1] earns an officer respect from his peers, and is an expectation of cultural assimilation. SOG do not consciously associate their violent actions with serving the state as the social compliance controller. Their acts of force upon the public are expected by peers to ensure each Operator is willing to protect his brother, exercise that option, and capable of remaining silent about it.

During an observation of Virginia SWAT Operators, they joke about violence experienced or inflicted upon civilians, and about violence that was not justified but inflicted for the sake of making a point. The conversation during this observation sounds contrived at times, but the effort to impress each other led to one Operator trying to outdo the other with their accounts of occupational violence. The observations and interviews provide numerous accounts of the aggregate desire of the SOG subculture to engage in physical violence. A SOG from Nebraska admits within a group of his peers that:

"...what matters is getting the job done and kicking the crap out of shitbags."

A Narcotics Agent from Arizona shared that:

"I think that's the thing most people do not understand. You have to defend yourself. Gotta take it to them. All they respect is force. That's their life. They got a saying about "taking your courage." Not me motherfucker. I'll take your life before you take shit from me."

An interview with a Louisiana SOG involved asking the question, what else do you enjoy about the job? His answer reflects the indoctrination to violence:

"Really? Cracking skulls. I whipped the shit out of some motherfuckers. Can't count the asses."

I do not know if state sponsored violence[2] was meant for the levels of "cracking skulls" though. This attraction to violence also earns Operators' respect within the ranks as a Louisiana SWAT commander earns his position because of experiencing violent situations. He shares that he was only 26 years of age, but he had survived the "shit" so the chief made him the commander. This incident is similar to claims that counter-institutional behavior results in higher rates of promotion[3] than other officers.

A Mississippi Operator states that there is a professional price paid for exacting levels of violence. He said,

"The worse we behave the more respect we earn from the street. I think that's why the rest of the agency looks down on us. We don't and not going to take any crap."

This Louisiana SOG also talks about the countercultural disposition towards the agency's internal integrity mechanism commonly known as internal affairs (I.A.). He states,

"Oh, I.A. Fuck them. Kick one ass and they think they own you. One douche said to me, 'you have established a pattern of violent and destructive behavior'. Like that's a fucking insult?"

These examples validate the dilemma of the SOG and their role in traditional policing. The one Operator displays the organizational reward for violent behavior; the second example shows how the violence causes separation from the rest of the agency, and the final example illustrates the adversarial relationship between SOG and institutional accountability.

A Colorado SOG was asked: Do you like being in the middle of the chaos and having others look to you? He says,

"Sure. I work my ass off to get here and stay here. I'm good at what I do and if everybody knows it, oh well. I don't mind the heat and I can take care of business. Most people are sheep looking for a shepherd. I'm the shepherd motherfucker."

The Operators promote the culture of violence because it is expected. Cops see themselves as society's shepherd, and they understand the necessity for applying violence to keep the flock intact and the attackers at bay. Another SOG Operator from Louisiana responds to my question to support the acceptance of violence. I ask; has being in SWAT changed your professional life? He replies,

"Yea my attitude changed, I don't take shit from nobody. My brothers got my back. I want to kick ass. Not just drive around all day trying for free tea."

The "free tea" statement is attributed to uniform patrol officers who usually receive free drinks at restaurants as an enticement for visiting the store or restaurant while on duty. Another example from an Operator in California also talks about how he changed:

"Probably. Who doesn't? You want to do a good job and be nice to the people but after a while of them disrespecting you, you learn to say fuck it. I used to try talking to people to help with their stupid problems. Now I just say shut up or you going to jail. Maybe I'm meaner or more of an asshole. My wife also said I was an asshole. Maybe she was right."

In 85% of the observations, Operators use physical force on each other by applying striking, kicking, or control hold techniques against each other. This application of violence is executed using strategic techniques taught to officers in the academy, in-service trainings and martial arts classes. Seldom does the Operator swing wildly to inflict the force, but instead, methodically applies control techniques to gain immediate compliance from the receiver of the force.

The constant physical contact with each other is an informal rehearsal of those techniques. An Arizona Operator said this interoffice behavior causes the group to become desensitized and more prone to violence towards the public. He states that,

"...The office then flows into the streets. This is one violent ass group. But

either we take it to them or they will bring it to us. This is proactive violence prevention. It gets out of hand sometimes, but that's the suppression aspect of it. Lay it on their ass."

Even beyond the office environment encouraging violence, this Operator explains that:

"Can't control the future but you can sure the fuck train to kick the shit out of it."

In my earlier career I was not aware of the role institutional force served in policing. After entering the SOG I came to understand the value of violence when applied in a controlled manner. To the uninitiated, SWAT Operators armored in dark colors and the seemingly fast and violent tactics are dangerous; but they are purposefully orchestrated. These displays of strategic force often prevent the criminal from reacting to cause injury to himself, officers and the innocent public during the course of executing a high-risk arrest. This distinction between violence and violence applied in a controlled manner is not often made in discussions[4] of state sponsored violence as a mechanism for acceptance but it is critical to distinguish that the use of "violence" in this study refers to justifiable and unjustifiable applications.

As a reminder, the term violence or force is inclusive of a wide range of contextual definitions. As an example; SWAT Operators' physical presence by surrounding a home with a barricaded suspect inside has influenced many offenders to surrender. On the other end of the spectrum, SOG violence includes the ability of an Operator to immediately and accurately subdue or neutralize a violent threat to ensure the safety of innocent victims and other Operators. The tactical use of force when executed as a means for controlling chaos is a skill set that I became proficient in, and served as a foundation for conversation with officers during my study. This concept is consistently illustrated throughout these interviews and observations.

Degradation of Women

The hegemonic masculinity dominating cop culture includes the male dominance over his environment to include women. In this masculine environment women are seen as weaker than men, and therefore in need of protection. Similar to the examination[5] involving the fraternal value system of despising any behavior perceived as feminine, the SOG relegates women into a second-class status where not fit for duty, is not good enough. Although they may feel the need to protect women, it does not equate to respecting them, and this leads to their degradation.

During my research, I chronicle in detail the relationship between officers and OMC in Chapter 11. The role of women in both subcultures is lowered to a submissive social standing. Women are objectified, and regularly used for sex among the members of each group. The term hegemonic masculinity[6] was coined to describe the heterosexist desire for domination over women as well as subordinated masculinities such as homosexuality.

A retired SOG's interview illustrates the view of women as resources for Operators to use at will. He shared with a sense of pride when I asked what else he enjoyed about SOG, to say:

"Really? Fucking. Fucking everything that walked, moved, breathed. Those whores would sneak out of dorm rooms, bedrooms, hell, even their old man's houses to fuck us. It was a party out of this world. Look. Not all skanks either. They had some fine mommas too. We would pass them around like pets. Shit we would all fuck 'em at the same time. I still see some of them today. I'm like don't act like you don't know me bitch. Bet if her husband knew the whore she was, she'd drop that fucking attitude. I'd never say a word. Them was some good fucking days."

Badge Bunnies, Siren Sluts & Holster Sniffers

There are groups of women that pursue officers similar to musicians' groupies that are called by various unflattering nicknames. Every rookie officer is warned that; "Your badge will get you pussy, but pussy will get your badge." Yet, officers are fully aware of the "Badge Bunny" phenomena and still they partake in the deviance of women willing to engage in sex with an officer if only for the fact that they are a cop.

While observing groups of SOG working in mid-western cities, they report the same policing ideals about women. These conversations were not localized to the mid-west, but similar slang terminology and "stories" are shared from Alaska to Ft. Lauderdale. There was usually a near disdain for women in their conversations as derogatory comments dominated their descriptions. A sampling of the most frequently repeated terms include; groupies, badge bunnies, house mouse, holster sniffers, siren sluts, uniform jumpers, pension hunters, and beat wives.

With the exception of "beat wife" the other terms refer to one-time encounters or relationships without meaning or emotion. The "beat wife" refers to the other woman who is visited regularly while the officer is on duty. I've heard the term "office wife" used regularly outside of the cop culture. That usually meant a female who works closely with the male during office hours, but the relationship does not extend into a sexual or emotional affair. The beat wife is a mistress, who during the course of an officer's on-duty time engages in a relationship. Because many officers without residency rules choose to live outside the jurisdiction they work, the beat wife (who lives in the working location) is insulated from the officer's real life. I was told by several officers in several states that these relationships have lasted for years.

I was also curious as to whether maintaining a separate committed relationship with a 'beat wife" is a condition manifested by the conflict of duality for living a double life by experiencing traumatic exposures at work, yet coming home to be husband and dad influences, or is just another relationship of convenience because the adulterer is wearing the badge? Nothing in their follow up answers revealed anything deeper in content than that their wives failed to understand the job they do and the stress they were under.

The hegemonic masculinity characteristic may prevail in the SOG, but the acts of degrading women come as an introduction to the fraternity. The Arizona SOG who struggles with his sense of morality admits:

"I'm not proud of it, but I've done some evil shit. I never knew we had groupies, like rock stars. Freaking women throw themselves at you. Like they stalk you to have sex with you. My first experience was with a house mouse. I'd only been in a few months and before leaving for a deal, the guys got real goofy.

Next thing I knew there was this girl going from office to office. Guys were piling up in the offices and coming out laughing. I was told she was there to take the stress off doing the drug deal. She was screwing or blowing every guy in the office. Hell, she wasn't even bad looking. What was I to do? I had to let her go down on me. They would have ridden my ass all night if I backed out. It became easier after that to run around. I justified it as part of the job."

While this is not meant to judge or justify the actions of the officers, but the availability of willing women promotes the temptation for engaging in illicit sexual behavior. It does not encourage the SOG to show respect to these women. Similar to the women that are property of the OMC, I witness a similar scene of women accompanying LEMC members. They are subject to a secondary role consistent with the fringe subculture's classification of women. They are not allowed to wear the same leather membership vests with rocker patches, but only wore "supporters" tee shirts and vests.

The negative on-the-job attitude towards women also relates to their personal relationships. An independent study[7] shows police officers suffer a divorce rate 60% higher than the national average and relates to the attitudinal experience towards women at work. I observe this devaluing attitude towards women by the Operators who are quick to dismiss female partners (wife or girlfriend) if they conflict with assignments. A Louisiana SOG discussed his divorce and the reasons he did not try harder to make the marriage work. I asked him, "Why didn't you tell her that?" He replies,

"By then I didn't care no more. Figured fuck it. She hates me so I'll go somewhere. Wanted me to quit the team and come home. For what? To hear more that shit? I'm fine without her."

I followed up by asking if SWAT meant that much to him, to which he responds:

"Why not? Women come around all the time. Who cares? I got hooked up after she left. Always some sniffer coming around. This shit makes me money. All she did was take it. She is better off. Go find some fag and tell him what to do. That's all she likes anyway. As to his divorce, he said: Only for my kids. Her, I don't care if she dis-a-fucking-pears."

Divorce and marital infidelity are common patterns and continues with an observation of four SOG in Kansas City. From my field notes, three of the four SOG were previously married but now divorced. The fourth SOG is still married, but the others assure him it would not be long until he was divorced. I pay special attention to him as the conversation moved to sex with other women. He reports having sex with women other than his wife and he did not seem too concerned about it. He even attempts to justify cheating by claiming that everyone engages in affairs, and that his wife did not understand the stress of his job.

The prevailing attitude towards illicit sex and their personal relationships is best illustrated by the Colorado Operator, who stated,

"My girlfriend says she don't even know me anymore. Who cares? Fuck her."

While women are minimally represented in SOG for a number of reasons, the degradation of women in both language and behavior remains pervasive. This type of stereotyping and projection is similar in the ways in which they think and act toward a wide range of individuals they cast as the "other."

Anti-Diversity / Anti-Homosexuality

As an ideal type, law enforcement officers are designated as society's moral entrepreneurs. The out-group homogeneity[8] identifies the SOG as the out-group that discourages and often prohibits participation of women, minorities, gays, and lesbians in policing. The homosexual lifestyle does not fit into the SOG because it is seen as abnormal[9]. The ideological imbalance between perceived deviant homosexuality and maintaining / enforcing society's laws supports the SOG ethos of anti-diversification.

I attempt to distinguish the data coded as physical contact between Operators from data coded with the hazing of Operators using homosexual gestures. It can become confusing to an uninitiated outsider to observe the behavior of SOG that includes taunting about homosexuality as a hazing method that result in touch or pretending to act out gay sex. This is used to shock the person receiving the hazing, but also establishes a hierarchy with the senior Operators hazing the junior members.

My field notes show the Operators of equal tenure were without inhibition in their physical contact ranging from traditional handshakes to simulating explicit sexual techniques on each other. These acts of physical contact would appear to contrast literature documenting the disdain of law enforcement officers towards homosexuality but the contact among these Operators is conducted to shock the other person.

Operators use terms associated with homosexuality while referring to each other. They also make suggestions of sexual acts towards each other. Similarly, these same observations are made at a Mississippi SWAT training session. Many Operators make lewd and sexual gestures towards each other. A Virginia SWAT training observation provides the same results. The language used is the same for all despite race and age. The verbal hazing includes suggestions and offers for performing homosexual acts on the Operator or accuses an Operator of homosexual acts, or inability to perform heterosexual acts.

This language goes beyond the "frat house" jabs associated with boys being boys. It establishes the subcultural fringe behavior and socially hierarchical positioning. The same Louisiana SWAT Operator I asked about the gay sex talk and acts reflects the defense of their actions and language. The question seems to catch him off guard, and he delivers a reply with defensiveness. He responds,

"Like suck my dick or I'm gonna fuck you? I don't freakin know. I guess to get under their skin. We say we gonna fuck your mom, don't mean we will. Just a way to test your heart. Too soft go home. We ain't gay, but it pisses people off to hear it I guess. We don't mean anything by it."

Despite the lewd language and actions, Operators are quick to distance themselves from anything seen as personally resembling homosexuality. A Louisiana SWAT Operator states:

"I played sports growing up. I like the individual sports now like running and triathlon. I was in the military. I guess that is like a team. No clubs or carnival krewes though. That is gay."

Although I never mention being "gay," the socialization process is so homophobic that any inclination of less than masculine activities are labeled as gay.

Relative to racism, I did not experience many instances within the ranks of the SOG. While being a white dominant subculture, overt speech and behavior about race are not present. Only one participant observation included a group of thirteen white males and one black male. During that opportunity, I only heard the black male refer to black people. Although he used terms like "cracker" and "uncle tom," he was not delivering or intending to be derogatory or racist. A group in Philadelphia included nine white officers and one black officer. Other than the color of his skin, nothing distinguished him from the others, nor did the other officers treat him or respond to him differently.

An interview of a Texas SOG presented a comment that I initially thought bordered on racist. Afterwards, he never elaborated nor used any other terminology resembling a race related comment. While he was describing the adrenaline of conducting a forceful SWAT entry into a fortified residential structure he said,

"Gotta be nice to this fucker and that one. This ain't like that. BAM, on the ground motherfuckers. Nothing like them spooks on the ground. Like what the fuck was that shit going off?"

As I reported earlier, the other exposure to race or anti-diversity was the North Carolina Operator, a black female who stated that her assignment selection was to "color it up." This is not said in an angry tone, but almost jokingly. While this is a small recognition of the deeper relations of race, it is an essential note.

The idea of hating others may appear as a strong indictment of the SOG Operators, but it is an accurate descriptor. The Operator fails to accept the diversity among others and refuses to coexist with them. Even remarks about non-SOG police officers who are white males are cruel and tainted with a tone of violence towards them. The imitation of homosexual speech and action are not admiration, but as an offense to the SOG Operator receiving the abusive hazing. Within the cop culture, this is a "circling of the wagons" against diversification, difference and change. Individually these men exercise social tolerance, but collectively they coalesce to protect what is perceived as traditional, true, and selfishly; "theirs." Why were there only two Chiefs of Police at that round-table?

Thus far we have uncovered a depth of understanding and meaning about the informal processes of becoming blue. It is naturally desired to want to belong, to fit into the ecology of your workplace. I trust you have begun to see why good cops go bad, and also understand that while the temptations are many, the opportunity to serve the core ideals of the organization are greater than the few officers succumbing to illicit behavior. We are not finished, as the next chapter will lead you through the final enculturation experiences of liminal transitions along the cultural path of becoming the darkest shade of blue.

17

FINAL SHADES OF BLUE

Deviant and Antisocial Behavior

Hate, violence, degradation of women, and the discrimination of others because of difference do not equate with the ideals of duty, honor, and service. Yet these are but some of the antisocial characteristics and actions of the SOG subculture. The alcohol-fueled violence and risk taking behaviors of the deviant Operator lifestyle support this. While this book focuses on the cop culture to include officers and SOG Operators, this final section gears more specifically on those special operations group members having becoming fully socialized into fragmented subcultures of isolated spheres for influence and purpose.

This is a phase I refer to as having become a darker shade of blue, or the darkest shade of blue. While not every officer experiences this depth of enculturation, it is a present possibility when organizations empower individuals with awesome authority yet fail to monitor, supervise and hold them accountable. A quote I have always used as a grounds for promoting integrity, transparency and accountability is "absolute power corrupts absolutely." Actually the entire quote by Lord Acton to Bishop Mandell Creighton in 1887 was, "Power tends to corrupt, and absolute power corrupts absolutely. Great men are almost always bad men."[1] Are great men almost always bad, or do they operate on an alternate plane of consciousness where a call to sacrifice and duty affects the normative understanding and practice of what is socially defined as "good?"

Who are these Operators and how do they arrive at this occupational status? Operators move through liminal phases of transition starting from the day they enter into the police academy as an idealistically naïve public servant and continue until becoming shaded as professional deviants. Becoming blue serves as a sliding scale for officers, and the darker the shade depends upon the number of thresholds crossed. SOG operates in the darkest shades of blue because of the subcultural fragmentation from institutional ideals.

I ask a retired Alabama Operator if his sense of serving the public had changed after becoming an Operator, and he replies,

"Yea. I used to give a shit. I realized they all got the same problem. They are constant complainers who don't raise their kids, don't pay their bills and want us to take care of their stupid asses."

His cynicism is typical of the responses I receive from Operators on this question. The Florida SWAT Operator similarly expresses,

"I guess the more hell I see the less I care. After a while, you either laugh or cry. I ain't crying for shit."

In every interview conducted, the subjects admit to experiencing an altered sense of duty since joining the SOG. They all express a disdain for the mundane duties of policing, such as addressing quality of life or traffic safety issues. The SOG with disgust uses the term "social worker," that their job was not social work. This liminal break from the policing ideals is what begins to sow the seed of deviant behavior.

I observe a group of 5 Louisiana SWAT Operators, of who three also serve as Narcotics Agents. To illustrate the antisocial attitude developed by the SOG, I include a portion of dialogue prompted by my question, Do you relate to your work peers the same in SOG as compared to previous traditional assignments?

Identities are assigned code numbers, and the question mark following the symbol for number represents a comment made, but I could not identify which Operator said it.

#1 - *Fuck no!!! You gotta watch your ass around the suits.*

They always looked to crack it off in your sweet ass.

#5 - *You ain't shitten. It's cool back here. We know whose*

boss hog, but he's one of us.

#? - *He came up like we did and if we ain't there for him,*

he's fucked

#5 - *Patrol is okay but it's a one man game. In the care of*

yourself all 12 hours. Fuck that anymore. Even

detectives can be squirrels sometimes. They got bosses

too.

#3 - *They not as bad though. You don't just start off deep.*

If you carry that crybaby shit in here your ass is back in the car.

#1 - *Cry alone motherfucker. Fucking sheep.*

This dialogue demonstrates a distinct separation from traditional policing assignments. These SOG realize their protection comes from a supervisor probably engaging in the same deviant practices and as they said, if they were not there for him, "he's fucked." Even within the subcultural brotherhood, there is an element of extortion or force for protecting the status. This discussion illustrates institutional fracturing from the patrol and detective sections.

This attack upon the hierarchy is an example of the organizationally internal "us versus them" paradigm. Since the issue of institutional isolation is established, I follow up with the question: "Describe being isolated from traditional policing assignments and how does it affect you personally and professionally?" Their collective replies were:

#1 - *You serious? It's fucking great. No bullshit. Nobody looking to bust your ass in IA*

#4 – *It's cool and all but sometimes I miss hanging out with the older guys. We did more shit like fishing and bowling. Them guys were okay.*

#? - *Yea, you just don't want to work with them though. I rather be away from that crap. No office hours, no report time, no fucking bosses after every little thing you fuck up.*

#? - *Then don't fuck up*

#1 - *That's right dummy. Do your shit and keeps the flies off your ass. Stupid bitch*

#4 – *It sucks sometimes because you don't know what's going on inside the place and fee like a derelict outsider. I'd rather be on the outs than getting crap from everybody.*

#5 – *That's the price you pay for freedom. It used to bother me but like anything else you get used to it.*

#? - *I think we mostly hang out with each other because we know each other and spend more time here than at home.*

#? – *It's like my family.*

ALL – *Laughing.*

It is also a recurring theme that many Operators express a sense of loss that comes with alienating themselves from the mainstream organization. Former friendships and activities no longer become available. The disconnection is that Operators express a loss of interpersonal relationships, but hate the assignments creating those initial bonds. These particular operators work for the same organization, but do not take the initiative to reengage former work friends. They spoke of the non-SOG officers as if only a memory. This further illustrates the depth of which SOG places itself while serving within the periphery of law enforcement.

The SOG account of antisocial behavior seldom mentions regret or repentance, but the retiree from Alabama admits when asked about that said:

"Sometimes I wish I didn't do some of the things we did ... Mostly, I'm proud of who I am and what I did in my life, but we can all do better right?"

The Mississippi Operator expresses the most regret about his moral conflict, but quickly justifies every action. He says,

"Yes, I have regretted some ass kickings but better them than me."

Other than these Operators, nearly all others express no remorse for their actions, words, and deeds. An Arizona SOG discusses work behavior in relation to the rest of his life:

"I've got a great family and wife, but I've done some stupid crap. Thank God she

understands what this job involves." and *"I ask myself that all the time. Where did my friends go? I'm so isolated to these guys, my wife and my boys. Not that it's bad, but man, where has everyone gone."*

In contrast, SOG are overly protective about their children and there were no negative comments about another SOG's children. I ask an Operator in Missouri if he behaves like this at home. He states,

"My personal life is nothing to do with my job. You have to be a certain way to survive and get along. I keep shit separate. My kids don't really know what I do. Best way to protect them. Everybody lives two lives."

The Arizona Operator held out hope that his eventual transfer out of

SOG and into the detective bureau would change his deviant behavior for the sake of his family. He said,

"I'm not that kind of guy. I guess after these last few years, I have become that guy. Makes me feel like crap for my boys. I'll turn it around in CID."

The SOG Operators showed little remorse for their actions, attitudes, or expressions. The few who say they regret some aspect of what they did were quick to distance themselves from the liability of the outcomes in those actions. This disregard extends to the way SOG Operators view and refer to the other police.

Apathy for Traditional Policing

Because SOG Operators separate themselves on many dimensions, their attitudes towards other police were often negative. SOG across the country expresses a genuine disregard for policing operations focusing on crime prevention and traffic safety. Their "us versus them" attitudes are consistent with "out-group homogeneity hypothesis."[2] I ask a Louisiana SWAT Operator if he relates to his peers differently than the non-SOG group. He says,

"Nobody fucks nobody. We know where to stick our dicks. Bitches in Patrol are always crying about their squad car being dirty or writing tickets, and something stupid."

Although most SOG began their career assigned to duty as corrections officers or uniform patrol officers, they recall the collective experiences with disdain. They do however; continue to relish the good memories with fellow non-SOG officers.

Similar to the Louisiana SWAT Operator's statement, a Pennsylvania Operator was similar in his apathetic perspective. Although he was attending a national conference focusing on traffic safety countermeasures to include detection and arrests of impaired drivers, he stated within a group of non-SOG officers,

"Fuck DWI arrests."

Another officer identified with the SOG Operator agrees silently by nodding his head and moving next to the critic to engage him in conversation centered on discontent with traditional policing operations such as making arrests for driving while intoxicated (DWI).

The National Highway Traffic Safety Administration (NHTSA) reports that in 2011 there were 32, 367 traffic related fatal crashes in the United States[3]. The Federal Bureau of Investigations (FBI) reports that 14,467 individuals were murdered during the same period.[4] Although nearly fifty-five percent more people are killed in traffic crashes than homicides in the United States, SOG Operators view traffic enforcement as not central in their mission.

A continuing theme of apathy towards traditional law enforcement missions was experienced in California. While preparing a room for a presentation I was delivering specific to traffic safety and enforcement inside the Anaheim Convention Center I encountered two sheriff's deputies. I welcome them and ask if they are there for my presentation. One of the deputies, Earl (name changed) states,

"Sorry. We really don't give a shit about this. SWAT is the next class in this room."

Remaining in the room during my presentation became a distraction as he and his fellow deputy, Dave (name changed) openly spoke to each other.

In the Midwest, the behavior of SOG Operators is similar. I joined six officers in the Skies Lounge atop the Hyatt Regency Crown Center. This is a lounge 42 stories high with a magnificent view of Kansas City. I enter into an ongoing discussion about the use of affidavits and search warrants to draw blood from a driver arrested for DWI, and refuse to submit to a chemical breath test by blowing into an intoxilyzer machine. As the seven of us discuss traffic enforcement strategies, Bob (name changed), a white male, twenty-seven years old states to the group,

"Who gives a fuck? I use that shit to find drugs."

His initial declaration of apathy for traditional police work is followed by a barrage of comments detailing his contempt for arresting drunk drivers because it took too long to process. He then asks the group:

"How we can arrest drunk drivers when everyone drinks and drives, especially us?"

His question was more rhetorical and he continued to criticize traditional policing duties. Carl, wearing grey slacks, dress shirt, and appears to be the oldest in the small group responds to Bob in a low toned voice and asks, "Then why in the hell would you attend this conference?" Bob replied with an even louder voice that he thought there would be courses on highway drug interdiction. Carl replies calmly that he should have checked the agenda before coming. This drew laughter from the others including myself. Bob's behavior, although not obnoxious, did not win favor from the group of seasoned officers.

This verbal exchange demonstrates an apathy extending beyond the normal work environment. The disrespect toward this older officer appears to show a genuine dislike for not only the traditional policing operations, but for individuals representing those functions. The disrespect for the traditional policing spills over to the individuals who perform these tasks when close personal friendships are not fostered between the SOG and non-SOG during prior assignments. The SOG condescension for non-SOG evolves into the ideological transformation of the SOG Operators.

Ideological Transformation

After fully actualizing the trajectory of socialization and the Operator assimilates into the subculture of the SOG, the individual perspective fades into a pack mentality. Prior individual creativity and initiative is replaced by following the rules, both formal and informal, and an ironclad code of silence. The ideological shifts manifest into various forms. While some may serve to improve an Operator's ability to cope with the stresses of the assignment, others become a detriment to their personal and professional lives.

I identify the following categories to demonstrate the differences in ideological transitions. Although change is imminent, the attitudinal adjustment takes different forms. These transitional forms include; Fuck the World (F.T.W.), SOG Over All, Attitude Adjustments, and Occupational Reflections. This collection of salient comments from Operators provides a description to demonstrate the manifestation of their ideological transformations.

F.T.W.

"Kings of the fucking world", "I used to give a shit about what they said", "I never fit in so I just said fuck it", "It was me against the rest of the ass kissers", "Fuck no. They don't have my respect", "you learn to say fuck it", "it's all of my bitches against your lying ass", "Fuck that anymore", "I'd rather be on the outs than getting crap from everybody", "Cry alone motherfucker", and "Fucking sheep."

The term F.T.W. originated with the OMC, but is adopted for use by the SOG, and further shows the relations between the OMC and SOG's outlier attitudes. The three letters are sewn onto OMC members' vests and tattooed into their skin for demonstrating their commitment to that ethos. The SOG liminal transition from social idealist to adversarial worldview is expressed in speech and by tattooing the three letters acronym.

SOG Over All

"Either SWAT or not", "My brothers got my back", "We are like a family who watches each other's back", "It's like another family but without the bullshit", "Don't like it go home. No bitches and no babies," "don't be sheep dude," and "I'm the shepherd mother fucker."

This ideological transformation ensures that Operators adhere to the expectant rules and behaviors that informally persist within the SOG to maintain internal and isolationist integrity. This category is similar to the metal dogs tags displaying our motto, "If Not Us, Who?" for my former SWAT unit.

Attitude Adjustments

"It makes you wild", "We're all cops but there is a difference in the way to act and do your job", "Yea my attitude changed, I don't take shit from nobody", "After a while you either laugh or cry. I ain't crying for nothing," "I used to try talking to people to help with their stupid problems. Now I just say shut up or you going to jail", "Maybe I'm meaner or more of an asshole. My wife also said I was an asshole. Maybe she was right", "when I'm in beast mode", "I think I don't worry so much about the small shit," and "Everybody lives two lives."

This category of observing the adjustments in the Operators' attitudes is necessary for understanding that the person entering the SOG does not arrive with this perspective. It is the result of an evolution of ideological transformations along the socialization continuum.

Occupational Reflections

"It's great if you fit in, it sucks if you don't", "Sometimes I wish I didn't do some of the things we did...", "Shit hits the fan and most of them bitches are calling us", "I always fought with the other commanders", "Everyday sucked having to deal with the political bullshit", "They don't do the job I do", "I guess my family doesn't understand what it takes to do this job'", "They rather me be a detective so I can come home at night and wear a suit", "want us to take care of their stupid asses?", "Gotta be nice to this fucker and that one. This ain't like that," and "BAM, on the ground motherfuckers."

This category highlights Operators who have the capacity to reflect upon their current occupational position, and articulate a justification for their actions and decisions. Additionally, their expressions about family or professional conflict demonstrate an awareness of the ideological transformations and their reluctance to digress. The trajectories of socialization illustrate the analogy of becoming blue, and the actualization of that process is demonstrated by describing the final shades of blue.

Transitional benchmarks during the SOG Operator's career cause the individual to experience ideological shifts in moral and professional perspectives. The series of liminal experiences present an opportunity for the Operator to color himself with the darkest, most deviant color of fraternal blue. The depth of commitment to these attitudinal shifts is examined in the analysis of the descriptive data discussed in the next chapter.

18

FINAL VERDICT

Effecting Change in Culture

We began this journey with the quest for discovering how good cops go bad. There are complicated sociological processes influencing organizational behaviors such as groupthink. There are also simple external forces causing the individual to see things from a different perspective such as liminality. The constant variable is that change will occur. How much or how far that change carries the officer depends on the individual, but make no mistake; there will be change. The analogy of becoming "blue" is used to illustrate the socialization process. I have identified definitive stages along the course of the process and use a "blue sliding scale" to visualize the concept of transformational stages and potential benchmarks.

Continuing with the strategy of describing, analyzing and interpreting data, this section focuses on the matrix[1] for analyzing the collected information. The foundation for scrutinizing this data is based upon the broader anthropological concept of liminality as it relates to the findings of cop culture. The importance of asking the correct questions in an investigation is the difference between confidence in your findings or just more questions. The answers demonstrate that officers experiencing their trajectory of socialization lead to perceptual and or ideological transitions. The slide or depth of those changes determine if and whether a good cop becomes bad, or just productively well-seasoned.

The research questions guiding this work are:

- Does assignment into the SOG cause perceptual changes specific to organizational allegiance that are detrimental to providing quality service to the public?
- Does a liminal state of ideological transition occur during the SOG socialization process preventing the transfer back into more traditional roles of policing?
- What are the effects of occupational socialization on the personal lives of law enforcement officers assigned to SOG?
- What are the effects of occupational socialization on the professional careers of law enforcement officers assigned to SOG?

Sliding Scale for Becoming Blue

By using the analogy of the sliding scale of becoming blue, it helps with visualizing the degrees which officers find themselves along the socialization experiences. While the police academy cadet finds himself at the lightest shade of blue, the sub-culturally socialized SOG Operator is located in the darkest shades of blue. This examination focuses on the segment of the cop culture where Operators evolve into the darkest shades of blue.

Basing my analysis on the descriptive data, I am able to show there are identifiable liminal benchmarks. Research[2] identifies distinct stages and outcomes in the descriptive works on fitting into the expected behaviors of different work cultures. This[3] shows that; becoming socialized is inevitable, and the commitment to fitting in affects the individual's ability to remain inside the organization.

Six Liminal Stages of Full Socialization

Police Organizations and Culture

From Civilian Prospect to Sub-Culturally Socialized SOG

There are six stages identified and each is associated with the sliding scale of color. The first three benchmarks are unique to the remaining three because they do not allow for the return to any of the previous stages. The first three stages can only happen for the first time, and once. Starting from a civilian perspective of no familiarity in the profession, the officer can only enter the profession, learn the culture, and complete the initial experience of training for the first time; once. The later three stages, though significantly affecting an individual have varying effects on the officer. The anti-institutional effects depend on whether the officers are accepted into a SOG assignment, the level of enculturation exposed to or participated in and the depth of commitment to the labelling of deviant. This oppositional relation is a cultural outcome of individuals solidifying ideologies for collective preservation[4].

Liminal Stages 1 – 3

Stage 1 - Pale Blue

The first liminal benchmark is the transition from civilian to police academy cadet. Societal preconceived notions of what policing involves are influenced by movies, media and myth. Cadets are immediately confronted with the reality that their expectations of what the job consist of contradicts the reality of policing. Cadets are forced to embrace a homogenous culture for the sake of success completion of the academy and the socialization process. There is no room for individuality, and this is indoctrinated by an authoritarian environment guided by policies and procedures for continued attendance and participation.

Though still a loose collection of transforming individuals, the core ethos begins to coalesce through the regimented drills and instructions. The "drill instructor" atmosphere is designed to instill a sense of severity in each lesson taught, tactic practiced or round fired. Physical punishment in the way of additional exercise is often incorporated as discipline when the rules are broken. Requiring the entire class to endure the discipline for the sake of one's error instills a sense of accountability for each other. Conversely, it teaches the cadets to watch each other's "back" for supervisory detection and becomes their first experience with bonding together against a "them."

The early introduction to the "us versus them" anti-authority / accountability ethos and no-rat rules continues throughout their career as a foundational baseline when communicating with organizational hierarchy or the public. The "all-pays-for-one" practice also demonstrates that there is an emphasis on punishment and not reward. This directly leads to the officers' attitude that there is no benefit for working work on the streets. If the simplest error is made, it might be met with disciplinary action resulting in the possibility for loss of pay, reassignment or termination. It is instilled in the rookie officer that there is no room for "making waves."

The cadet maintains strong ties to civilian anchors during this stage. The beginning effects of experiencing the bond of "brotherhood" are new and still in the future. The current efforts to reconcile this rapidly changing environment cements the cadet to pre-established civilian anchors that are familiar and welcoming. People such as a spouse, children, parents, family, friends, church, social and civic clubs or loose associations within the community can serve as stabilizing forces in the shifting perspectives of the cadet. These strong early occupation bonds, once severed cause high levels of resentment, stress and alienation from both sides.

Stage 2 – Light Blue

This stage will progress the individual through the remainder and graduation from an academy and the initial introductory phase of the Field Training process. The cadet has moved past the pre-employment misconceptions of policing and is engrained in the lessons and theory taught from trusted instructor's cadre. It is the value and reliance upon the academy staff leaving an indelible effect for influencing the civilian from the point of indoctrination to a culture where individual characteristics are forfeited for the sake of homogeneous cohesion. The trained cadet and soon to be rookie officer is more familiar with the concept of "us versus them," as it is practiced every day during the course of the academy.

Once graduated from the academy, the rookie officer enters a new phase of conflict and reconciliation. The demands of the street assignment, the FTO, the supervisory hierarchy and the peers create a toxic collection of stressors compared to the previously nurturing environment of the training academy. While primarily an observer at this point in the on-the-job training process, the rookie officer experiences the pressure to conform and willingly engages in risky behavior for the chance to establish personal relationships and peer clustering acceptance. The increased formal demands and informal expectations begin to create conflict within the officer's system of civilian anchors.

After weeks or months of eagerly listening to every detail the cadet has to share about their excitement in the academy, the sphere of civilians are less available for complete debriefings and the intensity of actual street work is too much for some (usually spouses) to bear. The rookie officer begins to conceptualize this draw to the job as a lack of relational empathy for their new experiences, and the beginning of the "they just don't understand what it's like" isolationist mentality.

Stage 3 - Blue

The third liminal benchmark occurs as the rookie officer progresses through the FTO phase. As they are required to begin conducting actual police work while under intense supervision from their FTO, another period of confliction arises. The training and theory learned during the academy is no longer taught, practiced or endorsed while working the "streets." Senior officers including the mentoring training officer instructs, if not threatens the rookie officer to forget the lessons taught at the academy. While the academy experience remains relatively present in the rookie's mind, the reality of the academy has never been more distant.

Upon completing an extensive period of field and peer training, the officer is now an independent and autonomously operating law enforcement officer. If they have successfully completed the FTO period, they have usually surrendered to the conformance of authority syndrome. This includes understanding the influence of each formalized rank in a sometimes confusing hierarchical system. An equally important understanding for the purpose of cultural acceptance is the appreciation and adherence to a social pecking order. The highest rated rookie in the force will soon fail professionally if tagged the "FNG."

The reality of peer influence and cultural expectancy dictates the identity of the officer. The job defines who they are, and he now embraces that definition. Although the officer perceives himself as having a career unique within the occupational society, he forfeits individual characteristics for the sake of sameness. To succeed at maintaining the job, the individual has accepted the mandate of fitting in by not "rocking the boat." Part of this fitting in is the exposure to and participation in illicit or illegal behaviors. The rookie is first introduced to abnormal behaviors during the FTO process by either their assigned mentor or another officer circulating within that sphere of influence. Now an independent officer, they are faced with daily decisions about engaging in illicit or illegal behaviors, and to what depth.

Finally, and since this is a major stage in the life and career of an officer, the earlier developing "us versus them" mindset becomes engrained through personal experiences and exposure to senior officers and the constant juggle of learning on the job and satisfying the unwritten "rules" of the profession. The desire for social acceptance, the understanding of what "brotherhood" means and requires and the newly discovered entitlements of carrying the badge begin tipping the scale where professional anchors outweigh previous civilian anchors. The officer is now less committed to resolving or compromising conflicts between civilian anchors, because their new "family" not only spends more time with them but experientially "understands" them.

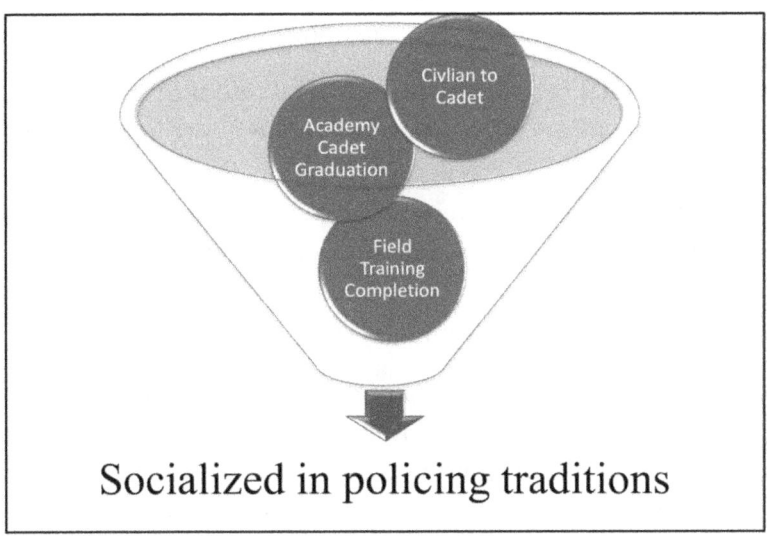

Table 18.1- Liminality Funnel showing initial stages of socialization. *Source:* (Original table produced by Dr. Scott Silverii for *Cop Culture: Why Good Cops Go Bad*.)

Liminal Stages 4 – 6

Stage 4 – Medium Blue

This stage includes an officer with over one year of operational law enforcement experience as they have already begun to develop a propensity towards the "social worker" or "crime fighter" paradigm of policing styles. As we have claimed before, neither is better; just different. The officer wanting to fight crime begins to desire more than a traditional police role. While the officer may not have formed a definite decision about the direction after leaving Patrol duty, they usually begin developing pre-conceived perceptions of SOG membership and entitlements associated with belonging. The officer also migrates through peer clusters towards a "supporter" role by beginning relationships with SOG Operators. Through this vicarious relationship, the officer desires future equal peer relationships with current members.

This fourth liminal benchmark includes the voluntary petition by the officer in the form of a transfer request or application for consideration into SOG. The decision to apply for SOG assignment is similar to the uninitiated external rational used to breach the initial liminal benchmark of entering into an unknown occupational ecology of policing. Through this formal request, the officer officially demarks separation desires from non-SOG assignments.

The perception of SOG entitlement encouraging application for the assignment begins to differentiate non-SOG officers into groups of those with a propensity for the fringe, risk taking lifestyle versus those honoring the core values of the institution. Those officers desiring an SOG assignment may experience one of two possible results:

- Acceptance - the officer will cross through the fifth liminal benchmark to begin a re-socialization process based on informal practices and culturally specific expectations congruent with the standards of the institutional fringe.
- Rejected - the officer, who makes the organizationally public profession of interest into SOG must deal with rejection. This rejection places the officer along a fringe area within the traditional policing culture, and creates a professional fissure leading to the disillusionment and segregation from the non-SOG ideas.

Because the desire to develop close personal friendships and peer clusters is so strong, rejection contributes to occupational isolationism and a continuation of darkening the shades for the non-SOG. The detrimental effects of occupational isolationism are a manipulative strategy for causing job dissatisfaction by preventing the opportunity to establish close relationships. The satisfaction experienced through the work performed by an officer sustains a positive correlation to occupational commitment. Those officers not accepted by the SOG, but remain in their non-SOG role may lose respect for the importance of their current mission, and experience a higher potential for quitting the job.

The seasoned officer has also chosen the path for current and future ethical behaviors. If earlier decisions to engage in bad behavior were made, it will either continue or progress into more serious abnormal behavior. The fully socialized officer understands the cop culture, and the lack of supervisory accountability leading to opportunities for deviant behaviors. Unless the officer is placed in jeopardy of discipline, termination and or criminal prosecution, there is no reason to discontinue this pattern of behavior. Consistent with the deeper slide along the scale, the officer identifies himself with the culture of policing and not the system of civilian anchors once helping define who they were. The officer rarely attempts to reconcile these civilian conflicts, and causes an environment of unfair sacrifice or compromise on the part of others for the sake of maintaining the relationship.

Stage 5 – Dark Blue

The officer accepted into the SOG crosses the fifth liminal benchmark as they experience the separation from the traditional institution, and are re-integrated into a new, animated environment with organizationally disparate ideologies. The officer, now categorized as Operator realizes a socialization distinction of title in addition to subcultural status. The completion of their initial indoctrination period provides sufficient time for fraternal acclimation and acceptance among their peers. Groupthink as defined embodies this fifth benchmark.

The re-socialization of the Operator into the SOG may occur quickly as the individual desires the collaboration with cohorts. This need for social clustering engrains the Operator into the singular mindset demanding the abandonment of autonomously operational ideas and independent action. This is possibly the point of no returning to the non-SOG assignment, or the stage of liminality where the regression of assignment becomes increasingly difficult if not impossible, and the darkening of deep blue shades begins.

Factors sliding the Operator towards a point of no return include the perception that former assignments and associations with non-SOG as "others." If the officer participated in bad behavior prior to SOG, the new Operator status and increased distance and layers of protection from supervisors promotes the propensity to continue the patterns. Conversely, if the Operator is initially introduced to irregular behavior at this stage, the decision to participate for purposes of assimilation causes internal conflict. Failure to fit-into this intimate and operationally independent unit causes isolation from SOG and potentially adversarial departure. By this time in an Operator's career, civilian anchors are severed, and the commitment to them now belongs to the SOG family.

Stage 6 – Darkest Blue

In the sixth liminal benchmark, the more years or greater the experiential intensity an Operator gains, the deeper a commitment to subcultural deviance becomes. The "outcomes"[5] stage relates to this point of full enculturation. The institutional socialization stage of "metamorphosis"[6] relates to liminality[7] and includes the individual adjusting into the environmental ecology of the assignment, providing a conceptual foundation for this benchmark.

This final transition of occupational evolution includes the emulation of fringe lifestyle characteristics and hedonistic behaviors associated with a disdain for traditional ideals and societal norms. The desire to shock the conscience of society through word, deed, or action becomes a personal standard of operation. The necessity to segregate from the core values of the organization begins to blur the blue lines and demand a continuing allegiance to professionally deviant behavior.

This final stage finds the Operator no longer struggling with moral confliction between the officer he used to be, and the SOG he now is. Although creating inter-personal conflict outside the job, this standard of behavior is no longer the exception, but the rule.

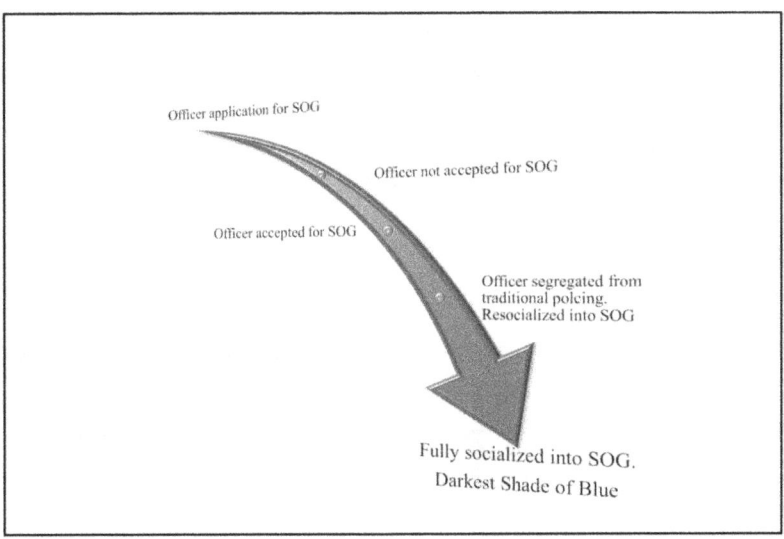

Table 18.2 - Path to full socialization into SOG. *Source:* (Original table produced by Dr. Scott Silverii for *Cop Culture: Why Good Cops Go Bad*.)

Additional Investigative Findings

Finding 1:

Answering the research questions, I find a majority of SOG assignments cause perceptual changes to agency allegiance. These perceptual changes are harmful to the personal lives of Operators as evidenced by divorces, domestic violence, alcohol abuse, and the detachment from traditional social networking anchors.

It is difficult to determine whether the quality of professional services is affected because of the subcultural characteristics. These challenges arise due to the nature of the SOG mission. For example, the assignment requires Narcotics Operators to frequently associate with felons and drug dealers for the purpose of gaining criminal intelligence and arranging undercover operations. These associations involve the nurturing of relationships with confidential informants to establish a basis of trust between them. The challenge is determining whether the professional effectiveness is measured by the levels of associational depth with their criminal networks for disrupting illegal activity, or by the standards applied to the non-SOG for assessing the Operators conformance to traditional social expectations.

Finding 2:

I found in cohesive groups, Operators may devolve into a deviant subcultural fraternity when associated with a purposeful segregation from the mainstream policing population, the homogenous environment of a high skill-set unit assigned to a unique mission, and an autonomous culture of limited institutional accountability. The slide into deviance is attributed to the daily exposure to the criminal elements they investigate, and the need to imitate the criminalistic, fringe lifestyle for the purposes of covert surveillance and undercover purchasing investigations.

Finding 3:

The labeling of deviance by the exposure to antisocial actions is also detrimental to the individual. Analysis shows a liminal state of ideological transition occurring during the SOG socialization process. I was not able to determine if this ideological transition prevents a transfer back into more traditional roles of policing, but the overwhelming consensus was that none of them would consider a return to strictly non-SOG assignments. As one Operator put it, "I'd eat a bullet."

Finding 4:

The descriptive findings express the negative effects of fitting in or occupational socialization on the personal lives of law enforcement officers assigned to SOG. Officers describe the harmful effects for families and friends as the Operator's commitment to the assignment requires them to choose the fraternity over civilian networks.[8]

Finding 5:

The characteristics associated with SOG fringe and deviant behavior suggests that their personal lives are limited to associations within that restricted group of companions. Most admitted to isolation from mainstream society, diminished relations with family and friends, and the desire to remain in the company of their trusted SOG "brothers."

Finding 6:

My findings, based on the Operators' admissions to the risky use of alcohol, infidelity, attraction to violence, and risk taking show behavior non-conducive to traditional civilian interpersonal relationships. This detachment from civilian moral anchors includes wife, children, family, and social associations beyond those of law enforcement.

Finding 7:

I find the effects of occupational socialization on cops assigned to SOG may not threaten or impede promotional opportunities. The main limitation to career advancement is the small number of Operators belonging to the specialized units. There can only be so much rank and supervisory authority among so few select individuals. The Operators assigned collateral duty and serve fulltime in non-SOG capacities demonstrate rank promotion at quicker rates as self-reported by association to their assignment to SOG SWAT.

This same effect is documented[9] to confirm aggressive officers traditionally referred to the EWS are actually promoted at faster rates than other officers are. I find the personal perception of the Operators relative to the negative attitudes of others directed to their SOG assignment was high, but there was no assessment method in my research design for determining the reality of biases or SOG discriminatory practices.

Finding 8:

Although the SOG is unique in its policing practices, the essentials of groupthink[10] make them similar to other sub-sects within policing's milieu and non-law enforcement professions characterized by the domination of hegemonic masculinity. An observation of the required execution of violence upon the public[11] distinguishes policing from other occupations. It is the operational ideological meshing of ideas, emotions and actions binding the white middle to lower class male to both realities.

Finding 9:

I found similarities between the SOG and other subcultures consisting of a restricted access membership, standards of similar dress, grooming and personal characteristics, common speech and behavioral patterns, and an identity formed by the collective momentum of the pack exercising groupthink. The important linkage between the SOG and similar groups wielding fallible power and substantial influence over others such as Catholic priests, OMC, athletic sports coaches, financiers, government leaders, or policy decision makers is the vulnerability in their respective groups for adopting faulty ideologies leading to detrimental actions.

Finding 10:

The characteristics of groupthink[12] create an environment contrary to legitimate, rational decisions leading to moral, ethical, and legal challenges for the collective cultural body. Because of the "sacred canopy" of policing, society assimilates to revere officers as dutiful servants. Demonstrating the parallels of perception and lifestyle characteristics between the deviant policing subculture and similar occupational features shines light into the dark blue environment of the SOG.

The analysis of qualitative data allows for the discovering of the above findings. These findings are possible because of the descriptive process detailed in Chapter 17, and also lead the way for the final chapter. The next chapter, 19 will address the interpretive process for presenting overarching themes and a new theory for explaining why good cops go bad.

19

IGNITING CHANGE

PERSONAL PERSPECTIVE

The initial inspiration for studying this topic occurred to me as I was describing my professional status and commented to a group of graduate students that I had "been on the outside" (from SWAT) for about two years. Prisoners have made that comment about their release from incarceration, as have former gang members after being "jumped out." That quick comment struck me as odd and it suddenly occurred to me that my informal speech had become infused with criminalistics street-style jargon.

Although receiving a Master of Public Administration, a Ph.D., and professionally serving as a city Chief of Police, I still had an attachment to the fraternity of SOG. At that time, I was unaware that the subcultural environment experienced over decades connected through academic research. Literature examinations and original data collections allowed me to vicariously relive the SOG experience. Most importantly, it provided the clarity through an objective distance for placing the data and my reality into perspective.

It is this lens making it possible to complete the method for digesting the volume of information by utilizing the process of description, analysis and interpretation. The following section documents my interpretation of the cop culture after having combined the previous research, the observations and interviews and the personal experiences within the SOG and policing's fraternity. Using my fraternal membership was the most effective method for exploring law enforcement, and for revealing a complex portrait of the cop culture.

Detrimental Homogenetic Entitlement

I came to understand the phenomenon of fitting into the darkest levels of the SOG's professional deviance by a term I refer to as *"detrimental homogenetic entitlement."* It applies to the characteristics of secretive groups shrouding their purpose of mission or profession within a mystique of autonomy. These select members participate in a culture of deviance contributing to destructive personal effects for the participant, the victim or both. These hedonistic subcultures consist of members sharing similar gender, race and interests in the initial core's legitimate purpose, but have unfortunately devolved into illegitimate or illegal practices. Finally, the unethical or illegal behavior is known to some degree by the legitimate organizational hierarchy, but a refusal to respond or inability to prohibit reinforces the abnormal behaviors.

This curiosity created by the secreting mystique of the SOG lends itself to an environment non-conducive to the traditional core values of duty, honor, and service. The detrimental aspect of this term is directed to the Operator, who may suffer great personal and professional costs by participation in the hedonistic subculture. I have illustrated this (Table 19.1) to link the connection between the SOG to other subcultures guided by the same principles of groupthink cohesion and hegemonic masculinity. Examples are provided of similar subcultures earlier in the work (Chapter 1) which when applied to this diagram, demonstrates the applicability of the general principles of detrimental homogenetic entitlement to more than only the SOG.

The significance is that within the most mainstream occupational or organizational cultures, the potential for subcultural deviance exists when the basics of detrimental homogenetic entitlement are allowed to foster. How does something so obviously detrimental to an organization's value system exist? It thrives in an environment of minimal to no accountability. These subcultures are often considered "special," "elite," "classified," or "secret," just to name a few of the monikers labeling them.

These labels begin the organizational segregation process. Along with labeling is the "halo effect" that this particular group owns a distinctive status requiring special handling. Within an institution of hierarchical command and accountability, these designations of being different or unique to the rest of the workforce become a signal for others to not interfere with the unit. Once having established the halo effect, these units seldom receive the objective and impartial supervision required for maintaining an institutional integrity.

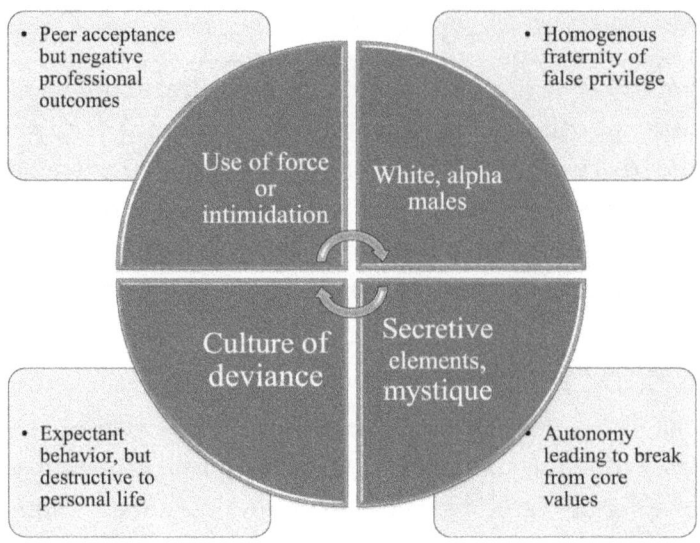

Table 19.1; the Detrimental Homogenetic Entitlement diagram illustrates the characteristics of assumed privilege within the circle, and the detrimental reality within the squares. *Source:* Original table created by Dr. Scott Silverii for *Cop Culture: Why Good Cops Go Bad*

The question begs to be asked; "Why does SOG participate in deviant activities?" Because it can. The assessment of police violence as a societal necessity is accurate, but the SOG Operator does not have the luxury of theoretical perspective[1]. Society submits to this violence as long as it is not too severely dispensed; not exposed through media; or, not used against someone closely associated to them. The SOG, whose mission it is to pursue the most violent criminals, are afforded operationally creative liberty to deliver their tactics centering on force meeting force. SOG Operators quickly realize the usefulness of violence as an occupational resource.

My interpretation of the descriptive information[2] and appreciation for the application of the series of liminal trajectories is that the SOG does experience ideological adaptations. Whether actual, perceptual, or imitative, the Operators experience levels of transformation. The concept of liminality[3] leaves the possibility open for the individual to experience changes in awareness, practice, or ideology.

Because of external forces such as peer clustering influence, and internal predispositions or expectations, the shades to which an Operator is colored dark blue are dependent upon various factors. The expectation is that the experienced law enforcement officer possesses the ability to prevent or limit the powerful seduction of the subculture that engages in professional deviance. It is their level of vulnerability and willingness to enculturate that determines the depth and deviance of the liminal transition.

I find that the effects of groupthink, pack mentality and attractiveness to the perceived freedom of the "others'" worldview, entices officers with certain personal characteristics to become SOG Operators. Occupational socialization is a powerful influence, and when metered out in unassuming stages of trajectories, it becomes difficult for detecting or preventing the harmful effects. There is an occupational dynamic associated with segregating specialized skill sets of Operators in an environment dominated by hegemonic masculinity. In my opinion, it does not appear that the subculture of deviance is a result of personal or moral defect.

Officers selected into the SOG are not made aware of the mental, physical, and social effects of the intense subcultural socialization. Peer clustering is a behavioral pattern practiced through a lifetime of social interactions. The patterning of behaviors change to reflect the synergy of individuals interjected into the social arena.

Violence, Silence and Risk

I find the subcultural SOG is a reflection of the manifestation of specialized skill set selection, the collective personal characteristics transformed during periods of liminal opportunities uniquely experienced in the SOG mission, and the institutionally autonomous operational environment of violence, silence, and risk. This overarching observation is detailed in the next section and includes practical suggestions to avoid the formation or substantiation of the subculture.

Opportunities for Sustaining Change

This urban affairs project focuses on cop culture and the SOG for examining personal and professional effects of socialization. The secretive subculture within an already isolationist institution presented a vibrant topic for study. This culture is entrenched within the profession of law enforcement but there are opportunities for affecting change. The individual begins the career with a sense of public service without knowledge of the detrimental potential associated with the job. It is this sincere willingness to serve their community that presents the opportunity to change the direction of each career, and collectively the culture.

The SOG Operators were often dedicated to a fault, by committing themselves to the ideals of the SOG in the esprit de corps instead of the institutional core values. The dedication to service is the crucial element, and it is the institution's responsibility to cultivate the direction that spirit of dedication goes. This change must pervade the entirety of the organization. The revelation that a distinctive divide exist between the various stratified levels within the organization allows for a comprehensive examination to bridge the gaps between levels in an effort for creating a cohesive, mentoring environment for change. The effects on the community, the agency and the individual are too great to ignore. The next section addresses these challenges with recommendations based on the personal and professional levels of obligation.

Personal Recommendations

To lessen the personal impact of the subcultural effects, the individual officer willing to enter the SOG should be encouraged to have the full support of their social networking system. The immediate and extended families, friends; both civilian and police peers, church and community service groups will anchor the individual in the civilian world.

Law enforcement agencies should educate all officers about the detrimental effects of terminating these civilian social anchors, and encourage network building within the community. If the officer accepts assignment into the SOG, law enforcement agencies must encourage boundaries and limitations for SOG personnel.

The SOG business office should be regarded as a professional work environment. The Operator will spend more time in that office socializing with his cohorts both on and off duty than with their respective families. This practice shows dedication to the team, but in actuality begins the process of selecting fraternity over family.

The degree of personal relationships with other Operators should be limited for maintaining a healthy separation of work versus play expectations by the peer group. The main factor for minimizing the detrimental effects to the officer's personal life is maintaining objective distance from the subculture of the SOG.

Professional Recommendations

Non-SOG Cop Culture:

The law enforcement profession cannot control what preconceived notions an individual may bring to the application and hiring process. The agency should immediately begin providing accurate information about what the job will involve; both formally and informally. The recruiting competition for quality candidates is no different from other industries, and the need to "hype" the process until the hiring is completed sacrifices the potential for attracting candidates with realistic expectations both before hiring and throughout the academy and training sessions. While some occupations allow for the new employee to gain a perspective of what their duties require, this is not a career best left to "on the job" training.

This examination shows that the academy training phase is vital to establishing a foundation for the remainder of an officer's career. While most police academies are based on a militaristic-style of instruction, discipline and evaluation, the failure of the organization to maintain that culture of rigid conformity and culture of accountable discipline creates a conflict of expectation. An example refers to the process mentioned earlier in the book whereby a rookie graduates from the militaristic training academy and reports to duty with a seasoned FTO. The rookie's training is rarely reinforced by this mentor or others. It is ridiculed and the impressionable rookie who is in the midst of a transitional phase and seeking peer approval is instructed to "forget the things" they were just taught as foundational principles in the academy.

While I agree that the initial academy environment is useful for providing an atmosphere based on military-style standards for behavior and performance, I suggest that the agency continue monitor the post-graduation training the rookie enters into. Monitoring the senior officers' formal and informal messages is equally important. I'll offer a simple initiative I began to prevent the rookie from becoming untethered to the academy. I also looked at why the military boot camp experience succeeds at initiating and enculturating the new soldier and law enforcement's training academy fail. The primary reason is that while both initiation experiences are valuable, it is the post-training that creates the difference in behaviors. The standard military environment is based on formal structure and rigid adherence to the policies and practices. Supervisors are trained to continue and advance upon the soldier's basic training foundation. Law enforcement officers are encouraged to forget what was taught to them in the standardized and structured training academy and adopt an informal behavior most conducive to the desires of the rookie's immediate professional social work cluster.

In an effort to reconnect senior officers to the standardized environment of the training academy, I assigned one officer to each cadet entering into an academy session. Serving as a "Big Brother or Sister" allowed the cadet to begin establishing peer relationships beyond the walls of the academy to help alleviate the stresses associated with assimilating into the next stage of the career. This also returned the senior officers to the academy element more regularly than the rare retraining or firearms requalification mandated by policy.

Once the cadet was graduated from the academy, the rookie officer is usually assigned to a series of experienced FTO for a defined duration of training and evaluation. This is the stage where the greatest conflict of expectation occurs. For the duration of the FTO period I mandated that each rookie be assigned to a member of the academy training staff with weekly communications / debriefings. The training staff members were the rookies' first level of contact upon entering the job. For the sake of balancing what they were formally taught, versus the informal education they were experiencing, the continued communications served as regular reminders about the value of the structured training and the disciplinary consequences of abnormal behaviors.

The cadre of academy trainers were also asked to recognize signs that FTO were influencing the rookies to "forget the things" they were taught. If revealed by the rookie to the trainer, I was able to take corrective action towards the FTO by either re-training in the purpose of the field training objectives, assign the rookie to another FTO, or remove the offending senior officer from the unit designated and compensated as a FTO. This initiative was effective for establishing networks of positive peer support and accountability at levels ranging from cadet, trainer to senior officer. Most importantly, it reduced anxieties for the cadet awaiting the field training stage, and minimized the confliction between what they were just taught and what they are now experiencing. The consistency of message and perceptions of performance will enculturate a more organizationally committed public servant.

SOG Cop Culture:

There is a point of diminishing professional work efficiency for the SOG in relationship to time-in-assignment. This relates to a peak window of opportunity between the energetic naïve rookie and the "been there done that" veteran. I spent twelve years in a multijurisdictional narcotics task force, with three of those years operating as an agent with the Drug Enforcement Administration Task Force. I experienced a point of enduring too much for too long, and needed to transfer out of the SOG for maintaining a productive work habit. In hindsight, I stayed in too long, suffering much personal loss for the sake of honoring the code and the SOG ideal.

Limited time in assignment:

The Operator should be limited to an established number of service years in the SOG; as long as the assignment is free of personal harm to the officer, organizationally productive and free of disciplinary actions. The subjects in my study appear to slide deeper into a commitment of social deviance as their career longevity increases and the experiential intensity rises. While transferring Operators out of SOG might sacrifice a level of expertise, the ability to sustain an ethically high level of legitimate performance may be enhanced. The assignment over time becomes damaging by allowing the Operator, while initiating criminal investigative cases, to cause irreparable personal harm.

I will note that the evolution of the SOG Narcotics Agent has changed the role for many officers entering into this assignment. During the era that I began, most undercover agents were hired directly into the assignment without undergoing formal academy training. This was to prevent detection by fellow officers, citizens and drug dealers. During my years commanding a drug task force, Agents conducted less actual undercover missions and served more as investigators and case managers. As the assignment becomes more volatile and technology continues to advance, Agents use techniques like wiretaps and surveillances while directing confidential informants and contract agents during undercover drug purchasing operations. While this decreases the direct interpersonal contact with drug dealers and less often requires the adoption of a secondary identity for undercover missions, the intensity of the operations remain high.

Rotating supervisory oversight:

An alternative or combination to the officer rotational practice based on time-in-assignment is the reallocation of command staff every two years to ensure a fresh perspective. The commander should come from outside the ranks of the SOG. As an example, I witness a clique-based occupational extortion used against a new supervisor for ensuring the continuation of status behaviors and deterring the potential for new levels of accountability. The narcotics section commander was promoted from within that unit. Operators were heard joking with him, while still making their point that they "knew what he had done." It is difficult, if not impossible for maintaining a degree of separation from the daily activities and practices of a cohort after being too closely associated with it.

The traditional thought process is that only an experienced SOG will know how to supervise such a unique assignment. This is perpetuated to protect the isolationist practices of the SOG. Scientific management practices supersede any claims of uniqueness or specialty. There are progressive agencies regularly rotating command level staff on a multiyear basis to prevent burnout, stagnant leadership and promote creativity with new vision and accountability of service delivery.

Policy and integrity compliance:

Additionally, policy should mandate regular integrity checks such as unannounced drug and alcohol screenings, criminal history and driving history records checks against personal and undercover identities to ensure no criminal actions have taken place against the Operator, and routine inspections of reporting, evidence collections, weapons and equipment inventories and assigned workspace and computers.

Supervisors should monitor take-home vehicle usage practices, relationships with confidential informants, expenditures of monies for undercover operations, drug purchases and payments for information. SWAT demands high levels of physical fitness, which pushes the Operator to maintain a state of readiness. Random steroid testing is rarely included in the standard panel drug screens. Officers realize this and may use performance enhancing drugs to maintain not just peak strength but to also enhance their physical appearance as a perceived demand of the masculine stereotypes.

Even the best of agencies tend to lean less heavily on the SOG. Their assignment is tough and allowing these units to operate with a high degree of autonomy does not diminish their capacity to succeed, it increases the individual's potential to fail. These personal and professional recommendations also provide opportunities for future studies of the SOG phenomenon. Included are a few areas for potential research that I discovered during my study.

Recommendations for Future Examinations

How long is too long:

The first recommendation for future study addresses the above topic of diminishing returns over years assigned to SOG. An examination of the number of years it takes assigned to the SOG before Operators begin experiencing the diminished returns on their assignment will benefit the law enforcement officer and profession.

Commonality of cultures:

The next suggestion for further research kept emerging during each observational opportunity. The question is, "How can police officers in Alaska act the exact same way as police officers in south Florida?" There is no standard training manual or unified national police academy. To explore the possibilities, I searched for an explanation of similarities among distant cultures to determine if there is applicable theory relating remote ancient cultural commonalities to the policing cultures.

Going back to the earliest days of anthropology,[4] similarities discovered in disparate regions and cultures was credited to either human mental processing or diffusion. Researchers believed that groups living on opposite ends of the earth, yet behaving in the same manner were because humans thought similarly. The domesticated use of fire, or the skills and tools invented to hunt and trap animals for food was found globally, yet without the possibility of contact between the cultures. The idea of diffusion credited evidence of contact among distant cultural regions (travelling missionaries for example) as the other explanation why cultures share traits yet distanced by continents. The exploration of disparate cultural similarities based on these theories would provide another opportunity for exciting future study.

Executive awareness:

A third suggestion is determining if policing's chief executives are aware of the deviant subcultures operating within the ranks of their agencies. There is an unofficial tolerance for the SOG since it is necessary for investigating the seriously chronic and violent offenders. If deviance is allowed within an organization because commanders do not have the SOG background for understanding the complexity of the subculture, it is the failure of the institution's executive level command.

Conversely, commanders having SOG experience, yet allowing operational latitude because of a relational history also demonstrate executive level failure. This future study would provide the opportunity for examining a top down ideology relative to acceptance of organizational segregation.

Universal Application of "Detrimental Homogenetic Entitlement"

My final suggestion for future research is to expand the sociological scope of the occupational and organizational groups I established in relation to the subcultures of countercultural deviance based on the characteristics of groupthink[5], neutralization theory[6], slippery slope[7] to deviance, and liminality[8]. I chose the SOG for the purpose of methodological suitability, but my description highlights the subculture's mystique and its ability for relating to other groups having characteristics of detrimental homogenetic entitlement.

Deserve Better

The existence of SOG in the public safety sector delivers a necessary service to both the institution of law enforcement and the community. The SOG targets the most dangerous criminals, yet their very existence causes concern for administrators and the public. The image of professional deviance is not always validated, but the actions of those setting the subcultural standard are recreated for popular public consumption in the media, movie and television fiction in programs such as "*The Shield*" and "*Training Day.*"

I trust that the cop culture and the salient influencing effects of the transitional stages become better understood. The demystification of the SOG, the influences promoting the substantiation of the subculture, and the detrimental effects to the individual committing their professional talents at great personal risk, demand a serious examination by the policing community. The officer, the agency, and the community deserve better.

Don't be sheep!

APPENDIX INTRODUCTION

I am including a series of seven brief appendixes in a theme of executive law enforcement leadership conversation starters. Each individual article is meant for the collective publishing in my work with cop culture. Based on my doctoral dissertation's research for the University of New Orleans' Ph.D. program, the pieces are written in a language of cop talk as compared to the rigid academic formats I've grown accustomed to.

The value of including the articles is the mix of professional experiences, formal research and the opportunity to informally reach out to an audience in a comfortable environment. Using straight talk and sometimes sarcasm and humor. Each theme is meant to challenge you to think about the way we do policing. I've learned that because it is the way it's always been done, does not mean it cannot be done better. Consider the way we continue repeating the same activities, customs and practices without ever stopping to ask why.

Is there a better of policing, of training, of mentoring, of holding ourselves and each other accountable? Yes there is! This book explores the influencing factors associated with the culture of policing, and shows were the stumbling blocks are along the career

Appendix Introduction

path from rookie to retiree. We started with the question; why do good cops go bad? I believe this book covers why, and more importantly how to prevent them from doing so. The following appendixes are offered to you as a challenge for reconsidering the way we treat one another on the job. You will recognize the stories as similar to work experiences and conversations you have probably shared along the way. Give them a quick read through and I trust you will begin asking yourself and others that most important one word question; "Why?"

APPENDIX A

Changing the Culture and History of Policing

The apple never really falls far from the tree, and this remains a truism of policing's reactive paradigm of responding to crime. The tree I'm referring to is England's tithing system begun in 648 A.D. that included groups of village men (usually 10) responding to the commission of a criminal offense. The group was summoned from the course of their daily routine by a "hue and cry" that beckoned a response to pursue the offender. Upon capturing the rogue, he was turned over to an authority and the group disbanded, returning to individual duties.

Fast forward a scant 1346 years later to observe today's Patrol shift in action. They randomly move throughout a subjectively drawn geographic beat conducting independent police and non-police actions. There is little explanation for the patterns they travel or the areas selectively chosen for conducting these random acts of policing. That is until the high-band radio cries out an offense in progress, and the non-cohesive actions of a clustering of officers' turns into a coordinated response.

Singular in mission and motion, these officers unite for pursuing the offender. Upon apprehension, he is delivered to the local authority and the unit disbands yet again into their non-choreographed areas of responsibility. We even still use the horse, domesticated dog and chase on foot during these actions while remaining close to the historical roots of our enforcement service delivery methods. Although I'm sure even the village idiot would appreciate today's police fleet advancements, whether it's the act of deploying ultrasonic sound to disorient an offender, or throwing a rock from the village cliff, the philosophy of reactive response remains unchanged.

The evolution has been slow to come, but it is coming. Citizens, elected officials and progressive law enforcement commanders are demanding efficiency and effectiveness from agencies entrusted with serving as peace keepers and social service providers. As a profession, policing assumes the responsibility for measuring levels of crime and perceived effectiveness in combating that crime. This is a dangerous combination, and is similar to asking the fox to keep a count of the chickens.

Recently, federal grant solicitations to law enforcement are including requirements for partnering with universities while conducting research designs to quantifiably examine the effects of enforcement efforts. This is a giant leap in the right direction. Not because police and quantitative statistics go together like gasoline and fire, but the ecology of law enforcement is entangled with internal performance requirements, external demands and political pressures. Anecdotal stories and back patting for a job well done does not allow the responsible internal partners and external stakeholders the accurate information specific to the successes of reducing social harms.

Analyzing data using various scientifically rigorous methodologies is the only manner for ensuring that police organizations are conducting their mission conducive to the mandates of the body they serve. Today's police executive handles an array of requests ranging from mundane to the impossible. The expectation that the chief of

Appendix A

police is aware of precisely how effective the organization operates without the use of data is unrealistic.

There is a body of expertise in law enforcement emerging from the traditions of "crime analyst" that are evolving from one-time number counters of post-events and activities to a progressive, scientifically based predictive policing professional. The International Association of Crime Analyst (IACA) leads the way for this truly emerging skill. With the use of statistical packages and geographic information systems, analysts provide the fuel for running the data-driven engine of modern law enforcement.

For the past four years I have had the great fortune to travel this country delivering workshops on behalf of the National Highway Traffic Safety Administration (NHTSA) that offers a progressive system for changing the culture of policing. My former agency participated in the pilot phase beginning in 2008, and as the model progressed along with my career, it is entrenched as the cornerstone of the city police department I serve as chief. Data analyst now replaces the rock throwing village idiot, and intelligence centered Patrol assignments replace randomized ineffective practices of patrolling without purpose.

The concept of proactive policing is known by various names including intelligence-led policing, hotspot policing, predictive policing and selective enforcement. My base of experience is rooted in the data-driven approaches to crime and traffic safety (DDACTS) philosophy. It is a business model effecting the efficient allocation of policing resources for the purpose of reducing social harms. Based on the analysis of crash and crime data, agencies affect the occurrence of both social harms with the application of highly visible traffic enforcement strategies.

The correlation of crash and crime occurring within close proximity allows the police executive an opportunity for addressing both challenges with a singular tactic. The use of highly visible enforcement (HVE) sustains a flexible and cost efficient method for reducing these social harms. By placing on-duty officers in geographic locations based solely on the statistical frequency determined by a micro-place and micro-time analysis, communities may enjoy the benefits of decreases in actual and perceptual fears of crime and victimization.

The cognitive nature of human beings as patternistic, and the ecological dynamics of placed-based victimization provide the foundation for law enforcement to capitalize on the historical routines of individuals as they move through time and space as either victims or victimizers. By mapping multi-year data sets of crashes and crimes, policing agencies begin to see the high frequencies of occurrences for both categories overlay within a jurisdictional map.

Simply put, create a map of crashes over the last three to five years. Now produce a map of crimes over the same period of time. Finally, lay one map over the other and like GIS-magic, the hotspots appear. Going a little further, agencies may examine these hotspots to determine the days of the week and times of the day when the highest levels for crashes and crime are happening.

This is where the executives become increasingly interested. There are zero addition expenses associated with the implementation of the DDACTS philosophy, strategy or tactic. Officers already assigned to Patrol are, or should be in these areas anyway. Reallocate their assignment to specifically target the hotspot. This assignment should include the days of the week and hours of the day illustrated through your mapping technology.

Proactive officers with no direction usually end up at internal affairs. The same officers provided a scientifically quantified and justifiable geographic assignment based on the micro-place and micro-time analysis of data usually result in significant reductions of social harms associated with crashes and crime.

A commitment to working smarter than hard requires the optimistic leader to exit the traditional reactive paradigm of running from one

Appendix A

call for service to the next. The "fire brigade" method of extinguishing small fires after small fires is not consistent with efficiently managing the resources entrusted you. By allowing your analyst or the 27 year old gen-X'er to geocode CAD and RMS data onto a jurisdictional map, you gain an overarching perspective of crime and crash challenges plaguing your jurisdiction for years past and to come.

There are numerous non-cost prohibitive resources available to law enforcement agencies. My cohort and current president of the IACA, Christopher Bruce claims, and then demonstrates that approximately eighty percent of the tools required for conducting quantitative data analysis are available within a basic Microsoft office suite. My agency uses an off-the-shelf software, CrimeReports.com for delivering a web-based mapping capability with public consumption applications. Positioned on our department website, and an accompanying smartphone app, this acquisition also allows for a command central component accessible by every employee for generating series of maps, data charts, trend tracking graphs and other tools capable of making every employee a data analyst.

The National Institute of Justice provides a free software download for CrimeStat III, and when combined with the power of GIS generates a level of sophisticated analysis promising police agencies the upper hand in battling social harms. These examples are just a few of the unlimited resources available to law enforcement and deliver a mechanism for breaking from the traditions of the reactive tithing system.

History is great when teaching about our nation or sharing the customs of one's family and culture. American policing has evolved through the political, the professional, and the community policing eras, and now stands at the horizon searching for the next direction. Never has data been so available to the policing profession. The irony is that we, by trade are documenters of fact, and those facts (data) are held hostage inside CAD and RMS systems. Despite the captured data, we fail to access, analyze, disseminate, and create actionable

Appendix A

enforcement items based upon it. In effect, we fail the communities served.

I challenge you to learn from the history of policing, but not repeat it, and explore our fraternal origins of reactive service, but not practice them. As the leaders of our nation's committed and capable officers, I encourage you to consider the application of data-driven practices; to refuse allowing one more shift to conduct directionless patrols; and to stop enforcement activities determined on the intuitive biases of race, socioeconomic or political entitlement.

Do you hear the hue and cry?

Source: Article written for Executive Leadership section by Chief Scott Silverii, PhD and posted October 9, 2012 at Law Enforcement Today online website. *Source:* Reprinted with permission of Dr. Scott Silverii for *Cop Culture: Why Good Cops Go Bad*

APPENDIX B

Beware the "Gift" of Socialization

Ernest Hemingway said that, "Certainly there is no hunting like the hunting of man, and those who have hunted armed men long enough and liked it, never really care for anything else thereafter." Is this where we are in the social evolution of our profession? How many family outings and trips do we by-pass, or rely upon "I'm on call" to skip the zoo adventure just because we are not interested?

Recently, while going through boxes of things stored at my dad's house, I came across hundreds of my pictures. I stopped to reminisce alone, as I was flooded by the vivid recall of memories. My first day on the job picture afforded plenty of laughs as I saw a much younger me in a blue faux cowboy hat holding a .38 revolver pistol and speed loaders. Thank God the Sheriff did not require we wear those hats, but I guess he distributed them for good measure and tradition.

The pictures of 12 years working undercover afforded as many "looks" as drug dealers arrested. The giant circular wire-rim eyeglasses and operationally fashionable mullet were my favorite era. Before laughing look at your 1980-90's collection of flipped up collars and

Don Johnson-inspired blazers. The biker period provided menacing images of a shaven headed, giant bearded psychopathic facade, or so thought my neighbors and church members. Nothing like having the pew to yourself.

The photos from Hurricane Katrina still sear sadness as we faced the storm sheltered in place at the heart of its arrival. The times following included SWAT deployments into the New Orleans metro areas' worse hit locations. While the background and heavy tactical gear looked more like movie fantasy, it was every bit real.

The latter-career pictures began to resemble the "me" of today. The trimmed down cyclist no longer looks like the 260 lbs power lifter, and the beards and long hair are replaced with civilianized flat-tops. I'd love to find that cowboy hat.

Then I stopped laughing and relishing the fond memories when I realized that over 22 years were stored in this box. I'd estimate that less than 10% of the hundreds of photographs from Polaroid to digital included my family. There are a few of them at law enforcement inspections and gatherings centered on the job, but where are the zoo, pool and birthday pictures?

We casually comment about spending more time with our law enforcement family than our own. It somehow becomes a badge of honor to miss the kid's party or the wife's date night. When did we stop regretting or feeling the guilt associated with absenteeism?

There is a process called occupational socialization that includes the organizationally informal dynamics of becoming blue that includes desensitization and detachment. It's the reason we don't cry over dead bodies or beat child molesters as opposed to reading them their rights. One of the tragedies, yet defense mechanisms this profession "gifts" us with is the ability to separate ourselves from the horrors we see for the sake of getting the paperwork completed.

Those photographs caused me to painfully recall the first time I administered CPR. I worked my tail off and gave it everything I had as the family stood there waiting for police magic to happen. My body burned with aching muscles, my lungs cried out over each dispelling of life-saving breath I offered, and my arms cringed with each forceful chest compression.

Back at home I called the hospital that night to check on my victory. He died. I was crushed. I cried at home and my family seemed surprised to see their knight in tears. I had only been on Patrol a few months, and had never intimately experienced death. The social and familial expectancy is that no matter your experiential level, you are supposed to be the cop portrayed in the movies. Really?

A few months later, I responded to an emergency call to find another person in cardiac distress. Without hesitation I began CPR, and they too passed away. Did I shed a tear for the loss? Now I joked about being 0 for 2, and laughed as the fellow officers cracked wise about being the messenger of death. Even recounting the incident to my family was more of a police report than an emotional breach. No one was surprised by the callousness, not even me.

This is the "gift" of socialization. There are stages to becoming fully indoctrinated into the fraternity, and although we are trained to "see" through the surface appearances of situations, we are curiously blinded to circumstances personally affecting us. I think personal suffering is a badge of honor we award ourselves. How injured are you, how much child support are you ordered to pay, how many hours have you been on duty, and how many months has it been since your saw your child. Do these badges of honor sound familiar? When did we take the oath of bearing the suffering albatross?

As a chief executive it is our responsibility to teach officers, especially young ones about the "gift" of socialization. It is our obligation to take action when we see the fraternal expectancies are overbearing the individual. It is our moral duty to mentor these officers and encourage them to spend more time with family than shift mates.

Earned time off is not a sign of weakness, and time spent with moral and social anchors such as family, friends and church builds individual strength. I used to boast that the first 10 years of my career were spent without ever taking a day off for vacation or sick. While God blessed me with good health, He balked on my common sense.

Socialization does have benefits such as teaching the organization's cultural expectancies and occupational mores. It ensures we understand how each other works, thinks and reacts. It builds morale, confidence and esprit de corps among the troops. It establishes the informal social pecking orders.

It also teaches you that if it hurts, suck it up. If it destroys your marriage, find someone new. If it causes you to drink, roll your gold if you get stopped driving home, and if you feel like you can no longer exist in this life, you are weak asking for help.

This "gift" of occupational socialization is a mystery. Peter Manning refers to the job as having a mystique veiled by a sacred canopy. The symbolism, pageantry and tradition make our calling noble. It is vital to maintaining the highest levels of loyalty that we see this low-wage earning, long-hour working and risk-taking job as a "calling." These badges of honor endear us to the service of policing.

Why is a police officer's line of duty death and funeral so impacting of an agency, a community, and a nation? Are there websites, ceremonies and engraved walls dedicated for fallen teachers, bus drivers or public works employees?

These acts of respect are symbolic insurances to officers, that if I also lay my life down in the service to others, that I will too be memorialized by pageantry and procession. Ceremonial symbolism comforts us to know that if our life is lost in the line of duty, we will be honored not for the way we died, but for how we lived. This phrase is inscribed at the Police Memorial site in D.C., and it is our reassurance policy that in our passing, our families will be cared for and we will be missed.

Instant, sudden or violent departure preparation is another one the "gifts" you'll receive upon achieving full socialization. Is running towards danger while others flee an innate behavioral characteristic? If that was the case, we could skip entrance exams and hiring practices and only test your fight or flight response. Those running this way are hired, the other group need not reapply.

Yes, our chosen calling, profession, occupation, job, grind, or whatever it's called is a mystery, but the systematic processes associated with occupational socialization are well defined and documented in the studies of organizations.

As chiefs of police and senior executive managers, we have either survived the turmoil to rise through the ranks, or are some of the luckiest s.o.b. on Earth. Regardless of the occupational trajectory landing you in position, we now have the obligation for creating environments free from detrimental fraternal hazing and cultural expectancies inconsistent with healthy work ecologies.

Please stop before calling this information or me anything you wouldn't call your closest family member. I do not ascribe to the tree-hugging warm and fuzzy school of police management. I actually have rightfully earned a reputation for strictness with zero tolerance for accepting anything less than everything you have. I also have lived, witnessed and studied for years the effects, both positive and negative of socialization's gift.

There are better ways of enculturation than repeating the sophomoric rituals from school days and dormitory life. Scientific, theoretical and practically applied management methodologies for engraining loyalty, respect, and longevity for the calling are more appropriate and sustainable than back slapping over pitchers of beer.

Be the moral, professional and exemplar compass for your officers. It doesn't require being perfect, it just requires being present. Your encouraging words and inquiries about their wellbeing carries so much more weight than we will ever understand. I've learned that compassion is strength when shown in leadership. I also know that once we have successfully traversed a section of pathway, it is not only important that we guide others from the front, but that we look back and caution for obstacles along the way. Don't allow the "gift" to become the rock that removes young officers from the trail.

Stop often along the path to take pictures, but also work harder to include your family in them. Say, "Cheese."

Source: Article written for Executive Leadership section by Chief Scott Silverii, PhD and posted January 7, 2013 at Law Enforcement Today online website. *Source:* Reprinted with permission of Dr. Scott Silverii for *Cop Culture: Why Good Cops Go Bad*

APPENDIX C

Cops and Cavemen; Come Out of the Cold

I was speaking with a Captain about an officer who just did not seem to grasp the agency's vision. Although clearly communicated over the last two years in agency-wide meetings, in-services, e-mails, social media, and personal conversations the officer just refuses to "get on board."

This Captain is fully committed to the city, the agency and the progressive vision of this administration. The officer, uh.....not so much. In our last conversation about this officer the Captain asked, "Why can't he just see what we are building here?"

I replied that he is a "laggard." He knew me well enough to understand that there was more, much more behind that term. Enjoying the dramatic pause, so I followed with "and you are an innovator!" He was still not convinced my response addressed the adversarial officer.

How do great ideas spread, what does it take for a product to catch the public's imagination or why do organizations adopt behaviors as acceptable? There is a term originating from the social sciences called Diffusion of Innovations.

The term seeks to explain how, why and at what rate do new ideas and technology spread through various cultures. Consider the domestic application of fire. Someone's great, great, great... grandfather had an experience with fire in a manner positively affecting the quality of his life. This also benefited the community, thus the culture of early human groupings and prosperity.

Had that innovation been quenched by an elder for the sake of maintaining tribal traditions, where would we be today? Literally; in the dark. Obviously this innovation was replicated by the few with a capacity for appreciation, understanding and promoting the domestic use of fire. Even though, how did a torch in Asia Minor spread to the Pacific Northwest?

Fire, like the progressive vision of an administration requires four elements influencing the adoption, implementation and sustainment of the vision.

1. Innovation

2. Communication channels

3. Time

4. Social systems

Relying on human capital to promote the wide-spread adoption of the new idea is critical for establishing it as a cornerstone of an administration. A Neanderthal passed that first torch, who then passed the next torch, and so on. A Chief of Police (sometimes called a Neanderthal) shares their fire with a new vision, an organizational ideal or an operational paradigm shift. Then they wait for the agency to openly embrace the progressive public service direction. Then wait and wait.

Stop wasting your time waiting for something to happen. It won't, and you will be like the solo caveman before the successful caveman who introduced fire to humanity. The first one probably sat in a cave alone thinking how awesome and hot his new idea was. He never shared that flame, that fire, that passion for improving the collective culture. He probably expired in the cold after that flash extinguished.

I understood this concept as a new Chief and strategically planned the introduction of my vision for organizational change. It was not wrapped around ego, but founded upon scientific principles of administration, theory, data analysis and old-fashioned accountability.

The Innovation element was the organizational reliance upon data with NHTSA's Data-Driven Approaches to Crime and Traffic Safety (DDACTS). This proven philosophy has realized significant reductions in social harms formerly plaguing communities deserving a better quality of life.

The Communications Channels used agency-wide introductions, e-mails, social media, public presentations and personal conversations to share the vision with actionable items for achieving quantifiable goals and performance standards. The element of time is the most difficult, because as Chiefs we want it done yesterday. It is our idea, so it must be great and accepted immediately.

Time is critical, as is timing. I always reassure my staff that I will not be out worked or out waited. If you have been on the job more than a year, you know what I mean. Time can be your friend or your enemy. In a fraternity where the primary goal becomes earning pension, they also know how to leverage "time" against your innovative ideas.

The final element required for achieving diffusion of innovations are Social Systems. Who do you go to lunch with regularly? How many mealtimes have you and posse in tow walked out past other officers? As the leader of any organization it is vital that you do not allow that sense of comfort to control your actions. The perception of

Appendix C

segregation or elitism spills water on the flame of your vision. Re-engage your team with your time and sincere attention.

Back to Officer Laggard. I explained to the Captain that an idea needs to reach a point of critical mass before becoming part of the culture. Reality is, not everyone will adopt your vision, as not everyone thought the "Flowbee" was great for cutting their own hair.

After convincing enough in your agency that the passion behind the vision produces sustainable results, they will also promote your vision and embrace it as their own. The good news is, you do not have to gain the support of every individual to obtain critical mass.

This is where I should have paid more attention in math and statistics courses, but here it goes. Remember the Bell curve that spared so many of us from failing grades? It's here again to demonstrate the phases and population adoption percentages for achieving critical mass (acceptance.)

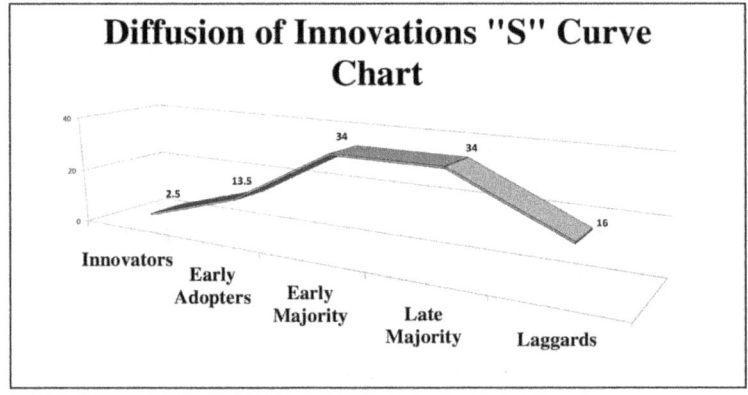

Appendix C

Table C.1 – The Diffusion of Innovations "S" Curve chart illustrates the percentages of cultural acceptance before an innovative idea reaches critical mass. *Source:* Table created by Dr. Scott Silverii for *Cop Culture: Why Good Cops Go Bad.*

Cultural innovation, be it fire or an IPhone involve four types of people. Only a small percentage of the culture is Innovators. Only one Steve Jobs, William Bratton, or you! These innovations are embraced by the Early Adopters. These are the officers embracing the new zero tolerance for DWI enforcement, or the first in line for the IPhone 76. They will carry the flag of your vision faithfully, regardless the cost or inconvenience.

Your first big slice of the culture's population is the Early Majority. Great news is, you are no longer the single voice preaching the powerfully positive influences of your vision. You've collected other Innovators and Early Adopters to carry your banner. You have now achieved critical mass, and your policies, practices and persona are eligible for cultural sustainment. Eligible I say, because nothing is guaranteed.

Rounding down the employee pool is the Late Majority who will comply because the others seem to be benefitting from it. This group will not respond to your motivational plea, only to your very specific directions for what it is you want them to accomplish. These employees are not contrary to the agency's objective, but they are a reality and must be included in the vision sharing.

Finally, Officer Laggard. He will only embrace your ideology when placed in personal jeopardy. Let off the pedal and they are back to a dead stop. While you may rejoice once Officer Laggard retires, resigns or finds employment in a scrapyard, it is short lived euphoria. There will always be a percentage, although a very small subculture of your population, as laggards.

Maintain your focus and your presence. Laggards drain your creative energies and distract you from providing your best positive mentoring attentions to those officers willing to trust the new direction.

Being successful in leadership also involves the wise expenditure of personal energy and equity investments. A sure way to fail in supervision is believing you can satisfy everyone. Don't neglect fanning the flames of your "team" because the laggard wants to sit out in the dark. Maybe the nocturnal wolf of unemployment will snatch him!

Source: Article written for Executive Leadership section by Chief Scott Silverii, PhD and posted March 25, 2013 at Law Enforcement Today online website. *Source:* Reprinted with permission of Dr. Scott Silverii for *Cop Culture: Why Good Cops Go Bad*

APPENDIX D

Old Bulls and Young Bulls

Who can forget Robert Duval's advice to a young LAPD Officer played by Sean Penn in the 1988 movie "*Colors*?" While Duval's character may have been referring to operational efficiency more than chronological age, the point is that better results are often associated with maturity.

Oakland's Chief of Police Howard Jordan recently announced increasing the Police Department's minimum hiring age from 20.5 years to 25 years old. I hope this draws the more experienced recruits with college, military or additional life exposure on their resumes.

Most importantly, I pray God blesses and protects the good people of Oakland. Next, the city is fortunate to have a chief executive willing to explore options and alternative solutions for solving violent crime. When we stop searching, we stop serving. Chief, here is wishing you the best of luck searching for what works in Oakland.

My concern is not with the age, the education, or the numbers of recruits. It is the organizational culture that these recruits are entering. I am not referring to the 2003 Negotiated Settlement Agreement (NSA) that followed the tumultuous period of "The Riders." I am not even referring to the fact that Oakland could become the first police department in the country put into federal receivership due to their lack of compliance with action items designed to improve performance, accountability, and responsiveness.

I am referring to the culture of the institution of policing. I am referring to the cultural phenomenon promoting mediocrity and minimal performance for fear of reprisal from supervisors and "brothers in blue." I am referring to a culture based on the antiquated, reactive policing models denigrating the values of self-initiative and community-serving enforcement activities. I am referring to an ethos of "do not rock the boat."

While I believe today's profession of law enforcement is transitioning into a data-driven model with emphasis on service delivery and effective responsiveness, I do know that the traditions of the past remain deeply rooted in the advice I and countless other rookies received from veteran officers, "Don't start no stuff, won't be no stuff." A leader in police culture studies, Van Maanen quoted a veteran officer during an interview who stated:

There's only two things you gotta know around here. First, forget everything you've learned in the academy because the street's where you'll learn to be a cop; and second, being first around here don't mean shit.

This is where the paradigm shift enters conflict as an out with the old means either changing the current ideology of more veteran officers, or encouraging their retirement before they uninspired yet another generation of hopeful, idealistic public servants. The most tragic event in one's career is to have your idealism doused like a wet flame. For those entrenched in the "accumulating time till pension" mentality of policing, it is critical that the dynamics of homogeneity remain strong.

Appendix D

The sense of sameness is achieved by ensuring everyone looks alike, acts alike and reacts alike. Mustangs, rebels, and visionaries need not apply. They are the "wave makers" whose proactive policing performances cause supervisors to pressure the rest for similar results. Because there is safety and security in similarity, those fighting to maintain their passion for public service are ostracized by the flock. Even those sharing the same race, gender, or religious characteristics are discriminated against because of idealistic actions, not demographic details.

My concern is not with the age, experiences, or quantity. It is the culture. It is not of the Oakland Police Department, but the fraternity of policing. Until there are enough "boat rockers" creating the tide of change, the old ways of "retired on duty" entitlement prevails. Researcher M. Britz also observed upon completing her seminal study of the socialization process resulting in the perpetuation of the mediocrity model that,

Traditional research in this area has suggested that the socialization process is so intense and the subculture so strong that individual characteristics are quickly overwhelmed.

The occupational socialization process, known as becoming blue is a powerful force. I am a product of socialization, but was fortunate to have progressive mentors showing me a path more productive than sitting on my ass accumulating years until retirement.

Chief Jordan's desire to increase the age for obtaining higher quality recruits will be met by just a few challenges. Of course, you can welcome college graduates to the fraternity, but unless you are competitively compensating them for that education, they will pursue better options. An arbitrary age such as 25 also leaves a time gap between most people finishing college and military service. Will they be recruited from current careers or expected to remain willingly unemployed until their 25th birthday?

Finally, several foundational studies reinforce the paradigm of occupational socialization out-influencing education and military experience. McKittrick describes the USMC socialization process focusing on satisfaction for mission as opposed to policing's personal self-actualization. The Marine is taught that becoming a Marine is the ultimate motivator, while law enforcement satisfaction derives from attaining self-recognition.

Another study (Van Maanen) shows stages of socialization including a benchmark where the field training apprenticeship introduces rookies to the expected attitudes and behaviors of veteran officers. While great for learning the job, it is also the point when the highly motivated and performing academy cadets (military and college) surrender to the mediocre levels of motivation of more seasoned officers. As an example, recruits with military backgrounds initially reported high levels of motivation, organizational commitment and needs satisfaction.

Within the first few months of actual police experience, those levels dropped sharply to parallel the measures of the recruits who reported no military experience. The decline is attributed to decreased expectations about what the job actually involved after graduating from the academy, and adopting the veteran officers' apathetic attitude that hard work is not linked to a system of reward or recognition.

A parallel study of institutional culture shows the need of individuals for social clustering and gaining peer acceptance. Ashforth and Saks' study would suggest that even the newest Oakland Police Department Officers aged 21 or 25, are also subject to this dynamic. Without a cultural revolution, officers willing to operate within a cultural expectancy outside of their ethical sphere to avoid institutional isolation from cohorts may compromise their moral character and deviate from the principles of true community-policing ideals sought by Chief Jordan and the city of Oakland.

In the course of my doctoral dissertation research, I identified the term "detrimental homogenetic entitlement" detailing the adverse

Appendix D

effects of officers isolating themselves from public accountability for sustaining a self-serving culture. Finally, I provide thoughtful recommendations for assisting the senior executive's decision to ignite the revolution of change. Whether you chose to walk down the hill, or run down the hill, make sure the valley is filled with a positive culture awaiting your new bulls (recruits).

Source: Article written for Executive Leadership section by Chief Scott Silverii, PhD and posted January 22, 2013 at Law Enforcement Today online website. *Source:* Reprinted with permission of Dr. Scott Silverii for *Cop Culture: Why Good Cops Go Bad.*

APPENDIX E

I Quit

Johnny Paycheck popularized this song originally written by David Allen Coe in 1977, and despite having been his only #1 hit, we recall with clarity those famous words, "*Take this job and shove it.*" He sings about the dissatisfaction and hurt of a man who gave his life to his work without reciprocation of reward.

Ok, I'm not quitting, but it gets your attention. It also gains the attention of supervisors, Chiefs and Mayors who ask, "Why?" Well, there are many reasons why, but I'm going to share with you several of the real reasons, despite what the nice resignation letters say about "learning a lot, enjoyed serving with people, it is with regret that I inform you, ..."

Quitting what you love is a terribly emotional event. Whether it is a relationship, a food, a vice or a calling to serve, the act of physically, mentally and emotionally separating yourself only happens after much thought, turmoil and reconsideration. We are not discussing ice cream, alcohol or chewing tobacco. We are discussing the separation from an occupation requiring that you give no less than everything you have to ensure your survival, success, and socialization.

There are individuals who enter the fraternity, only to realize it was not their calling and quit. I admire those people for accepting a reality and not jeopardizing the others because of less than a total commitment. Those selfishly clinging to the job because it's better than serving in the manual labor industry, or enjoy the perks (abuse) coming with the shield, should be encouraged to quit immediately. Because they are cloaked behind a badge, they are a greater threat to officer safety than the victimizers.

I examine the reasons cops quit in my research, and after studying the culture of organizations, interviews, and observations of officers across America have discovered a common variable. The most common factor is that officers do not associate hard work and risk with a system of reward. The reward did not mean monetary, and is often associated with self-satisfaction through the appreciation of others. I'm talking to you – Chief. Who knew a simple pat on the back or sincere thank you could reverse the tradition of attrition?

Unfortunately, it is not that simple, but human decency goes a long way. The USMC promotes an indoctrination for new recruits teaching that the act of becoming a Marine is the most rewarding part of becoming a Marine. Because many mission-based objectives are not pleasant, the USMC attaches the higher ideal of service to satisfaction.

Law enforcement attaches the outcome of self-actualization to the officer's perception of value or importance to the work conducted. Researchers look to understand why individuals enter the profession, endure the difficult assimilation processes, seek the social clustering, yet become so alienated leading to early separation.

Officers are highly influenced by the occupational assimilation process, or "fitting in" as it contributes to self-actualization. It also shows officers care more about intrinsic values (duty, honor and service) than extrinsic values (monetary compensation, or public opinion). Officers also value close friendships and peer clustering opportunities.

The desire to establish close relationships is valuable for esprit de corps, but is also a weapon used against officers seen as going against the flow or not fitting in. Officers ostracized and isolated from peers soon experience a fragmentation from the organizational core, a sense of dissatisfaction and soon the desire to quit.

Officers have been tempted to operate within a cultural expectancy outside of their ethical sphere to avoid institutional isolation from cohorts. They soon find themselves compromising their moral character and become vulnerable to professional deviance. This duality of conscience versus fitting in leads to either quitting the job, or remaining within a realm of great dissatisfaction.

During the course of my ethnography, I spoke with an officer from Arizona about his feelings about "fitting in" with his new Narcotics Task Force. I do not identify he, or anyone in my research to honor my promise of maintaining confidentiality. An excerpt from my research describes his feelings;

An undercover narcotics agent in Arizona shares his struggles over maintaining the integrity he desires versus being pulled into a lifestyle he wants to avoid:

"I'm not like some of these cats who just do it for the rush, or the pain. They live to chase women and tell war stories after each night of partying. Hell, I find myself at the center of these stories, and I'm like, this ain't the me I want to be."

He exemplifies the strain of subcultural socialization when he states:

"Just the peer pressure ... is crazy. Worse than any college frat I saw. I used to think if it's that bad then the guys should just quit. Then I realized that you can't. In a way you're trapped. It's a dishonor to quit.

Another reason cops quit is unrealistic expectations of what the job actually involves. We grow up admiring cops while we pretend to be them, dress like them for Halloween, even bachelor(ette) parties have been known to receive visits from "officers."

Movies, television, books, and video games glamourize the profession of policing. Who would not want to become one? Yet these preconceived expectations quickly dash once the cadet enters day one of the academy.

The daily gun battles, bank robbers, and detonating bombs don't happen. You are not swept into an undercover role driving a Maserati, and the awesome goatee and earrings are replaced by strict grooming policy, old fleet Crown Vics and sweeping spent brass from the range.

The hopes of being mentored by a crusty old Sergeant, treating you like crap because he cares for you is realistically replaced by the FTO who just completed the process himself and is stuck with training you because his recent training is still "fresh" in his mind.

The only thing you'll hear from old crusty is to forget the stuff they taught you in the academy, because the streets are where you learn to be a cop. Raise your hand if you have heard that fairy tale before. Now, strike yourself with that hand if you were the one saying it to the rookies.

Academy life instills homogeneity as a crucial element for maintaining the standardization and rigors of policing. Everyone is forced into a similar square peg through policy, practice, and pressure. In a profession of over 70% white and male, it is easy to see how looking, acting and thinking the same is so important for maintaining the "traditions" of policing's culture. This does not only refer to race, gender, religious or sexual preference.

Become the highly proactive officer on your shift and see how quickly your dispatchers' cheerfully respond with requested information and lunch invites from your buds diminish. Anyway, police work is truly about public service, and that includes directing traffic so little Jill may safely cross the street, to taking someone's life as they try taking yours.

The key is to attach the ideal of policing to a higher calling. No not, the ministry, but to a true sense of service and satisfaction. The process of self-actualization for becoming an officer must mean more to the individual than an hourly wage or the year of the fleet unit issued.

As chiefs and senior leadership, we must create an environment producing an affective and cognitive attachment to the job and the organization, as it relates to higher levels of career satisfaction, organizational commitment and identification, and the reduced intentions to quit.

What does that mean? Stop being such an a-hole and show someone you care about the important work they do. Just kidding about that, but please do take the time away from budgets, lunches, research, lunches and policy review and lunches to express your appreciation.

The more you say thank you, the less you will hear, "I Quit!"

Source: Article written for Executive Leadership section by Chief Scott Silverii, PhD and posted January 30, 2013 at Law Enforcement Today online website. *Source:* Reprinted with permission of Dr. Scott Silverii for *Cop Culture: Why Good Cops Go Bad*

APPENDIX F

Breaking Up Is Hard To Do

I want to follow up to my last article "I Quit" by sticking with the musical theme. I highlighted Take This Job and Shove It, last time and promise not to use Chipmunk Love the next. Let's explore why it is so hard to "break up" from a job you love and love to not love.

Before beginning, I was approached by a lady Saturday night while monitoring a downtown nightclub crowd following the Ambrosia Mardi Gras parade. She is not associated with law enforcement and I am not sure who she is. She was kind enough to share having read the entire "I Quit" article. Even emphasizing that she read the whole thing. I was curious if she meant it was interesting, or long! Either way, it was a kind gesture. If you read this; thank you and owe this inspiration to you.

I realized then, that in addition to the many e-mails I receive from all of you in support of our cultural revolution, these principles apply to everyone. I write to encourage sincere public servants, but also know that cultures exist in all aspects of society.

Appendix F

Who knows, we may ignite a "change" reaction in another industry while recreating ours. I believe dedicated professionals are ready for a change, and desire a singular vision directing their energy. I believe "we" are the soldiers of evolution, and in our generation of service, a new era of fraternity will emerge.

Occupational entitlement has long allowed others to exist on the efforts of others. Accumulating "time" waiting to retire is the bane of those who will give their best effort and their last breath to this beloved profession.

I was told by a junior ranking officer that leading to your 20 years of service you add upwards. After making your 20, you count downwards to your retirement 30. I was guilty! I no longer shared that I had 15 years on, or 19 years on the job. I began saying I have 9 years left or 7 years left…

The difference is; he is counting down the years left for working to escape work. I am cherishing my remaining years left for effecting creative and positive change for our profession. How will your countdown contribute to policing? Are you dying to gain your pension, or living to gain perspective?

Let's discuss perspective. That's why I began writing this piece anyway. Why is breaking up so hard to do? While I examine the areas in need of improving in my study of cop culture, I fully appreciate the many wonderfully amazing qualities of this job.

The most amazing aspect is you. I was taught in 1991 while attending a SWAT school in Amarillo, Texas that you can "do" SWAT with a knife while wearing a loin cloth. Not sure about wearing the loin cloth, but I understood the point. Strip away everything black, ballistic and bought because there were lightning bolts and eagles affixed to the tag. It comes down to you. The officer willing to train, respond and sacrifice on-call for no extra compensation. You are what is special about this profession.

The Best of Times

Appendix F

My starting pay was around $11,000 a year while working out of a dilapidated wooden school house stuck next to the detention center. The men I worked with were older and much more experienced, yet they were in the truest sense of the word; public servants.

There were no take-home units, portable radios, in-service trainings or pay raises. Yet after blessed to rise through the ranks, earn a Ph.D., become a Chief of Police, travel this country and author a book, my fondest times were spent in that white wooden shack.

My first week on the job was spent with the greatest supervisor a public servant could ask for, Lieutenant Leo Naquin. A compassionate and fiercely loyal leader, he drove me by each officer's home and their families' homes ensuring I knew exactly where they lived.

This instilled the sense of family and fraternal obligation to care for each other. Not a message of looking the other way to illegitimate behaviors. He explained how important each officer was, and not as a law enforcer, but as a father, son, brother, and friend to the community.

Have you known a supervisor like that? Have you been a supervisor like that? If not, it's not too late to make an enormous difference in another person's life. It is an eternal investment. I will attest to you that though he had only met me, there was no way of knowing the effect he would have on my life.

What Is So Special

I am collecting my thoughts while writing this in an effort to present the other great elements making our job hard to leave. The new cars will age, the new radio will lose battery life, the new station house will lose the new station house smell, and the cool new color-coded handcuffs you paid too much for will chip and rust like the first pair I bought and still carry.

Make a list of what keeps you coming back to duty every shift, even after throwing your rig on the bed and saying this was "it!" Next, scratch off anything that is black, ballistic and bought because there are lightning bolts and eagles affixed.

It is you. It is him. It is her. It is them. It is you. You make breaking up hard to do. Someone depends on you to be there. You may not know it, or realize it, but you do sense it. You sense the draw to each other, that no matter how bad conditions get, you belong there.

You belong to something greater than yourself. You are why I stay, and why I write. I know that because of me, someone else stays. Although I do not know who, it is my and our moral obligation to always mentor and encourage. You may just become the reason another one stays. Breaking up is hard to do. It is not because there are no other professions out there. It is because no other job in this world values you the way we do. It is you.

Source: Article written for Executive Leadership section by Chief Scott Silverii, PhD and posted February 13, 2013 at Law Enforcement Today online website. *Source:* Reprinted with permission of Dr. Scott Silverii for *Cop Culture: Why Good Cops Go Bad*

APPENDIX G

What Should Chiefs be Thinking About

Recently, while speaking with a sergeant from another jurisdiction about calling my Patrol Division lieutenant, he suggested that contact would be made over the radio. The sergeant then asked; "What band is he on?" Band? I honestly have no idea. I know that when I push the power button, the light comes on and I hear radio traffic. Because I did not know the radio band, does that make me a bad chief?

Then I thought, well I bet the sergeant does not know the employee pension contribution percentage or the average overtime rate for determining expenditure allocations associated with state and federal grants. While that allowed a temporary relief from the sting of the "radio band" debacle, I immediately realized the banality to this line of rationalization.

Truth is, the above illustration is not a completely accurate reflection of my response to this fine sergeant's question, but it did prompt me to think. I considered the various strata of professionally intimate knowledge and the organizationally relevant issues based on an individual's path along the para-militaristic hierarchy. Obviously our focus shifts through the years and responsibilities. I was challenged by this to ask what is important to me as the chief of police.

As a patrol officer, I recited the criminal ordinances verbatim and communicated exclusively using the 10-code. As an undercover agent, I knew precisely how many grams made an ounce, how many ounces made a pound and how many pounds made a kilo. As a division commander, I was focusing less on the adrenaline-producing accounts of arrests, pursuits, and seizures, and more on budgeting, total quality management, and alternative scheduling solutions. As we move up the ranks, time is spent wrestling less over arrests and more over the employees affecting them.

The areas of concern most important to me at this stage in my career are various, but the singular topic monopolizing my focus is the employees. The challenge of investing in human capital yields the greatest institutional returns for you as the leader, for the individual officers in their quest to serve with dignity and longevity, and for the community in their desire to live unencumbered by the fear of victimization.

If employees knew the depth of consideration given to their safety, training, education, mentoring and general well-being, there would be plenty of crow to eat. Obviously, how could they know? Without the relational experiences as a senior law enforcement executive there is no substitute for understanding the objective perspective required for surveying the comprehensive nature of the organization as it relates to the employee.

The difference in the expected and the experienced creates the traditionally adversarial nature of employee / employer relations leading most to view this fraternal caste system through a Marxist lenses. The senior law enforcement executive becomes the oppressive bourgeois, while the proletariat officers bust butts as their labor is exploited as a commodity to be reassigned, promoted, transferred, and disciplined. However unrealistic this analogy is, perception for some becomes their reality.

Appendix G

Breaching the institutional stratification of rank, assignment, classification or perception may be accomplished by articulating a clear organizational vision focused on equity of opportunity and ownership. Will the rookie officer attend your command staff meetings? Probably not, but if their voice is represented, then they become an invested resource for the institutional ideals and operations.

The truth is, while we care about the well-being of the individual and their ability to communicate on the proper radio band, our focus also considers the operational integrity and effectiveness of the organization. This may segregate us from the rank and file, but objective distance is necessary for ensuring a sustainable natural balance of labor and demand contributing to long-term and productive employment.

Bridging this perceptual divide also promotes employee longevity as they balance a need for external motivators (fair compensation) and internal satisfiers (selfless service). Is harmony achieved with increased pay that encourages employee's retention? Possibly for a brief period, until the next material purchase beyond their means, and then it is back to pay rate complaints.

It seems that every employee terminating their service is offered a job elsewhere making at least twice their law enforcement earnings. Really? I want a job like that. Of course, most soon return because of their "love of the job." It is what we call unemployment.

Materialism does not create deeply committed careers in progressively challenging workplaces. The luster of new vehicles wane as the miles accumulate, SWAT gear gets forgotten as the activations go fewer and farther between, and the reassignment to narcotics fails to satisfy because it doesn't live up to what was learned watching "Training Day."

The material and external appeals to self-satisfaction are temporary, and like forecasting the market or predicting the next YouTube video to go viral, law enforcement executives cannot continue guessing when the motivational rollercoaster will adversely affect the institutional core. A sound foundation is laid when leaders focus attention to the internal motivators appealing to the altruistic nature of public service.

Listen quietly as the chorus reigns down, "You cannot pay bills with altruism." No, but without an ethical anchor or altruistic attachment, meaningful institutional commitment fails to develop and diminishes the individual's potential for meaningful long-term employment.

The contrasting of personal values creates fissures between the employee's desire to serve and reasons to remain. There are occupational points of departure when employees become disenfranchised with the altruistic ideals of duty, honor and service. The socialization process of "becoming blue" includes the period when a new officer is introduced to the traditions, codes, and cultural expectancy of fraternal membership.

Researchers struggle to decode the mystery of the thin blue line, and their attempts end with mere speculations about what occurs behind the veil. Peter Manning's seminal research into the meaning and symbolism of police work describes the powerful mystification of policing as the "sacred canopy."

Researcher Marjie Britz concluded after attempts to identify dynamics involved in the enculturation process that; "Traditional research in this area has suggested that the socialization process is so intense and the subculture so strong that individual characteristics are quickly overwhelmed." Top academics focusing on what makes us; us, can only venture about the informal processes creating such loyalty yet so much discontentment.

The years of research I invested for my doctoral dissertation focused on the occupational socialization of policing. During this time I learned that the initial disenfranchisement from the organization begins once the individual joins the agency. They immediately realize that the preconceived notions established through external influences, such as media and myth are in actuality not what policing involves.

The next major point of departure happens once the cadet graduates the academy. Senior training officers fail to reinforce the lessons taught in the academy by encouraging the rookie to forget what they just learned there. The senior officers impose their ideology of "not making waves" thus ensuring a continuation of the homogenous nature of the organizational ethos. This further alienates the officer from the original altruistic motivators such as duty, honor, and service. Homogeneity is critical to maintaining the status quo as evidenced by the lack of minorities and females throughout the classified ranks of the profession.

The combination of these stages produce the fully socialized officer who learns to acclimate to the occupational environment by embracing mediocrity for the sake of avoiding isolation from peers. Police observer John Van Maanen captured the essence of the fraternal unity by stating: "Consequently, the police culture can be viewed as molding the attitudes, with numbing regularity, of virtually all who enter."

My best observation for remedying the contrasts between what senior law enforcement executives want for their employees, and the perception employees have towards organizational altruistic ideals is found in the "why." Core commitment is not cultivated in the "what" or "how" things are done, but "why" we do it. As it relates to addressing institutional investment, officers know how to do police work and what to do when situations arise requiring their services. What they either never knew or forget over time is "why" they do police work.

Simon Sinek explains it succinctly in his work, and attaching meaning to their need for "why" establishes a cause greater than themselves, their pay, or their current condition. The sense of sacrifice and service is as relevant today as ever. It is incumbent upon us as leaders of our organizations to discover the voice for relaying this message to our employees and re-introduce them to the reasons they played cops as kids, admired them as teens and joined them as adults.

Chiefs, if you are wondering what you should be thinking about, please take note. Catch them early in the career, do not overlook the significance of your influence and opportunity to meet with potential candidates, recently hired cadets, proud graduating rookies, and fully field trained officers. Brief one-on-one moments spent sharing your vision and level of expected commitment burn an indelible image on the public service psyche of these officers.

Does "what" I think about matter? Maybe not. What does matter is "why" I think about it. That is because we have been commissioned to grow the next generation of public servants, and without specificity of focus on the core tenants of sacrificial service, we remain numbingly regular and amazingly ineffective. That's why.

Source: Article written for Executive Leadership section by Chief Scott Silverii, PhD and posted November 12, 2012 at Law Enforcement Today online website. *Source:* Reprinted with permission of Dr. Scott Silverii for *Cop Culture: Why Good Cops Go Bad.*

AFTERWORD

I look back over the more than 25 year career, and yet I can recall my meeting with the Sheriff who gave me that first opportunity in law enforcement. Remaining vividly in my memory is that day and still my stomach begins to pine with the same sense of nervousness it did that morning as I pinned the Silver Star to my freshly pressed uniform shirt.

I love the job. I love the career. I love the experiences I have enjoyed, created and survived. I hope I have made a positive difference in the lives of the public I served and the fellow officers I served with. Sure, there has been plenty of heartache and difficulty, but that is the case in any life fully lived.

I began this book with an account of a crisis leading me on this journey of exploration as to why cops behave the way we do. Although the years have passed since the day of lifting my arms to see pools of blood staining my uniform shirt, I remember that event with a clarity of focus. It continues to inspire me.

It was not a stab or gunshot wound, but it was just as damaging. I was sitting in the office looking through my cell phone. I realized that within the hundreds of contacts, there were only five civilians who were not friends or family. At that very moment I realized I had become a victim to the cop culture's greatest enemy; isolation. I had unknowingly fell for the hype "that no one understands but my brothers," and eventually, ever so gradually, I eliminated anyone not related or associated through policing from my personal life.

The blood source was much less dramatic than other serious injuries I have sustained through the years, though it remains a wound requiring healing. After 16 years working special operations groups, placing myself in the most dangerous situations for the sake of ensuring the safety of my officers and community, I now sat behind a desk.

The field work, the adrenaline, the risk and the rush were gone. I had become an administrator, and alone at my desk. The blood came from the open wounds from the friction caused between the arms of the executive office chair and my elbows. The blood stains and the cell phone contact list became a reality almost too much to accept. It was not the question of who had I become, but what happened to the person I was? Sitting there in silence as the busy hallway outside my office door buzzed with activity, I asked the one word, life changing question; "Why?"

This culture is surely an interesting thing. It is even more so when examined from a lens of intimate experience, objective distance and studied reference. It serves the purpose for bringing us together, pulling us apart, and moving us in a direction despite the natural confluence to flee danger.

We can revolutionize the process of becoming blue with thoughtfulness of action and clarity of vision. We can redefine the cop culture by focusing on the most positive elements of public service. This generation of dark blue officers can be the last. Share this vision by joining the cultural revolution.

Stay Blue

I wish to thank the officers who have trusted me with their stories, their secrets and their hopes for a better way. I have honored our agreement; and your names, agencies and identities will never pass my lips. The job we do is difficult enough, without skepticism from those who have never bloodied the uniform giving it everything or willing to give it all. Thank you for your service to our country and community.

Mostly, I thank my family and friends who have known my passion for policing was also my burden. Your patience and interest in this multi-year journey, and my multi-decade adventure is a testament to your shared commitment to improving the culture of policing.

To my sons, I apologize for being cop more than dad, and I only trust that you will see my sacrifices as noble and benefiting the greater good.

ABOUT THE AUTHOR

Chief of Police Scott Silverii, Ph.D. is passionate about positive change. Over twenty-five years in policing gives Chief Silverii the experience and vision to believe there is always a better way. Scott spent 16 years working in policing's special operations groups (SOG) with years of undercover narcotics and SWAT missions.

His passion for the public service flourished while growing up in south Louisiana's heart of Cajun Country. His life is seasoned by the Mardi Gras, hurricanes, oil spills, humidity, and crawfish boils. This gumbo of experience serves up a unique perspective in his writing.

Dr. Silverii attended the University of Southern Mississippi

(Hattiesburg, MS.), then completed his Bachelor's Degree from Nicholls State University (Thibodaux, Louisiana). Twelve years later, he earned a Master of Public Administration (University of New Orleans, Louisiana) and a Ph.D. (University of New Orleans, Louisiana) all while working as a full-time law enforcement officer, then Chief of Police. He shares that perseverance and sacrifice can accomplish anything if you want it badly enough.

Research for his doctoral dissertation, A Darker Shade of Blue: From Public Servant to Professional Deviant forms the core for this book, and is complimented by the years of cross-country travel for interviews and observations. He combines these experiences with academic research to bring you the best and most compelling details of what life is like behind the thin blue line.

Lets Connect:
scottsilverii.com
scottsilverii@gmail.com

INSERTS & CREDITS

- Insert 1 – Photograph from Scott Silverii
- Insert 2 – Photograph from Scott Silverii
- Insert 3 – Internet image from anonymous source
- Insert 4 – Blue Line T-Shirts & Products
- Insert 5 – Blue Line T-Shirts & Products
- Insert 6 – Photograph from Emily Schwarze (Staff/houmatoday.com, 4-29-11)
- Insert 7 – Photograph from Emily Schwarze (Staff/houmatoday.com, 4-29-11)
- Insert 8 – Photograph from Emily Schwarze (Staff/houmatoday.com, 4-29-11)
- Insert 9 – Photograph from Scott Silverii
- Insert 10 – Image from AR15.com (anonymous Operator)
- Insert 11 – Image from driodforums.net
- Insert 12 – Image from Scott Silverii
- Insert 13 – Image from Scott Silverii
- Insert 14 – Image from Scott Silverii
- Insert 15 – Image from Blue Line T-shirts & Products
- Insert 16 - Photograph from Emily Schwarze (Staff/houmatoday.com, 4-29-11)

INSERTS & CREDITS

- Insert 17 – Six images from public access sites on World Wide Web.

BIBLIOGRAPHY

- All Family Resources, (2005). Depression: A serious but treatable illness. Retrieved June 20, 2011, from http://www.familymanagement.com/aging/depression.html
- American Foundation for Suicide Prevention, (2010). Risk factors for suicide. Retrieved October 19, 2010, from: http://www.afsp.org
- Americas Most Wanted, (2012). Fugitives: Dan William Hiers. Retrieved July 18, 2012, from:http://www.amw.com/fugitives/case.cfm?id=30956
- Armakolas, I., (2001). A Field Trip to Bosnia: The Dilemmas of the First-Time Researcher. In M. Smyth & G. Robinson (Ed.), Researching Violently Divided Societies; Ethical and Methodological Issues, 165-184. Tokyo, New York, Paris, United Nations University Press.
- Ashforth, B, and Saks, A., (1996). Socialization tactics: longitudinal effects on newcomer adjustment. The academy of management journal, 39(1), 30. August 3, 2011, from www.stopthemadness. org/cops.html
- Babbie, E., (2007). The practice of social research. California: Thomas Wadsworth Publishing.

- Barker, J., (2005). Danger, duty and disillusionment. Los Angeles: McGraw Hill.
- Bassler, W., (2011). FACTfinding: How often do police commit sexual offenses? Retrieved June 8, 2012, from: http://constitutionaldefense.org/?p=3779
- Bauer, K., (2011). Cop pulling dare trailer charged with dui. Retrieved August, 11, 2011, fromhttp://www.wave3.com/story/15170315/cop-pulling-dare-trailer-chargedwith-dui
- Beede, B., (2008). The roles of paramilitary and militarized police. Journal of Political and Military Sociology, 36(1), 10.
- Beidelman, T., (1991). E.E Evans-Pritchard; International Dictionary of Anthropologists. New York: Garland Publishing.
- Benjamin, B.E., & Werner, R. (2012). You and your nervous system: How stress affects your body. Health Touch News, 6, 1-4.
- Birzer, M., (1999). Police training in the 21st century. F.B.I. Law Enforcement Bulletin, p. 68.
- Birzer, M., (2003). The theory of andragogy applied to police training. Policing: An International Journal of Police Strategies and Management, Vol. 26.
- Birzer, M., (2008). What makes a good police officer? Phenomenological reflections from the African-American community. Taylor and Francis Publishing
- Boas, F., (1940). Race, Language, and Culture. Chicago: University of Chicago Press.
- Brannan, T., (2001). When the batterer is a cop: Domestic violence in police families. Retrieved November 8, 2010, from: http://www.purpleberets.org/violence_police_families.html
- Britz, M., (1997). The police subculture and occupational socialization: exploring individual and demographic characteristics. American Journal of Criminal Justice, 21(2)
- Brown, L., (2009). Memphis police Officers charged with dui

Bibliography

will get a second Chance. Retrieved August 8, 2011, from http://www.wmctv.com/story/11705724/Memphis-police-officerscharged-with-dui-will-get-secondchance?redirected=true100
- Canberra, A. National Drug Strategy, (1996). National drug strategy household survey: survey report 1995. Canberra, Australia: Australian Government Publishing Service.
- Cao, L., (2002). Curbing police brutality: What works? A reanalysis of citizen complaints at the organizational level. Michigan: Eastern Michigan University
- CBS 2 Chicago, (2013). Two Investigators, BGA: Suburban Cops Form Motorcycle Club. Retrieved June 19, 2013 from http://chicago.cbslocal.com/2013/02/19/2-investigators-suburban-cops-form-motorcycle-club/
- Klockars, C., Kutnjak-Ivkovich, S., Harver, W. and Habrfeld, M. (2000). "The Measurement of Police Integrity." National Institute of Justice in Brief: pp. 1 - 17.
- Carter, P., (2011). Rapists with badges. Retrieved July 17, 2012, from: http://www.copblock.org/1813/rapists-with-a-badge/
- CBS Local Media., (2011). Update: Outrage after drunk cop gets 8 years for dui that killed four. Retrieved August 2, 2011, fromhttp://stlouis.cbslocal.com/ 2011/03/11/former-sunset-hills-officer-gets-8-yearsfor-dui/
- CBS Modesto, (2012). Former Modesto police officer charged with sexual assault 03/15/former-modesto-police-officer-charged-with-sexual-assault-while-on-duty/ while on duty. Retrieved June 17, 2012, from: http://sacramento.cbslocal.com/2012/
- Center for Disease Control, (2011).Injury prevention and control: Motor vehicle safety. Retrieved August 10, 2011, from http://www.cdc.gov/ motorvehiclessafety/impaired_driving/impaireddrv_factsheet.html101
- Chemerinsky, E., (2001). An Independent analysis of the Los Angeles Police Department's board of inquiry's report on the

rampart scandal. Loyola of Los Angeles Law Review, January edition, Vol. 34:545, pp: 545-656.
- Clark, J, Jackson, M, Schaefer, P, and Sharpe, E., (2000). Training swat teams: implications for improving tactical units. Journal of Criminal Justice, 28.5: pp. 407-413
- Cornell University Law School., (n.d.). 42 USC § 16911. Retrieved June 18, 2012, from:
- Country=en_US&PageId=4615
  http://www.law.cornell.edu/uscode/text/42/16911
- Crank, J., (1998). Understanding police culture. Cincinnati: Anderson Publishing Company.
- Creswell, J., (1994). Research Design: qualitative and quantitative approaches. SAGE Publications, Inc., ISBN 978-0-8039-52546.
- Creswell, J., (1998). Qualitative Inquiry and Research Design; Choosing Among Five Traditions. London, New Delhi, Thousand Oaks, Sage Publications. ISBN 978-1412916073
- Creswell, J., (2002). Educational research: Planning, conducting, and evaluating quantitative and qualitative approaches to research. London, New Delhi, Thousand Oaks, Sage Publications. ISBN 978-0131367395
- Creswell, J., (2003). Research Design, qualitative, Quantitative and Mixed Methods. Second Edition, SAGE Publications, Inc., ISBN 0-7619-2441-8.
- Creswell, J., (2007). Qualitative inquiry and Research design. Choosing among the five approaches. Second Edition, SAGE Publications, Inc., ISBN 978-1-4129-1607.
- Creswell, J., (2009). Research Design, qualitative, quantitative, and mixed methods. Third Edition, SAGE Publications, Inc., ISBN 978-1-4129-6557-6.
- Department of Mental Health, (2006). Erasing the stigma of mental illness. Retrieved June 22, 2011, from http:www.state.sc.us/dmh/erasing_stigma.htm
- DePaulo, J. R., Jr., & Horvitz, L.A., (2002). Understanding

depression: What we know and what you can do about it. Hoboken, NJ: John Wiley & Sons, Inc.
- Diamond, D., (2003). Departmental barriers to mental health treatment: A precursor to police 54-65). Springfield, IL: Charles C. Thomas.
- Douglas, R., (1997). Death with no valor. Keener Marketing, Inc.
- Edds, K., (2010). Anaheim cop notches three dui arrests in a year - and is still on
- enforcement suicide. Minnetonka, MN: Global Health Care Systems. Retrieved August 2, 2011 from http://taxdollars.ocregister.com/2010/03 /12/Anaheim-cop-notches-three-duisin-a-year-while-on-payroll/53067/ payroll.,
- Farkus, G., (1986). Stress in Undercover Policing. Psychological Services for Law Enforcement. Washington, DC: United States Government Printing Office.
- Farmer, S., Beehr, T. and Love, K., (2003). "Becoming an Undercover Police Officer: A Note on Fairness Perceptions, Behavior, and Attitudes." Journal of Organizational Behavior 24: pp. 373 - 387.
- Feagin, Orum and Sjoberg, (1991). A case for the case study. The University of North Carolina Press. February 22, 2013, from: http://health-information.advanceweb.com/Features
- Federal Bureau of Investigations, (2009). Some good news, crime is declining. FBI Unified Crime Report for 2008, FBI website; http://www.gov/news/stories/2009/ january/ucr_stats011209
- Federal Bureau of Investigations, (2009). National Gang Threat Assessment. The National Gang Intelligence Center, Jamestown,
- Feldman, D., (1976). A contingency theory of socialization. Administrative Science Quarterly, September, 19.
- Fetterman, D., (1998). Ethnography: Step by step. 2nd edition. Newbury Park, CA: Sage.
- Fitzgerald, P., (2002). Crisis Manual: Crisis Intervention Plan

for Police Departments and Undercover Law Enforcement Personnel. Police Crisis Intervention Manual. Chaminade University. Honolulu: Chaminade University.
- Fitzgerald, P., (2002). Undercover Officers at the Honolulu Police Department. Behavioral Survey. Chaminade University. Honolulu: Chaminade University.
- Gall, M., Borg, W. and Gall, J., (1996). Educational Research: An Introduction (6th ed.). White Plains, NY: Longman.
- Girodo, M., (1991). Drug Corruption in Undercover Agents: Measuring Risk. Behavioral Sciences and the Law, 9, 9. Pp. 361 - 370
- Girodo, M., (1997). Undercover agent assessment centers: crafting vice and virtue for imposters. Journal of Social Behavior and Personality, 12(5), 23. Pp. 237-260
- Girodo, M., (2002). Dissociative-type identity disturbances in undercover agents: socio-cognitive factors behind false identity appearances and reenactments. Social Behavior and Personality, 30(7), pp. 631 - 644
- Girresch, L., (2012). Belleville detective, found passed put behind the wheel in Mascoutah, said he was on cold medicine. Retrieved March 02, 2012, from www.bnd.com /2012/03/02/2082643/belleville-detective-found-passed.html#disqus_thread
- Gruber, J., (1970). Ethnographic Salvage and the Shaping of Anthropology. American Anthropologist, New Series, Vol. 72(6).
- Hazer, J, and Alvares, K., (1981). Police work values during organizational entry and assimilation. Journal of Applied Psychology, 66(1), 6.
- Heim, C., Nater, U.M., Maloney, E., Boneva, R., Jones, J.F., & Reeves, W.C., (2009). Childhood trauma and risk for chronic fatigue syndrome: Association with neuroendoctrine dysfunction. Archives of General Psychiatry, 66(1), pp. 72-80.
- Henry, V., (1995). The police officer as survivor: death

confrontations and the police subculture. Behavorial Sciences and the Law, 13, 19.
- Henry, V., (2004). Death work: Police, trauma, and the psychology of survival. New York: Oxford University Press.
- Henry, V., (1995). "The Police Officer as Survivor: Death Confrontations and the Police Subculture." Behavoioral Sciences and the Law 13: pp. 93 - 112.
- Hill, C., Knox, S., Thompson, B., Nutt Williams, E., Hess, S. and Ladany, N., (2005). Consensual Qualitative Research: An Update. Marquette University: Education Faculty Research and Publications.
- Hughes, F. and Andre, L., (2007). Problem Officer Variables and Early-Warning Systems. The Chief, 74(10).
- Illescas, C., (2011). Aurora panel reinstates cop fired for off-duty DUI arrests. Retrieved August 16, 2011, from: http://www.denverpost.com/news/ci_18203984?source=rss
- Illinois Secretary of State, (2012). Driving under the influence: Zero tolerance/underage driving. Retrieved February 14, 2012, fromwww.cyberdriveillinois.com/departments/drivers/traffic_safety/driving_under_under_the_influence/uselose.html
- Illinois State Police, (2012). Illinois state police murderer and violent offender against youth is key. Baltimore, MD: Retrieved July 1, 2012, from: http://www.isp.state.il.us/cmvo/cmvofaq.cfm
- Ivkovic, S., (2003). To serve and collect: measuring police corruption. The Journal of Criminal Law and Criminology, 93(23), 57. Pp. 593 - 650
- Jacobs, B., (1997). Contingent Ties: Undercover Drug Officers' Use of Informants. The London School of Economics and Political Science, 48(1), 19. Pp. 35-53
- Jamison, K., (1999). Night falls fast: Understanding suicide. New York: Vintage Books.
- Janis, I., (1972). Victims of groupthink: A psychological study

- of foreign policy decisions and fiascoes. Boston: Houghton Mifflin Company. ISBN 978-0-3951-40444
- Janis, I., (1982). Groupthink: A psychological study of policy decisions and fiascoes. Boston: Houghton Mifflin Company. ISBN 978-0-395-31704-4
- Johnson, L., (1991). On the front lines: police stress and family well-being. Proceedings of the House of Representatives, 102st congress, first session. hearing before the select committee on children, youth, and families (pp. 32-48). Washington, DC: United States Government Printing Office.
- Johnson, O., (2011). Blue wall of silence: Perceptions of the influence of training on law
- June 3, 2012, from: http://ezinearticles.com/?Is-Your-Child-a-Sex-Offenders-Target?-
- Kappelar, P., (1997). Militarizing American police: the rise and normalization of paramilitary units. Society for the Study of Social Problems, 44(1), 18.
- Kessler, R., Chiu, W., Demler, O., & Walters, E., (June, 2005). Prevalence, severity, and comorbidity of twelve-month DSM-IV disorders in the national comorbidity survey replication. Archives of General Psychiatry, 62(6), pp. 617-627.
- Klockars, C., Kutnjak-Ivkovich, S, Harver, W. and Habrfeld, M., (2000). The Measurement of Police Integrity. National Institute of Justice in Brief, 17.
- Kolman, J., (1982). A guide to the development of special weapons and tactics teams. Springfield: Springfield: Charles C. Thomas Publishing.
- Kraska, P., (1997). Grounded research into U.S. paramilitary policing: Forging the iron fist inside the velvet glove. Policing and Society, No. 7.
- Lauder, M., (2003). Covert Participant Observation of a Deviant Community: Justifying the Use of Deception. Journal of Contemporary Religion, 18(2).
- Levenson, J. & Harris, A., (2011). 100,000 sex offenders missing...or are they? 2012, from:

Bibliography

- http://www.ovsom.texas.gov/docs/100000-Sex-Offender-Missing-or-Are- Deconstruction of an urban legend. Criminal Justice: Policy Review. Retrieved July 17,
- Librett, M., (2006). Biker: Wild Pigs and Outlaws - What's the Difference and Are the Police a Deviant Subculture? American Society of Criminology, New York: SAGE Publications. Pp. 257 - 269
- Lincoln, Y. and Guba, E., (1985). Naturalistic Inquiry. Newbury Park, CA: Sage.
- Lincoln, Y., and Guba, E., (2000). Paradigmatic controversies, contradictions and emerging confluences. In N. K. Denzin & Y. S. Lincoln (Eds.), Handbook of Qualitative Research (2nd ed., pp. 163-188). Thousand Oaks, CA: Sage Publications, Inc.
- Longthorne, J., (2010). Traffic fatalities in 2010 drop to lowest level in recorded history, National Highway Traffic Safety Administration, NHTSA journal 05-11, website; http://www.nhtsa.gov /PR/NHTSA-05-11
- Los Angeles Times, (1999), "A Secret Society Among Lawmen", Orange County Edition.
- Manning, P., (1980). Violence and the Police Role. American Academy of Political and Social Science, 45(2), 19. Pp. 135 - 144
- Marx, G., (1988). Undercover police surveillance in America. Berkley: University of California Press.
- Maslow, A., (1943). A theory of human motivation. Psychological Review, 50(4), 26.
- Matza, D. and Sykes, G., (2009). Delinquency and Drift. New Brunswick: Transaction Publishers. Originally printed by John Wiley and Sons (1964).
- Matza, D. and Sykes, G., (1957). Techniques of neutralization. American Sociological Review, 22:664-70.
- Maxfield, M and Babbie, E., (2005). Research methods for criminal justice and criminology (4th ed.). Belmont, CA: Wadsworth.
- Mayo Clinic, (2011). Depression (major depression):

Definition. Retrieved June 19, 2011, from http://www.mayoclinic.com/heath/depression/DS00175
- McCaslin, Metzler, Best, Liberman, Weiss, Fagan and Marmar, (2006). Alexithymia and PTSD Symptoms in Urban Police Officers: Cross-Sectional and Prospective Findings. Journal of Traumatic Stress, Vol. 19 (3), pp. 361–373
- McKittrick, R. Major, (1984). An Analysis of Organizational Socialization in the Marine Corps. The United States Marine Corps Command Staff and College, Quantico, Virginia.
- Medical College of Wisconsin, (2012). Public safety: Sex-offenses forcible. Retrieved June 21, 2012, from: http://www.mcw.edu/display/docid20082.htm#.UAXwmI5DufQ
- Merleau-Ponty, M., (1962). Phenomenology of perceptions (C. Smith, Trans.). London: Routledge. Millstadt, IL: PCT Research Publications.
- Moghaddam, A., (2006). Coding issues in grounded theory. Issues In Educational Research, Vol. 16. The University of Western Ontario.
- Moore, J., (2004). Visions of culture; an introduction to anthropological theories and theorists. Lantham: AltaMire Press, Rowan and Littlefield Publishers, Inc.
- Moore, J., (2009). Visions of culture. United Kingdom: AltiMira Press.
- Moustakas, C., (1994). Phenomenological research methods. Thousand Oaks, CA: Sage.
- Myers, K., Forest, K. and Miller, S., (2004). Officer Friendly and the Tough Cop: Gays and Lesbians Navigate Homophobia and Policing. Journal of Homosexuality, 47(1), 20.
- National Center for Missing and Exploited Children, (2012). Number of registered sex
- offenders in the U.S. nears three-quarters of a million. Retrieved July 17, 2012, from:
- http://www.missingkids.com/missingkids/servlet/NewsEventServlet?Language

Bibliography

- Country=en_US&PageId=4615
- National Criminal Justice Reference, (2008). United States Department of Justice, Office of Justice Programs. Women and policing Washington, DC: National Center for Policing and Women. Retrieved from www.http://womenandpolicing.org/violenceFS.asp>
- National Highway Traffic Safety Administration, (2010). Alcohol-impaired driving. Retrieved August 1, 2011, fromhttp://www-nrd.nhtsa.dot.gov/Pubs/811385.PDF
- Johnson, O., (2008). National Police Suicide Foundation. Introduction: Understanding the problem is key. Baltimore, MD.
- Johnson, O., (2009). National Institute of Mental Health. The numbers count: Mental disorders in America. Bethesda, MD
- National Tactical Officers Association, (2008). NTOA SWAT Standards for Law Enforcement Agencies.
- Neddermeyer, D., (2012). Is your child a sex offender's target? – Learn the ruse. Retrieved Learn-Their-Ruse&id=262274
- Neidig, P., Russell, H. and Seng, A., (1992). Interspousal Aggression in Law Enforcement Families: A Preliminary Investigation." Police Studies, 8.
- Obst, P., Davey, J. and Sheehan, M., (2001). Does Joining the Police Drive You to Drink? A Longitudinal Study of the Drinking Habits of Police Recruits. Queensland University of Technology. Queensland: Taylor and Francis Publishing.
- Pelfrey, W., (2007), Local Law Enforcement Terrorism Prevention Efforts: A State Case Study. Journal of Criminal Justice, Vol. 35, Issue 3, May – June, 2007, pp. 313 - 321.
- Polkinghorne, D., (1989). Phenomenological research methods. In R.S. Valle & S. Halling (Eds.), Existential–phenomenological perspectives in psychology (pp. 41–60). New York: Plenum.
- Punch. M., (2009). Police corruption: deviance, accountability and reform in policing. Willan Publishing; United Kingdom. ISBN 978-1-84392-410-4

Bibliography

- Queen, W., (2005). Under and Alone. New York: Random House.
- Quinn, M., (Performer), (2004). Police work corrupted by culture of silence [Radio series episode]. Minnesota Public Radio. Minneapolis: NPR. 28 October 2004
- Quinnet, P., (1998). QPR. FBI Law Enforcement Bulletin.
- Rudd, E. and Descartes, L., (2008). The changing landscape of work and family in the American middle-class. United Kingdom: Lexington Books.
- Sanders, G., (2002). Good Officer's Gone Bad: PTSD Issues for Police Officers. pp.1-3.
- Seattle PI Investigations, (2007). A broken systems works in favor of cops busted for DUI. Retrieved January 12, 2012, fromwww.seattlepi.com/news/article/A-brokensystem-works-in-favor-of-cops-busted-for-1245747.php#photo-677368
- Seebohm, T., (2004). Hermeneutics; methods and methodology. Netherlands: Kluwer Academic Publishers.
- Senna, J. and Siegal, L., (2010). Introduction to Criminal Justice, Twelfth Edition. Wadsworth, Cenage Learning; Canada. ISBN 978-0-495-599977-7. sensitive pedagogy. London, ON: The Althouse Press.
- Siddle, B., (1995). Sharpening the warrior's edge: The psychology & science of training.
- Simon, B, and Pettigrew, T., (1990). Social identity and perceived group homogeneity: evidence for the in-group homogeneity group. European Journal of Social Psychology, 20, 19.
- Sipkoff, M., (2006). Depression in the workplace costs employers billions per year: Employers take lead in fighting depression. Managed Care Magazine, 1(1), pp. 1-22.
- Smith, M., Jaffe-Gill, E., Segal, J., Segal, R., (2011). Preventing burnout: Signs, symptoms, and coping strategies. Retrieved June 22, 2011, from http://www.helpguide.org/ mental/ burnout_signs_symptoms.htm

- Stack, C., (1974). All our kin: Strategies for survival in a black community. New York, NY: Haper & Row, Publishers.
- Stopthemadness.org, (2011). *Stop the madness: Cops busted for drunk driving.* Retrieved
- Strategies & Management, 30(2), 168-88.
- Sun, I., Triplett, R. and Gainey, R., (2004). Social disorganization, legitimacy of local institutions, and neighborhood crime: An exploratory study of perceptions of the police and local
- The Hammer Law Firm, LLC, (2011). Former Missouri police officer sentenced for fatal dui crash. Retrieved August 2, 2011, fromhttp://www.missouricriminallawattorney.com /2011/03/former-missouri-police-officersentenced-for-fatal-dui-crash.shtml-They- 2011.pdf
- Turner, V., (1967). Forest of symbols. Ithica: Cornell University Press.
- Tylor, E., (1865). Researches into the early history of mankind and the development of civilization. London.
- U.S. Census Bureau, (2010). Map of registered sex offenders in the U.S. Retrieved July 17, 2012from: http://www.missingkids.com/en_US/documents/sex-offender-map.pdf
- Ulmer, J., (1994). Revisiting Stebbins: Labeling and Commitment to Deviance. The Sociological Quarterly, 35(1), 22. Pp. 135 - 157
- United States Department of Health and Human Services, (2010). Depression. Retrieved June 20, 2011, from http://www.athealth.com/Consumer/disorders/nih_depression.html
- United States Department of Justice, (2010). Justice News, Office of Public Affairs, December 10, 2010 at World Wide Web:http//justice.gov
- United States Department of Justice, (2011). Justice News, Office of Public Affairs, September 14, 2011 at World Wide Web:http//justice.gov
- Van Maanen, J., (1975). Police socialization: a longitudinal

examination of job attitudes in an urban police department. Administrative Science Quarterly, 1975, 21. Pp. 207-228.
- Van Maanen, M., (1997). Researching lived experience: human science for an action
- Vroom, V. (1964). Work and motivation. John Wiley and Sons, Inc., New York.
- Walker, S., (2005). The new world of police accountability. Sage Publications, Inc., Thousand Oaks: California.
- Walker, S. and Katz, C., (2008). The police in America: an introduction. Sixth edition. New York: The McGraw-Hill Companies, Incorporated.
- Walker, S., Alpert, G. and Kenney, D., (2011). Early Warning System: Responding to the Problem Police Officer. Research. United States Department of Justice. Washington, D.C.: Office of Justice Programs.
- Walker, S., Milligan, S. and Berke, A., (2005). Supervision and Intervention Within Early Intervention Systems: A Guide for Law Enforcement Chief Executives. United States Department of Justice. Washington, D.C.: Office of Community Oriented Policing Services.
- Walker, S., Spohn, C. and DeLone, M., (2000). The color of justice: Race, ethnicity and crime in America. Stamford, CT: Wadsworth.
- Warner, S., (2012). Feeling chronically unappreciated can lead to burnout. Retrieved June 16, 2011, http://health-information.advanceweb.com/Features/Articles/Feeling-Chronically-Unappreciated-can-Lead-to-Burnout.aspx
- Washington University School of Medicine. (n.d.). Depression facts. Retrieved June 16, 2011, from http://www.psychiatry.wustl.edu/depression/depression_facts.htm
- Wasilewski, M., & Olson, A., (2010). Depression in law enforcement: What is it & what do you do about it? Retrieved June 20, 2011, from http://www.lawofficer.com/article/leadership /depression-law-enforcement

- Waters, J.A., & Ussery, W., (2007). Police stress: History, contributing factors, symptoms, and interventions. Policing: An International Journal of Police
- Weber, M., (1947). The theory of social and economic organization. Translated by Henderson, A. and Parsons, T. The Free Press.
- Weiss, R., (1994). Learning From Strangers; The Art and Method of Qualitative Interview Studies. New York, The Free Press.
- Weiss, S., (2005). Study: U.S. leads in mental illness, lags in treatment. Retrieved June 21, 2011, from http://www.washingtonpost.com/wp-dyn/conetent/article/2005/06/06/
- Westwood, J., (2002). Police Culture and the "Code of Silence." Police Act and Code of Professional Conduct, 8.
- Wolcott, H., (1994). Transforming qualitative data. Description, analysis, and interpretation. SAGE Publications, Inc., ISBN 0-8039-5280-5.
- World Health Organization, (2011).
- Mental Health: Depression. Retrieved 6-22-11 from http://www.who.int/
- Worth, T., (2010). Why is your job making you depressed? Retrieved 6-20-11 from http://www.cnn.com/
- Yin, R., (1993). Applications of case study research. London, New Delhi, Thousand Oaks, Sage Publications
- Zerubavel, E., (2006). The elephant in the room: Silence and denial in everyday life. NY: Oxford University Press.

NOTES

1. The Blue Line Mystique

1. Manning, P. (1980)
2. Manning, P. (1980)
3. Librett, M. (2006)
4. Turner, V. (1967)
5. Turner, V. (1967)
6. Punch. M. (2009)
7. Punch. M. (2009)
8. Matza, D. and Sykes, G., (1957)
9. Janis, I. (1972)

2. Special Operations Groups

1. Fitzgerald, (2002)
2. Gironde, (2002)
3. Clark, (2000)
4. Clark, (2000)
5. Colman, (1982)
6. Kreskas, & Appealer, (1997)
7. Appear, (1997)
8. Bede, (2008)
9. Palfrey, (2007)
10. Appear, (1997)

3. Studying a Secret Culture

1. (Ivkovic, 2003; Klochars,(2000)
2. Klochars (2000) and Ivkovic (2003)
3. Ivkovic, S. (2003)
4. Ivkovic, S. (2003)
5. Walker, S. and Katz, C., (2008)
6. Klockars, C., Kutnjak-Ivkovich, S, Harver, W. and Habrfeld, M., (2000)
7. Girodo, M. (1991)
8. Girodo, M. (1991)
9. Librett, M. (2006)
10. Girodo, M. (1991)
11. Fitzgerald, P. (2002)

12. Barker, J. (2005)
13. (Department of Justice, (2011).
14. Federal Bureau of Investigations (2009)
15. Federal Bureau of Investigations (2009)

4. History of Policing in America

1. Hess and Othman (2009)
2. Hess and Othman (2009)
3. Walker and Katz (2008)
4. Silver (1967)
5. Walker and Katz (2008)
6. Walker and Katz, 2008
7. Walker and Katz (2008)
8. Bailey (1996)
9. Walker and Katz, (2005)
10. Sienna and Siegel, (1990)
11. Walker and Katz (2008)
12. Sienna and Siegel (1990)
13. Lang worthy and Travis (2007)
14. Sienna and Siegel (1990)
15. (Sienna and Siegel, (1990, p. 187)
16. (Walker and Katz, (2005, p. 28)
17. Walker and Katz (2005)
18. Walker (1999)
19. Walker and Katz (2008)
20. Walker, (1999,p.32)

5. Occupational Socialization

1. Feldman, D. (1976)
2. Feldman, D. (1976)
3. Johnson, L. (1991)
4. Neidig, P.H., Russell, H.E., and Seng, A.F. (1992)
5. Quinnet, P. (1998)
6. Feldman, D. (1976)
7. Ashforth, B, and Saks, A. (1996)
8. Hazer, J, and Alvares, K. (1981)
9. McKittrick, R. Major (1984)
10. Van Maanen, J. (1975)
11. Ashforth, B, and Saks, A. (1996)
12. Van Maanen, J. (1975)
13. McKittrick, R. Major (1984)
14. McKittrick, R. Major (1984)

Notes

15. Van Maanen, J. (1975)
16. Hazer, J, and Alvares, K. (1981)
17. Feldman, D. (1976)
18. Hazer, J, and Alvares, K. (1981)

6. Why Cops Quit

1. Hazer, J, and Alvares, K. (1981)
2. Maslow, A., (1943)
3. Hazer, J, and Alvares, K. (1981)
4. Van Maanen, J. (1975)
5. Van Maanen, J. (1975)
6. Van Maanen, J. (1975)
7. Van Maanen, J. (1975)
8. Turner, V. (1967)
9. Van Maanen, J. (1975, p. 207)
10. Vroom, V. (1964)
11. Vroom, V. (1964, p.224)
12. Van Maanen, J. (1975)
13. Van Maanen, J. (1975, p. 225)
14. Van Maanen, J. (1975)
15. McKittrick, R. Major (1984)
16. Ashforth, B, and Saks, A. (1996)

7. Anti-Diversity In the Ranks

1. Simon, B, and Pettigrew, T. (1990)
2. Britz, M. (1997)
3. Myers, K.A., Forest, K.B., and Miller, S.L. (2004)
4. Armed Forces and Society (2000)
5. Simon, B, and Pettigrew, T. (1990)
6. Simon, B, and Pettigrew, T. (1990)
7. Britz, M. (1997)
8. Myers, K.A., Forest, K.B., and Miller, S.L. (2004)
9. Britz, M. (1997).
10. Britz, M. (1997, p.01)
11. Britz, M. (1997)
12. Myers, K.A., Forest, K.B., and Miller, S.L. (2004)
13. (Connell, 1997)
14. Myers, K.A., Forest, K.B., and Miller, S.L. (2004)
15. Armed Forces and Society (2000)
16. Feldman, D. (1976).
17. Van Maanen, J. (1975).
18. Ashforth, B, and Saks, A. (1996).

Notes

8. Police Culture

1. Crank, J. (1998)
2. Walker, S. and Katz, C., (2008)
3. Walker, S. and Katz, C., (2008)
4. Walker, S. (2005)
5. Ivkovic, S. (2003)
6. Ivkovic, S. (2003,p. 593)
7. Klockars, C., Kutnjak-Ivkovich, S, Harver, W. and Habrfeld, M., (2000)
8. Westwood's (2002)
9. Westwood (2002)
10. Westwood, J. (2002)
11. Quinn, M (Performer) (2004)
12. Quinn, M (2004,P.27)
13. Obst, P., Davey, J. and Sheehan, M. (2001)
14. Manning, P. (1980)
15. Ulmer, J. (1994)
16. Librett, M. (2006)
17. Obst, P., Davey, J. and Sheehan, M. (2001)
18. Canberra, A. National Drug Strategy, (1996)
19. Canberra, A. National Drug Strategy, (1996)
20. Obst, P., Davey, J. and Sheehan, M. (2001)
21. Barker, J. (2005)
22. Janis, I. (1972)
23. Ulmer, J. (1994)
24. Ulmer, J. (1994)
25. Girodo (1997; 2002)
26. Girodo, M. (1997)
27. Girodo, M. (2002)
28. Girodo, M. (2002)
29. Bennet v. Commonwealth of Virginia (1997)
30. Girodo, M. (1997)
31. Fitzgerald, P. (2002)
32. Fitzgerald, P. (2002)
33. Fitzgerald (2002)
34. Farkus (1983)
35. Fitzgerald (2002)
36. Fitzgerald (2002)
37. Grossman, (2009)

9. State Sponsored Violence

1. Manning, P. (1980)
2. Manning, P. (1980)

Notes

3. Manning, P. (1980)
4. Van Maanan, (1975)
5. Librett (2005)
6. Walker, Alpert, and Kenney (2001)
7. Librett (2005)
8. Bittner (1970)
9. Bittner, (1970, p. 100)
10. Gallagher, Maguire, Mastrofski, and Reisig, (2001)
11. Mastrofski, (1988)
12. Manning, (1980)
13. Manning, (1980, p. 135)
14. Rosenblatt, (2001)
15. McEwen (1996)
16. National Institute of Justice (2009)
17. Manning (1980)
18. Manning, (1980, p. 136)
19. Manning, P. (1980)
20. Manning, (1980, p.142)
21. Clark, Jackson, Schaefer and Sharpe (2000)
22. Clark, Jackson, Schaefer and Sharpe, 2000
23. Kraska and Kappeler's, (1997)
24. Pelfrey's (2007)
25. Manning (1997)
26. Ulmer (1994)
27. Westwood (2002)

10. Policing the Police

1. Walker, S., Alpert, G. and Kenney, D. (2001)
2. Hughes, F. and Andre, L. (2007)
3. Frontline Report (1996)
4. Walker (2001)
5. Walker (2001)
6. Hughes and Andre (2007)
7. Hughes and Andre (2007)
8. Hughes, F. and Andre, L. (2007)
9. Walker, S. (2005)
10. Manning, P. (1980),

11. Cop Culture and OMC

1. Librett, M. (2006).
2. Librett, M. (2006), p. 258
3. Queen, W. (2005).

4. Queen, W. (2005)., p. 251
5. (Librett, 2006; Janis, 1972)
6. Queen, W. (2005).
7. Manning, P. (1980).,
8. Librett, M. (2006).
9. Librett, M. (2006).
10. Librett, M. (2006), p. 257
11. Librett, M. (2006).
12. Ulmer, J. (1994).
13. Janis, I. (1972).
14. Queen, W. (2005).
15. Queen, W. (2005). P. 256
16. Queen, W. (2005).
17. Queen, W. (2005). Pp. 258-259.
18. CBS Chicago, (2013)
19. Federal Bureau of Investigations (2009).
20. Federal Bureau of Investigations, (2009).
21. Federal Bureau of Investigations (2009). P.8.
22. Librett, M. (2006).

12. Driving Drunk Behind the Badge

1. NHTSA, (2010)
2. Center for Disease Control, (2011)
3. Bauer, (2011)
4. Edds, (2010)
5. Illescas, (2011)
6. Illescas, (2011)
7. Brown, (2009)
8. Brown, (2009)
9. Stopthemaddness.org, (2009)
10. Seattle P-I Investigations, (2007)
11. Seattle P-I Investigations, (2007)
12. Seattle P-I Investigations, (2007)
13. Illinois Secretary of State, (2012)
14. Seattle P-I Investigations, (2007)
15. Garish, (2012)
16. Girresch, (2012)
17. Belleville News Democrat, (2012)
18. Zerubavel, (2006)
19. The Hammer Firm, LLC, (2011)
20. CBS Local Media, (2011)
21. Zerubavel, (2006)
22. English, (2012)

Notes

I. Stress

1. Warner, (2012)
2. PSF, (2008)
3. Waters & Ussery, (2007)

II. Depression

1. National Institute of Mental Health. (2009)
2. Weiss, (2005)
3. Mayo Clinic, (2011, p. 1)
4. Kessler, Chiu, Demler, & Walters, (2005)
5. World Health Organization [WHO], (2011)
6. Treating depression", (2009, p. 580)
7. World Health Organization [WHO], (2011)
8. DePaulo, J. R., Jr., & Horvitz, L.A. (2002).
9. Washington University School of Medicine, (2011).
10. Department of Mental Health, (2006)
11. Johnson, (2010)
12. All Family Resources, (2005); U.S. Department of Health and Human Services, (2010)
13. Worth, (2010)
14. Diamond (2003)
15. C. Willard, personal communication, June 20, (2011)
16. Heim et. al., (2009)
17. Wasilewski & Olson, (2010)
18. Siddle, (1995)
19. Wasilewski & Olson, (2010)
20. Benjamin & Werner, n.d; Smith et al., (2011)

III. Suicide

1. AFSP, (2010)
2. Zerubavel, (2006, p. 58)
3. Jamison, (1999, p. 135)
4. Jamison, (1999, p. 26)
5. Brannan, (2001)
6. Douglas, (1997)
7. Siddle, (1995, p. 12)
8. National Police Suicide Foundation [PSF], (2008)
9. Johnson, (2011)
10. Zerubavel, (2006, p. 62)
11. Henry, (2004)

Notes

12. Zerubavel, (2006)
13. Henry, (2004)
14. Zerubavel, (2006, p. 11)

14. Investigative Strategies

1. Creswell, J. (2009)
2. Denzin and Lincoln (1994)
3. Flick, (1992, p. 398)
4. Gall, Borg and Gall (1996)
5. Creswell, (1998, p. 16)
6. Creswell, (1998, p. 15)
7. Creswell, J. (2007)
8. Creswell, J. (2007, P.68)
9. Stack, (1974, p. xxi)
10. Fetterman (1998)
11. Creswell (1998)
12. Creswell, J. (2009)
13. Lauder (2003)
14. (Lauder, 2003, p. 187)
15. Creswell, J. (1994)
16. Creswell, J. (1994, p.524)
17. Creswell, J. (2003)
18. Creswell (2003)
19. Creswell, J. (2009)
20. Creswell, J. (2009)
21. Creswell, J. (2007)
22. Creswell (2003)
23. Creswell, J. (2003)
24. Wolcott, H., (1994)
25. Wolcott (1994)
26. Wolcott (1994)
27. (Walcott, 1994, p. 24)
28. Wolcott (1994)
29. (Walcott, 1994, p. 36)

15. Just the Facts

1. Van Maanen, J. (1975)
2. Obst, P., Davey, J. and Sheehan, M. (2001)
3. Simon and Pettigrew, (1990); Britz, (1997); Armed Forces and Society, (2000); and Senna and Siegal, (2010)
4. Barker, J. (2005)
5. Myers, K.A., Forest, K.B., and Miller, S.L. (2004)

Notes

6. Britz, M. (1997)
7. Van Maanen, J. (1975)
8. Turner, V. (1967)
9. Los Angeles Times, (1999)
10. Quinnet, P. (1998, July)
11. Obst, P., Davey, J. and Sheehan, M. (2001)
12. Van Maanen, J. (1975)
13. Manning, P. (1980)
14. Janis, I. (1972)
15. Feldman (1976) and Ashford and Saks (1996)

16. Hating Others

1. Manning, P. (1980)
2. Manning, P. (1980)
3. Walker, S., Alpert, G. and Kenney, D. (2001)
4. Manning, P. (1980)
5. Myers, K.A., Forest, K.B., and Miller, S.L. (2004)
6. Connell (1997)
7. Quinnet, P. (1998, July)
8. Simon, B, and Pettigrew, T. (1990)
9. Myers, K.A., Forest, K.B., and Miller, S.L. (2004)

17. Final Shades of Blue

1. Baron John Acton (1887)
2. Simon, B, and Pettigrew, T. (1990)
3. Longthorne, J. (2010)
4. Federal Bureau of Investigations (2009)

18. Final Verdict

1. Wolcott, H., (1994)
2. Feldman (1976), Van Maanen (1975), Ashford and Saks (1990), Hazer and Alvares (1981), and McKittrick (1984)
3. Feldman (1976), Van Maanen (1975), Ashford and Saks (1990), Hazer and Alvares (1981), and McKittrick (1984)
4. Janis, I. (1972)
5. Feldman, D. (1976)
6. Van Maanen, J. (1975)
7. Turner, V. (1967)
8. Queen (2005) and Librett (2006)
9. Walker, S., Alpert, G. and Kenney, D. (2001)

10. Janis, I. (1972)
11. Manning, P. (1980)
12. Janis, I. (1972)

19. Igniting Change

1. Manning, P. (1980)
2. Wolcott, H., (1994)
3. Turner, V. (1967)
4. Tylor, E. (1865)
5. Janis, I. (1972)
6. Matza, D. and Sykes, G., (1957)
7. Punch. M. (2009)
8. Turner, V. (1967)

www.ingramcontent.com/pod-product-compliance
Lightning Source LLC
Chambersburg PA
CBHW031138020426
42333CB00013B/432